FOR THE POOR

AND

DISENFRANCHISED

FOR THE POOR AND DISENFRANCHISED

AN INSTITUTIONAL AND HISTORICAL ANALYSIS
OF AMERICAN PUBLIC INTEREST LAW
1876-1990

by

Robert Sauté

qp

QUID PRO BOOKS

New Orleans, Louisiana

Published in 2014 in the *Dissertation Series* by Quid Pro Books.

ISBN 978-1-61027-281-0 (pbk)
ISBN 978-1-61027-282-7 (ebk)

QUID PRO, LLC
5860 Citrus Blvd., Suite D-101
New Orleans, Louisiana 70123
www.quidprobooks.com

qp

Publisher's Cataloging-in-Publication

Sauté, Robert.

    For the Poor and Disenfranchised : An Institutional and Historical Analysis of American Public Interest Law, 1876-1990 / Robert Sauté.
        p. cm. — (Dissertation series)
    Includes bibliographical references.
    ISBN 978-1-61027-281-0 (paperback)

1. Public interest law—United States. 2. Practice of law—United States—sociological aspects. 3. Law firms. 4. Legal assistance to the poor—United States. I. Title. II. Series.

KF299.P23.S31 2014   2014599871

Author photograph © by Rie C. Sauté, used by permission and with the thanks of the publisher and author. Cover design © by Quid Pro, LLC.

CONTENTS

PREFACE

For the Poor and Disenfranchised is an historical and institutional analysis of the public interest bar in the United States that traces how the legal profession delivered on the legal system's promise of equal justice for all by making the legal system available to all and a vehicle for substantive justice. It describes three types of public interest practices – direct service, political mobilization, and entrepreneurial lawyering – and analyzes how those practices influenced the availability of legal representation for the poor and disenfranchised, as well as its degree and the type of advocacy involved. The book also examines the evolution of *pro bono publico* from a professional responsibility of individual attorneys to an institutionalized expression of large commercial firms' uneasy commitment to non-market forms of legal service.

This book shows, through case studies of early twentieth century legal aid societies, the Legal Services Corporation, the ACLU and NAACP (and NAACP-LDF), and public interest law firms, how legal reformers have attempted to resolve tensions between formal and substantive justice. Under the bar's elite leadership, the profession institutionalized a form of direct service based on noblesse oblige, good government, and a form of citizenship that stressed order and conformity to wage labor. The formation of the Legal Services program was a reaction by legal and policy reformers to that model. It saw law as a means to end poverty and drew upon a service ideology that stressed lawyers' autonomy and zealous advocacy. The NAACP and ACLU were political organizations forced to the courts by a lack of democratic opportunities. As political mobilization lawyers they defined their service ideal through commitments to politics and the Constitution. Unlike the NAACP and ACLU, entrepreneurial lawyers used litigation as a primary strategy for social change. They used their expertise to represent the public interest and create legal market niches. In addition, in the 1970s and 1980s, large law firms became involved in providing legal services to the poor in response to threats to the profession's legitimacy and autonomy. They embraced *pro bono* as a service ideal compatible with their business model.

This book is based on my Ph.D. dissertation in sociology from the City University of New York Graduate Center, completed in May 2008. Although it is adapted for the present, it is primarily an historical work and further updating it would little change its argument. In the Introduction I note the disparity in commercial law firm revenues and funding for the

i

largest public interest organizations, New York Legal Aid Society and the Legal Services Corporation for the year 2000. The dozen law firms with the highest revenues for 2000 had revenues ($7.6 billion) approximately fifteen times greater than the combined budgets of New York Legal Aid Society and the Legal Services Corporation. Fifty-one private U.S. firms had higher revenues than the Legal Services Corporation. For 2013, the twelve U.S. law firms with the highest revenues had $17.85 billion in revenues (http://en.wikipedia.org/wiki/List_of_100_largest_law_firms_by_revenue). The budget for the Legal Services Corporation in FY 2013 was $340.88 million (http://www.lsc.gov/congress/lsc-funding), and for New York Legal Aid Society total expenses were $283.37 million in FY 2013 (http://www.legal-aid.org/media/187753/las_annualreport_2014.pdf). Seventy-nine private U.S. law firms had revenues higher than the budget of the Legal Services Corporations in FY 2013.

As the disparity between the legal haves and have-nots continues to grow, it is all the more important to understand how and why the legal profession has come to represent the poor and disenfranchised as it has. I hope this volume will contribute to that understanding.

ROBERT SAUTÉ

New York, New York
November 2014

ACKNOWLEDGMENTS

This book started as a dissertation. My committee, Cynthia Fuchs Epstein, Carroll Seron, and Paul Attewell, offered support, encouragement, and much useful advice. They displayed tremendous patience and were generous with their time. Cynthia Fuchs Epstein, my advisor, mentor, and friend, taught me about sociology, the legal profession, and even more about research. The best parts of this book could not have been accomplished without her assistance. Besides her intellectual guidance, she provided years of material support through research work. Finally, she put in practice her commitment to gender equality by making it easier for me to be a father.

Jack Levinson read every word of the manuscript, made useful editorial suggestions, helped me frame arguments, and urged me to brevity. His psychological insights into the process of writing were enhanced by a sociological understanding of the barriers to and rewards of finishing. He knew the importance of praise and the utility of well placed blame.

Many others deserve credit for helping me to complete this study. Donna Ellaby encouraged me almost daily. Michael Farrin read and edited a chapter that never quite made it to the book and continually asked interesting questions. Ras Price was candid about what did not make sense and always had a sympathetic ear. Terrence Blackman inspired me with his commitment to justice.

I met many lawyers in the course of research on the legal profession. The "direct service" lawyers at New York Legal Aid Society who were so generous with their time and advice, even though the interviews they granted never formally made it into this dissertation, made me understand the political importance of institutions and organizations. Their commitment to serving the poor makes this a better world. Michelle Fox offered insights into the quotidian life of public interest law and helped me understand the law.

Lee Scheingold at Quid Pro Books provided impeccable editing.

I would never have written this book were it not for my parents. When I was growing up my father worked seven days a week, fifty-two weeks a year, and my mother worked almost as many hours in the family pharmacy, as well as her "second shift" at home. Their hard work was not much different from the work that other parents did for their children. They provided my siblings and me with love, material comfort, and a respect for learning. Most important, though, and relevant to this book, is that they gave me the moral support and psychological strength to reject the commercial values that direct so much of American society. The sense of justice that motivates this research could only be realized because their hard work of running a business was a means but never an end.

A last word for Youngmi, and my daughters, Aya and Rie: Youngmi, without your faith and sacrifice this work would never have been completed. In our family everyone deserves credit for writing this book.

R.S.

FOR THE POOR

AND

DISENFRANCHISED

1

INTRODUCTION

How does the legal profession fulfill its commitment to justice? "Equal Justice Under Law," inscribed on the façade of the United States Supreme Court, is the mandate of the legal profession and symbolic of its ultimate values. Yet in a system in which legal services are distributed through the market, the ability to pay determines access to "Equal Justice." In a legal system based on partisan and adversarial representation in which the duty of a lawyer is "one-sided partisan zeal in advocating her client's position" (Luban, 1983: 57), the large private firms that serve the legal needs of wealthy individuals and corporations devote seemingly limitless resources to that end.[1] The poor face very different circumstances. Unable to afford private attorneys, they must rely on charitable or government-funded services, and their legal needs are less frequently met.[2] Even so, what are called the public interest and poverty bars are an important part of the profession because they put in place those values that make the institution of law a profession with an ethos of service to society and the production of collective social obligations.

This book analyzes the historical development and transformation of the public interest and poverty bars, examining the institutional response of the legal profession to American society's changing definition of its own responsibility to the "deserving" poor and to other issues of social justice and the role of forces and institutions outside the profession that reinforce its public service mandate. It explores the social organization of public interest lawyering from its first organizational appearance in the last quarter of the nineteenth century in New York and Chicago to the present. Three types of public interest practices – direct service, political mobiliza-

---

[1] For example, in 2000 the top dozen law firms in the United States each had gross revenues of over $500 million, for combined gross revenues of $7.6 billion. Those same twelve firms earned combined profits of slightly more than $3 billion (derived from *American Lawyer*, July 2001).

[2] New York Legal Aid Society, the nation's largest public defender, had a budget of $143 million in 2000. One-hundred and eighteen private firms had higher revenues than NY Legal Aid. For Fiscal Year 2000 Legal Services Corporation had a budget of $305 million. Fifty-one private firms had greater revenues than the LSC budget. (*Legal Aid Society Annual Report*, 2001: 58; Legal Services Corp. Press Release, http://www.lsc.gov/pressr/pr_00a.htm; *American Lawyer*, July 2001; see also Luban, 2002: 54).

1

tion, and entrepreneurial lawyering – will be examined, including those practices that have influenced the availability of legal representation, that is, the degree and type of advocacy available to the poor and disenfranchised. In addition, the book examines the evolution of *pro bono publico* representation from a professional responsibility of individual attorneys to an institutionalized expression of large commercial firms' uneasy commitment to non-market forms of legal service.

The demand for legal services for the poor has always outstripped the supply. Neither the legal profession, private charity, nor the state has ever provided resources to meet the need. Moreover, the problem of providing legal services is exacerbated in a democratic society because the very expectation of universal and equal treatment creates a potentially unlimited need (Lipsky, 1980). In order to provide legal expertise for those unable to participate in the market, certain sectors of the legal profession, advocates for the poor, and the poor themselves have created institutions to provide legal expertise for those who cannot participate in the market. While this book focuses on the poverty and public interest bars and other ideas about helping the poor gain access and substantive justice (see Weber, 1978 [1921-22]), it is worth noting that the high cost of pursuing justice for the disenfranchised and the relatively powerless, especially when they contest the state, makes much of the American populace functionally "poor."

Through the twentieth century the organized bar, the state, and organizations of civil society attempted to deliver legal services to poor individuals and to socially and politically disenfranchised groups. Several factors internal to the profession have influenced the supply of public interest attorneys. They work under difficult conditions. The bar is highly stratified with public interest lawyers ranking at the bottom in pay and prestige (Abel, 1989; Heinz and Laumann, 1982; Kornhauser and Revesz, 1995; Sandefur, 2001), and they typically have fewer resources than their counterparts in the private sector.[3] There are also factors external to the profession which have affected the growth and decline in the public interest bar, especially the demands of social movements (Handler, 1978; Katz, 1982), and the varying efforts of private firms, philanthropists, and law schools (Epstein, 2002).

Yet, while the supply of legal services for the poor has never met the demand, the public interest and poverty bars are an intrinsic part of the profession. They have litigated many of the landmark cases in civil liberties, civil rights, and criminal law. They have drafted historic legislation and led campaigns for political and social reform. Finally and most fundamentally, they have provided poor individuals with their only recourse

---

[3] See notes 1 and 2, above, comparing such budgets.

against the depredations of the state and more powerful economic interests.

The first type of public interest practice, direct service lawyering, including indigent criminal defense, is the dominant form of public interest law. Originally organized through privately funded legal aid societies during the Progressive Era, its civil law component is now mostly publicly financed through the federally funded Legal Services Corporation and through state funding. LSC continues to serve more poor individuals and employ more attorneys and resources than other types of public service practice. State and local governments fund constitutionally mandated indigent criminal defense, which is the second largest sector of the poverty bar.

The second type, political mobilization lawyering had its start around the time of World War One in organizations such as the American Civil Liberties Union (ACLU) and the National Association for the Advancement of Colored People (NAACP). It relied on a relatively small but geographically dispersed number of politically committed lawyers backed by constituent groups that provided political direction and funding. The lawyers tended to volunteer or work for nominal fees. Some of the groups had legal staffs that directed legal strategies at the appellate level, and, by the 1970s, many of these same groups became public interest law offices with expanded legal staffs through foundation support but separated from their constituent groups.

Entrepreneurial lawyering, the third type of public interest practice, came into being in the late 1960s and 1970s. It relied on small staffs of lawyers with highly specialized skills. These organizations tended to be directed by charismatic leaders with few or no constituents. As "public interest entrepreneurs," they sought to identify legal needs that were not being met in the for-profit market but could be fulfilled otherwise with support from foundations or that generated by court fees.

Even though employment opportunities in the public interest field are severely restricted, many attorneys find fulfillment and career opportunities in pursuing this vocation. *Pro bono publico* has been the traditional way in which individuals have answered the profession's calling to provide all members of the public with equal access to the law. Law students also express interest in pursuing *pro bono* work either to supplement the work they expect to do in the private sphere, or as a way to increase their career options should they later opt for public interest jobs.

Throughout this book I address the broad and historically important role law schools have had in the production of public interest lawyers and their impact on the reinforcement of the profession's commitment to its service ideal. During the Progressive Era, the legal aid societies of Boston and New York recruited students directly from elite and local law schools.

Prominent educators such as Roscoe Pound, Felix Frankfurter, and Karl Llewellyn encouraged students to consider careers outside of the large corporate firms, especially in government. Schools responded to the demand for public interest relevant curricula and in the 1930s and 1940s, initiated programs in administrative and public law. Some provided internships in federal agencies. In the 1960s, a movement to provide clinical education in law schools proved to be a breeding ground for public interest lawyers. Its institutionalization provided an important "transmission belt" from law school to the public interest and poverty bar. Some law schools bolstered the ranks of the public interest bar because they trained groups of students whose life circumstances channeled them into public service. For example, at the turn of the twentieth century, NYU Law School trained a large proportion of the women attorneys in New York (Drachman, 1998: 120-22). Many of them worked at New York Legal Aid or pursued other public interest jobs, sometimes as volunteers, because they had so few other employment opportunities. In the 1930s and 1940s, Howard University Law School trained a generation of black attorneys who staffed the legal wing of the civil rights movement. In the 1970s and 1980s, law schools, ABA- and non-ABA-accredited, incorporated with the mission to train public interest lawyers.

The Public Interest and Poverty Bars, Social Rights, and the Welfare State

The American political system promises and is premised on equality before the law, yet within that ideal there is a tension between procedural and substantive law, types of law that lead to formal or substantive justice. In the first instance equality before the law requires a formal equality of treatment in which all are "governed by general rules or principles" and there is a distinction drawn between legal and political or ethical principles. The law, according to Weber, is formally rational and thus can be applied equally to all when it

> represents an integration of all analytically derived legal propositions in such a way that they constitute a logically clear, internally consistent, and, at least in theory, gapless system of rules, under which, it is implied, all conceivable fact situations must be capable of being logically subsumed lest their order lack an effective guaranty (Weber, 1978 [1921-22]: 656, 812-13).

Procedural law "infringes upon the ideals of substantive justice": it works to the advantage of those who possess economic power, for those whom calculability is their guide to the permissible limits of freedom rather than ethical goals or an equitable distribution of resources (Kronman, 1983: 92-95).

This tension between formal and substantive justice has played a role in the development of the poverty bar and shaped the definition of the legal profession's ethical obligations to represent all equally. The early legal aid movement's commitment to provide the poor with their "day in court" followed, according to Reginald Heber Smith (1919), from the bar's "legal and ethical obligation to see that no one shall suffer injustices through inability, because of poverty, to obtain needed legal advice and assistance." Smith was a graduate of Harvard College and Harvard Law School who worked his way up from intern to staff member to general counsel of the Boston Legal Aid Society. The Carnegie Foundation commissioned him to conduct a national legal aid survey, which they published as *Justice and the Poor* in 1919. Although he resigned from Boston Legal Aid shortly after its publication to join the prestigious Boston firm of Hale and Dorr, Smith became the legal aid movement's chief spokesman and most dynamic leader. He found little to complain about in the law. Like many other Progressive Era legal reformers, he thought the most pressing task for the legal system, in the words of his mentor, the eminent jurist Roscoe Pound, was "to *administer* the law to meet the demands of the world that is." (cited in Grossberg, 1978: 28). As Smith explained in *Justice and the Poor*:

> [T]he body of the substantive law, as a whole, is remarkably free from any taint of partiality. It is democratic to the core. Its rights are conferred and its liabilities imposed without respect of persons.... The substantive law, with minor exceptions, is eminently fair and impartial. In other words, the existing denial of justice to the poor is not attributable to any injustice in the heart of the law itself. The necessary foundation for freedom and equality of justice exists. The immemorial struggle is half won (Smith, 1919: 13, 15).

The institutional response to the problem of procedural versus substantive justice could never be as cleanly settled as Smith and other leaders of the legal aid movement imagined. The daily encounters that attorneys had with clients illustrated clearly the gap between the "necessary foundation for equality of justice" and the power of employers, landlords, and the judicial system. Procedural justice could work, and frequently did, for those with resources, and this did not escape the notice of those most familiar with the work of the societies. Attorney J.T. Schmidt remarked that it was difficult to raise funds for New York Legal Aid Society because "the rich did not know and never felt the distress caused by injustice, because when unjustly treated they have the power to assert their rights, and for that reason do not appear to appreciate what it means to be wronged and to be without redress" (Schmitt, 1912: 22).

The call for substantive justice would eventually get a hearing and be fulfilled to a limited extent, especially in the field of criminal law. Changes in the law that were often driven by racial struggles for equality extended the reach of the federal constitution over the states and increased the rights of individuals. These court rulings, culminating in the landmark case *Gideon v. Wainwright*, 372 U.S. 335 (1963), asserted the right to legal counsel and created an institutional demand for indigent criminal defense that expanded the ranks of public defenders. They led to a similar expansion of individual rights, attempts to address continued racial divisions, and the expansion of what T.H. Marshall (1992) would call "social citizenship" through the War on Poverty, which spurred the development of the federally funded Legal Services Program.

In both of these areas, the bulk of responsibility for attempts to bridge procedural and substantive law is carried out by those serving in institutions of direct service lawyering: lawyers employed by Legal Services Corporation-funded programs or public defenders, as well as the large-firm lawyers who provide *pro bono publico* services to the poor.

This book is a return to an institutional analysis of the field of public interest law. Much recent literature on the field has centered on analyses of individual strains of dissidence or ideological outliers. It celebrates the role refusal of lawyers who reject service as officers of the court or disinterested service to individual clients (Sarat and Scheingold, 1998, 2005; Scheingold and Sarat, 2004). While cause lawyers may be the ideological bearers [*traeger*] of a "critique" of the law, their efforts at advocacy tend to be outside of the everyday "practice" of the law. The viability of their efforts is subsumed by political forces over which they have little control. The irony of cause lawyering is that in "normal times" its transgressive advocacy of substantive justice cannot sustain itself as a political project and instead becomes a moral voice of individual lawyers in opposition.

Political Lawyering as an Institutional Response to the Demands for Democracy

The legal profession has played a contradictory role in America's democratic life. In the first half of the nineteenth century, Tocqueville argued that the profession was uniquely suited to overcome the democratic excesses of the people. Lawyers had "habits of order, a taste for formalities, and a kind of instinctive regard for the regular connection of ideas" that put them in a position to counteract the "unreflecting passions of the multitude" (cited in Scheingold and Sarat, 2004: 98). A little more than a century later Talcott Parsons would find that same moderating effect in the manner in which lawyers carried out the functional specificity of the legal profession and acted as a "mechanism of social control" by standing between legal authority and its norms and private individuals or groups and their desires (Parsons, 1954a: 39; 1954b: 382). To those structural explanations there should be added the historical observation which bears repeating here, that lawyers have more often than not served the powerful (Abel, 1985; Auerbach 1976).

In contrast, segments of the bar have responded to and shaped democratic movements to expand the rights of individuals and social groups. Lawyers in these domains have relied on the idea that the legal system has a degree of independence from naked political interests. The judiciary in its claim of independence from the political passions of the crowd and from the venality of vested interests has always held out the promise of introducing reason into governance. In interpreting the Constitution the judiciary brings the protean world of politics under legal norms. Yet the possibility of social change through the legal system exists because reason is a plastic concept, historically shaped and applied in partisan ways. Political movements, which exist to pursue substantive issues, have for much of the twentieth century relied on the courts as their leverage into civic participation. Justice Jerome Frank has characterized these alliances as attempts to make law "more responsive to social needs" (Levi, 1963; Nonet and Selznick, 1978: 73; Scheingold, 1974).

The institutional impetus for lawyers to expand democracy, though, has largely come from *outside* of the profession. Like the legal aid movement, the organizations we most identify with politically-engaged lawyering were not founded by lawyers. They include the case studies for this research, namely the NAACP and the ACLU. They were originally political organizations that sought to challenge state policies. Because their goals, opposition to racism and militarism, challenged the core of the political system and because their constituencies – blacks, pacifists, and the left wing of the labor movement – were socially and politically marginal, they turned to the courts out of necessity. Politically, they often opposed the executive power of the state, and representing minority and often stigmatized social groups, they lacked influence in legislatures so they could expect to gain little power there.

Both organizations provide case studies of the institutionalization of politically engaged lawyering. The institutionalization was contingent upon (1) legal strategies and tactics that could advance the particular organizational goals, (2) changes in the law that provided opportunities to apply such strategies and tactics, and (3) a supply of lawyers who could put them into effect. Public interest lawyers have often depended on political and social movements because they provide not only opportunities for legal activism, and sometimes employment, but also generate what Durkheim (1995 [1912]) called "collective effervescence," the excitement of working for a cause that is larger than an individual's interests. Social movements appear sporadically and do not last forever: collective effervescence is fleeting at best. They are of limited duration with a natural history of their own (McAdam, 1982). Yet for all its dependence on social movements, political-mobilization lawyering has also had a separate life, that is, it has often existed prior to movement mobilization and has continued after the social movements have subsided. The same can be said of public interest lawyering in general, which (as this research describes) drew political and cultural energy from various social movements. Of course, it is the story of its institutionalization that really explains its perseverance in the profession.

For most of the twentieth century, political mobilization lawyering consisted of a corps of volunteer lawyers whose engagement with organizations such as the NAACP and ACLU was sporadic and locally based. Attorneys' commitment was usually the result of ideological affinity with the organization's goals, but in some cases attorneys, often nationally prominent, took on cases because of a commitment to their *professional* role as officers of the court or defenders of the Constitution. Attempts to carry out legal strategies and exert control over tactics often failed because of local political independence. In other cases, lack of local resources prevented legal interventions (Meier and Rudwick, 1976; Tushnet, 1987; Walker, 1990; Wasby, 1984).

Entrepreneurial Lawyering: The Profession Steps In

If lawyers' initiatives in constituting the public interest bar were late in coming in cases of direct service and political mobilization lawyering, the same cannot be said for what has been variously dubbed the "new public interest law," "public goods law" (Comment, 1970), "second wave public interest law" (Rabin, 1976), or "newer breed of public interest lawyers" (Halpern, 1970). These efforts to reform the law and enlarge the public's voice in government had attorneys spearheading new uses of the law and courts and new organizational forms for delivering these legal services.

I call this form of public interest lawyering "entrepreneurial lawyering" because of its emphasis on creating small organizations to address specific niches in the public interest "market." Lawyers alienated from commercial and mainstream public interest practices but with political passions congruent with the times and arcane expertise in the law and government regulations set up numerous organizations to challenge the government and corporations via the legal system. They took advantage of the federal courts' affirmation of the public's right to be heard in the administrative arena. Lawyers concerned with law reform appropriated academic critiques of laissez-faire liberalism and New Deal policymaking and responded to popular mistrust of bureaucracy. They often worked "at the intersection of corporate power and governmental responsibility, in those administrative and executive agencies where decisions affecting large numbers of private citizens used to be often quietly if not casually made" (Halpern, 1976: 159).

The prototypical entrepreneurial lawyer was Ralph Nader. He and his "Raiders," young recent graduates of law schools driven by the political zeal of the 1960s, took low-paying jobs in Washington, D.C., formed organizations to battle the political establishment, and stepped into the breach. Nader's Raiders carved out a legal voice for the consumer and pursued the public interest in the administrative arena. Issuing a series of reports on the Federal Trade Commission, the Interstate Commerce Commission, the Federal Communications Commission, and the Food and Drug Administration, Ralph Nader became a household name (Rabin, 1976: 224-25).

Again, different from the earlier manifestations of public interest lawyers, those practicing entrepreneurial lawyering rarely had constituents – in fact, their clients existed primarily to fulfill the technical requirements of the court: for standing, one needed a client. It is probably more accurate to say that private foundations such as the Ford Foundation were the constituents for entrepreneurial lawyering. Indeed, the Ford Foundation was the major actor in this area, giving support to an array of diverse three- to six-lawyer public interest law firms. Changes in the law and court rulings allowed the new public interest firms to fund their legal efforts through litigation via a mechanism called "fee-shifting," thus encouraging public interest lawyers strategically to pursue redress in the courts with questions of substantive justice and organizational well-being in mind (Bradford, 1995; Halpern, 1976: 170; Rabin, 1976: 228-30; Trubek, 2002: 577).

Professionals and Service

Many, if not all, occupations claim to serve the public. Yet, only professionals claim to serve *for* their patrons, even to go so far as to overrule their clients' wishes. Professional ideology claims a "devotion to a transcendent value which infuses its specialization with a larger and putatively higher goal which may reach beyond that of those they are supposed to serve" (Freidson, 2001: 121-22; see also Parsons, 1954). By claiming to serve a transcendent value, professionals assert their independent judgment and freedom of action and justify their privileged position. In a veritable quid pro quo, the state sanctions professional self-regulation in exchange for its commitment to "serving both the client's interest and the public good" (Solomon [1992], quoting ABA, 1986: 10).

This study explores how the legal profession has provided institutional means for fulfilling the service ideal. The ideological claim to public service calls forth a collective responsibility, but its fulfillment in the legal profession is brought about by both individual and collective mechanisms.

Individual attorneys face expectations that they will provide *pro bono*, free or reduced-fee legal services (Maute, 2002). In addition to individual expectations to serve the poor, lawyers and others have created organizations to provide legal services that are not typically provided through market mechanisms.

The problem of whom the service ideal addresses has vexed the profession throughout its history. Ideas of charity and desert have been at the heart of direct service lawyering. The institutions that provide legal services to individuals have been marked by attempts to balance the demands of the poor, conceptions of class responsibility and society's obligations, and the need to ration resources. Political mobilization lawyering faces similar problems, although those problems are not refracted through the cultural lens of the "deserving poor"; instead, they tend to be understood as strategic political choices.

Plan of Chapters

For the Poor and Disenfranchised sketches the shape of the public interest and poverty bars to show how they have structured opportunities to practice law as a public service calling. It analyzes the origins, development, and functioning of three types of public service lawyering: direct service, political mobilization, and entrepreneurial lawyering. The field of public interest lawyering, like most institutional arrangements, has a taken-for-granted feel to it (Jepperson, 1991). To move beyond the taken-for-granted nature of the field I will employ an historical and functional deconstruction. In a Mertonian vein, I will explore how the "humanly significant aspects of social reality came to be and to track their diverse consequences ... for society, for social sectors, and for individuals within those sectors" (Merton, 1995: 13).

This monograph consists of six additional chapters and a conclusion. Chapter 2, The Origins of Direct Service Lawyering, explores the dominant form of public interest practice, direct service lawyering, from its origins in the movement for legal aid societies prior to the Progressive Era until the creation of the federally funded Legal Services Corporation. It includes both civil and criminal defense. The first organizations providing legal services for the poor emerged from immigrant mutual aid societies and social service groups. They were intended to offer legal aid to "deserving" groups of immigrants and victimized women and children. Demands from the poor themselves and the limited financial resources of the original sponsoring organizations forced those agencies to expand their scope beyond their original clientele. The German Legal Aid Society (Deutscher Rechts-Schutz Verein) (founded in 1876) became the New York Legal Aid Society (1890). In Chicago the Protective Agency for Women and Children (founded in 1886) and the Bureau of Justice (1888) merged and became the Legal Aid Society (1905). They came under the leadership of the elite corporate bar: initial patrons of the Boston Legal Aid Society (1900) were members of the city's insular, Harvard Law School-educated elite. As such they mimicked the corporate bar's form of organization, operating in offices with salaried full-time attorneys specializing in specific areas of the law, and servicing a defined group of clients (DiMaggio and Powell, 1991). They reflected the concerns of the elite bar and segments of Progressive Era reformers in discouraging litigation, encouraging assimilation, and offering their particular version of the legal system as a bulwark against radicalism and the lower echelons of the urban bar.

Changing conceptions of the profession's ethical obligations to the poor and pressure from the urban poor to confront the effects of urbanization encouraged an institutional response to a lack of legal resources for the indigent. Legal aid societies provided limited representation to a small portion of the poor, and they relieved individual members of the profession from serving the poor. They incurred few costs: the history of the early legal aid movement was one of unmet budgets and increasingly stringent forms of rationing.

Initial attempts to provide indigent criminal defense proved difficult to fund through private contributions, and some bar associations and legal aid organizations opposed government funding for legal services. Leaders of the bar justified their refusal to accept government funding by appealing to the profession's autonomy from the state. They claimed that state-supported legal services would fall victim to political pressures and blunt the charitable impulses of the bar and legal aid supporters. Voluntary defender organizations found it difficult to extend the service ideal to the disreputable poor, rarely challenging criminal law or embracing zealous advocacy for their clients.

A major aim of the early legal aid movement was to provide the poor with their day in court: a minimal and frequently unmet requirement of procedural justice. Attempts to institute forms of substantive justice met with mixed results. The early legal aid societies involved themselves in various law reform efforts, but over time, especially as they came under the leadership of local bar elites, their ambitions narrowed to the provision of access to the courts and defensive efforts at curbing the worst excesses of urban life. Chicago, which had the deepest roots in reform movements, offered the liveliest opposition to limiting its mandate to access to the courts, but it, too, abandoned prohibitive policies that restricted the scope of business activity for permissive legislation that encouraged free market solutions to social problems

In the field of criminal law, reform came from outside of the traditional legal aid organizations. The first public defender offices were geographically and socially distant from the elite bar, in Oklahoma and Los Angeles.

The expansion of the legal rights of criminal defendants came not from legal aid attorneys but primarily from politically-engaged lawyers operating under the auspices of political organizations such as the NAACP. The federal courts began to recognize the right not only to representation in criminal cases but to effective counsel, with *Downer v. Dunaway*, 53 F.2d 586 (5th Cir. 1931). Three decades later, in *Gideon v. Wainwright* (1963), the United States Supreme Court mandated counsel for criminal defendants and finalized the institutionalization of indigent criminal representation throughout the nation. It was part of a steady, if uneven, broadening of individual rights and legal protections for less powerful sectors of society. And it seemed to augur the coming of an era in which the poor, social minorities, and the disenfranchised would find solace in the legal system.

In Chapter 3, The Origins of the Legal Services Corporation, I show how maverick attorneys, social scientists, and foundations, all with the intent of ending poverty, mobilized the elite of the bar and members of the Johnson administration to undertake an ambitious plan to provide free legal services to the nation's poor. This campaign took as its starting point a critique of the legal aid movement. They intended to move beyond the model that Boston Legal Aid Society director and leading spokesperson for the legal aid movement Reginald Heber Smith championed of insuring the poor "their day in court." By locating their services in poor communities, embracing holistic approaches to ending poverty (combining social work and/or political activism), they redefined their service ideal to provide the zealous advocacy that they saw lacking in the traditional legal aid societies.

With the financial backing and institutional imprimatur of the Ford Foundation, attorneys in New Haven, New York City's Lower East Side, and Washington, D.C. joined community-based organizations in programs to combat poverty. These attorneys were part of a resurgent liberalism that took its energy from three sources: (1) the civil rights movement, (2) Kennedy's election to the presidency, and (3) a growing sense of idealism among the young (Rossinow, 1998). The Ford Foundation described a "comprehensive attack on human problems of urban 'gray areas' – changing neighborhoods of low-income families, racial minorities, and migrants from rural areas and other cities" (Ylvisaker, 1963: i). This plan provided an opportunity for a sector of the legal profession to engage in the nation's incipient anti-poverty movement.

Extending the experimental neighborhood legal services program to a national level involved the kind of political maneuvering that the legal aid movement had generally avoided in its seventy-five year history. The Johnson administration's War on Poverty provided a home for a legal services program, and Administration figures such as Sargent Shriver were willing sponsors. The early advocates for government-funded legal services had to overcome the hesitance of the organized bar and neutralize opposition from traditional legal aid societies. These advocates won the organized bar to the legal services cause by appealing to the elite bar's sense of professionalism, to its exclusive claim to a knowledge mandate and the autonomy that entailed, and to a newly refined service ideal that recognized individual voluntarism was insufficient to address the needs of the poor. Leaders of the ABA recognized that to secure support at the local levels where state and city bar associations had influence over individual members of Congress, the Legal Services program had to incorporate local bar associations in the initial design and governance of individual projects. This move to incorporate local bar leadership expanded the number of parties with an interest in the success of Legal Services. But this expansion forced the program's early advocates to ratchet back their radical aspirations of including activism and the poor in the program's structure.

The passage of Legal Services legislation created a program with widespread support in the legal profession, but its constituency was narrow. From its inception it created opposition among powerful agricultural interests and conservative politicians, who used it as a symbolic target in their "law and order" campaigns and in general efforts, especially during the Reagan era, to "de-fund the Left." Like much of American welfare policy, it never provided sufficient coverage to build up a constituency with the political desire or wherewithal to defend it. As a result, it has been suffering death by a thousand funding cuts and experienced a political defeat in 1996 when Congress passed legislation restricting the clients Legal Services attorneys could serve and the types of law they could practice. Ironically, traditional legal aid societies advised against government entanglements precisely because of fear that the independence of lawyers would be compromised, but those legal aid societies had already largely disappeared when their position defending the poor in court was usurped by Legal Service attorneys.

Chapters 4 and 5 outline the changing forms of political mobilization lawyering from the Progressive Era through to the end of the "sixties," primarily through case studies of two organizations, the NAACP and the ACLU. The two organizations, founded within a decade of one another, came from similar political milieus, had founders from the same social background, and started as political organizations that advocated for unpopular people and causes. Lawyers founded neither organization, nor was the primary focus of the ACLU or NAACP shaping a legal strategy to effect change. Political, financial, and organizational factors – some structural, some contingent, some that they shared, and some that were different – provided opportunities and motivations to embrace legal strategies.

The NAACP's leadership sought to advance the interests of blacks through suffrage, "securing justice in the courts, education for the children, employment according to their ability and complete equality before law." Unable to mobilize voters and with a leadership that was socially distant from its constituency, the NAACP's political opportunities were restricted. Its initial organizational work involved publicity and legal tactics, but in the face of increasing racial violence and entrenched discrimination it gravitated toward activism. That activism was mostly defensive and frequently had a legal component.

The NAACP's legal work was initially done in an ad hoc fashion and relied on white volunteer attorneys who saw their work as their professional obligation to advocate for the defenseless and uphold the Constitution. In this aspect they resembled their colleagues in the ACLU – in fact, several of the same attorneys played pivotal roles in both organizations. Pressure from middle-class members and an increase in the supply of black lawyers from institutions such as Howard University allowed the Association to increase its lawyering, especially in the South. The promise of a large grant from the Garland Fund encouraged the NAACP to hire an in-house legal staff and to devise a long-term strategy that would attack the legal basis of segregation. The Garland Fund was to be one of the first of several instances when foundations would act as catalysts in the development of the public interest field.

The ACLU's initial trajectory was similar to the NAACP's. It, too, began representing a constituency that confronted a hostile majority. Facing government repression from the executive branch, it was forced into the courts. The ACLU's founding context provided motivations and opportunities for politically engaged lawyering. Pacifism, labor strife, and ethnic prejudice created needs and constituencies that an organization with political goals could address. Because of repression, however, the social distance of its leadership from its natural allies, and an expectation that its social networks would prove persuasive, the ACLU emphasized education and publicity rather than mobilizing large numbers. Its pacifist organizing against the World War I draft expanded its contacts with lawyers, and its desire to aid radicals in the labor movement forced it to engage state repression in the courts.

Like the NAACP, the ACLU started with a small core of legal advisors from the elite of the bar. Those advisors often identified with the underdog and held strong positions on constitutional guarantees of freedom. Unlike NAACP lawyers, though, the ACLU had a strictly legal approach to civil liberties that they thought should take precedence over political and educational activities, a strategy they pushed the organization to pursue. Much of the Union's litigation, successful and not, produced considerable publicity, if not gains in membership, and eventually found a receptive audience in the federal courts.

As a political force the ACLU had limited influence outside of the corridors of urban liberalism. But by the 1930s, under the leadership of Roger Baldwin, it deepened its commitment to a legal strategy for change and broadened its political mandate to oppose racial discrimination, police brutality, and various forms of censorship. Unable to mobilize its paltry membership, it instead relied on its resources of expertise, primarily legal but also educational, and social capital.

The legal work of the NAACP and the ACLU gained momentum in the 1930s in a context in which sectors of the legal profession moved to the left. A growth of radical social movements, a more interventionist and redistributive federal government, and law school professors eager to apply the doctrine of "legal realism" beyond the lecture hall encouraged the formation of organizations such as the National Lawyers Guild. Lawyers who came of age in the 1930s would provide much of the human capital and social infrastructure for public interest law of the following decades.

While Chapter 4 argues that the ACLU and NAACP were forced to the courts, Chapter 5 shows how, in the case of the NAACP, engagement in the legal system itself depended on and shaped the political mobilization of its constituents and by extension the civil rights movement. The legal strategy to overturn segregation that Nathan Margold, Charles Houston, Thurgood Marshall, and others devised in the 1930s and carried out in the 1940s and 1950s was shaped by political pressures from the ranks of the NAACP, including the push to use black attorneys, and from the African American community. The victory in *Brown v. Board of Education* required more litigation to enforce it and to combat the campaign of civil insubordination in the white South that greeted desegregation. Defending protesters and conducting test-case litigation kept the NAACP Legal Defense and Education Fund (LDF) close to the civil rights movement. The formal separation of the LDF from the NAACP became real as it developed and defended its own set of interests, which were related to fundraising, symbolic capital, and the functional requirements of practicing law instead of conducting protest politics. As the civil rights movement waned in the late 1960s, the LDF leveraged its reputation and fundraising skills and adapted to changes in federal law to weather the decline in activism. Taking advantage of Title VII employment discrimination cases and a Supreme Court ruling that awarded attorney fees to successful litigators in civil rights cases, the LDF increased its staff to 28 attorneys and for the first time pursued cases where a successful outcome in the immediate conflict was the principal justification for representation.

The ACLU's fortunes in the 1940s and 1950s also depended on the politics of the era (anticommunism and the antifascist mobilization of World War II) and political and organizational dynamics of the Union. The anticommunism of some board members, political pressures from Congress, and long-standing conflicts with rivals on the Left over how to conduct legal campaigns produced a controversial purging of Communists from the ACLU board. The ACLU's role in World War II was contentious as well. The organization's lonely defense of the civil liberties of dissidents and Japanese-Americans produced considerable organizational and ideological role strain as political factions and regional affiliates debated how best to defend the Constitution in the fight against fascism.

In the 1950s with the retirement of Roger Baldwin, the ACLU embarked on a campaign of national membership growth. It replicated much of what the NAACP had done in the late 1910s and 1920s by hiring a national organizer and granting greater autonomy to regional affiliates. Membership skyrocketed and chapters opened throughout the country. From 1950 to 1955 membership had more than tripled to 30,000, and at the end of the decade had doubled again to 60,000. In 1974, membership passed 275,000 in 375 local chapters in forty-nine states. In his first national speaking tour in 1951, the new executive director, Patrick Murphy Malin, listened to members and constituents. He found that there were strong concerns for (1) the Cold War's effects on civil liberties, (2) increasing censorship, (3) a need for a strict separation of church and state, and (4) a renewal of commitment to civil rights. Despite the repression of the Cold War – the Supreme Court seemed to be reversing itself in the area of political dissent – the ACLU alone and with other legal groups created a new body of law that extended civil rights, freedom from censorship, and strengthened the separation of church and state and the provisions of due process.

By the 1970s, the national office, increasingly funded by large foundations and sophisticated direct mail appeals, had moved away from volunteer attorneys. It built up a staff of attorneys who functioned less as "generalists" directing volunteer litigators and more as project attorneys in areas such as juvenile, women's, and prisoner rights, abortion, or sexual privacy. The organization also shifted gears away from a policy of filing amicus briefs to direct representation of clients. Local affiliates determined their own policy priorities and had tenuous ties to the national office.

Chapter 6 analyzes the transformation of *pro bono* services from an individual obligation to its institutionalization in large firms. It suggests that large law firms became involved in providing free legal services to the poor in response to threats to the profession's legitimacy and autonomy. They embraced a model of *pro bono* involvement that stressed a service ideal compatible with their business model. Faced with the need to recruit and retain attorneys, with demands from the courts for mandatory *pro bono*, and with pressure from the ABA and other bar associations to make up for cuts in government funded legal services in the 1970s, large firms began a massive shift in how the profession delivered *pro bono* services.

Moving away from the idea that *pro bono publico* was the responsibility of individual attorneys, local bar associations with the participation of large firms first created organizations to mobilize lawyers for *pro bono* service and then nurtured – sometimes prodded – the same firms to organize those services in-house. Legal Services Corporation funding for Private Attorney Involvement (PAI) provided the resources for the initial organizational attempts at encouraging private firm involvement in the field of legal aid to the poor. Firms increased *pro bono* service to head off populist distrust of the profession. This was fueled by a newly established and aggressive legal press that wrote for a general audience and reported on lawyers' venality and corruption.

Chapter 7 continues an examination of non-market legal services by exploring the creation of a third form of practice that had its origins in the 1960s: "entrepreneurial lawyering." This new form of entrepreneurial practice appeared as the response of a sector of the legal profession to (1) the political climate, (2) changes in the demographics of the profession, (3) the continued involvement of foundations in attempting to effect liberal policies, and (4) rulings from a sympathetic federal court. A group of entrepreneurial leaders identified areas in which they could apply the law to social needs and, in the words of Joseph Schumpeter (1991: 412-13), "get things done."

While the NAACP and the ACLU had been forced into the courts to carry out their work, the entrepreneurial lawyering movement voluntarily and eagerly undertook litigation as their primary strategy for political change. From the mid-1960s to the mid-1970s a largely middle-class political movement, believing that power was increasingly out of the hands of the "public" but disdaining the confrontational politics of the New Left and poor people's movements, found expression in a congeries of law firms, research centers, lobbying groups, and membership associations. These groups, gathering together what Simon Lazarus called the "Genteel Populists" (1974), attempted to limit the power of business. They were a part of a long American tradition of the "common people" standing up against entrenched elites (Pollack, 1962; Vogel, 1980-81: 607).

They created a form of public interest lawyering that sought to make the state more responsive to the will of the people by expanding the realm of public goods, goods that once they were provided cost no more to provide and could not be denied to subsequent "consumers." Entrepreneurial lawyering relied upon a high degree of legal expertise and insider knowledge of the workings of the regulatory state. It combined this expertise with a diffuse commitment to an expanded sense of democracy and access not just to the courts but to the political system. This combination of expertise and populist politics allowed entrepreneurial lawyering to take root and flourish in a context of liberal politics. Even so, it was unmoored from a political base and lacked a constituency or "natural clientele" outside of the fickle world of foundations. For these reasons, it has largely been unable to sustain its base of intellectually and politically committed individual lawyers in the face of a legal system moving increasingly to the right.

Methods

This study relies on socio-historical methods using data primarily from secondary sources. Several chapters also incorporate primary documents. Chapters 2 and 3 refer to material from (1) the *Annual Reports* of the New York Legal Aid Society, (2) histories and reports written by individuals involved in the legal aid movement, for example Reginald Heber Smith's *Justice and the Poor* (1919), and (3) contemporary accounts from the *New York Times* and popular magazines. Chapters 4 and 5 use material from memoirs, especially Jack Greenberg's account of his years in the NAACP-LDF (2004); a contemporary account of the ACLU from the *New Yorker*; and a report from Charles Houston to Harvard Law School Dean Roscoe Pound. Chapter 6 makes use of contemporary accounts of the legal profession from general circulation newspapers such as the *Wall Street Journal* and *New York Times*, publications of the legal press, and other contemporary journalistic accounts.

2

THE ORIGINS OF DIRECT SERVICE LAWYERING

Direct service lawyering, including indigent criminal defense, is the dominant form of public interest practice in the United States, serving the greatest number of poor individuals and employing the most attorneys and resources. About three-quarters of direct service lawyers work on civil law matters. In 2002, there were 3,845 lawyers in Legal Services Corporation funded-programs, including those funded with state, private, and other funds, or one lawyer for every 6,861 low-income people. In 2004, the number of attorneys declined almost five percent to 3,657. Non-LSC-funded organizations accounted for 2,736 attorneys who worked in organizations that provided civil legal services to the poor (Legal Services Corporation, 2005: 16).[1] Another quarter (approximately 2,300) of publicly funded attorneys who service the poor provide constitutionally mandated criminal defense (Sandefur, 2006: 8). Although it is now mostly publicly financed through the federally funded Legal Services Corporation and through state funding, the origin of direct service lawyering in the Progressive Era was through privately funded legal aid societies. This chapter examines the formation and institutionalization of this type of non-market-based mode of delivering legal services to the poor and disenfranchised in the United States.

The Origin of Legal Aid Societies

Throughout much of the nineteenth century, many problems of the poor never became legal problems. When they did, lawyers, especially in small towns, might be available for free or reduced fees. In the years following the Civil War, the courts were increasingly the venue in which individuals confronted and addressed social problems. With rapid urbanization, the swelling city poor faced problems that either led them to or could only be resolved through the legal system. Workers sued employers for unpaid wages, tenants faced evictions, credit agencies and consumers wrangled in court over debts as low as $8. Husbands and wives litigated

---

[1] Using the National Survey of Lawyers Career Satisfaction, Sandefur (2006: 8) estimates that in 1997 there were 3,350 lawyers providing legal services for the poor outside of criminal defense and LSC-funded organizations. In the same year there were 3,494 attorneys salaried by LSC.

over domestic problems, and parents filed charges against their children for being "unruly" or refusing to bring home wages (Grossberg, 1978a: 22; Willrich, 2003: 4-5, 21). The first organizational responses to the poor's needs for legal representation came not from the legal profession but from immigrant groups and social work organizations. These sprang up in New York, Chicago, Boston and other large cities. In 1876, the German Society in the City of New York founded the Deutscher Rechts-Schutz Verein (German Legal Aid Society), the first legal aid society in the United States. Its mission was "...to render gratuitously legal aid and assistance to such persons of German birth in the City of New York as may appear to be worthy thereof, but from poverty are unable to employ legal assistance...." In 1890 the Society expanded its "object and purpose ... to render legal aid and assistance, *gratuitously if necessary*, to *all* who may appear worthy thereof and who, from poverty, are unable to procure it" (Maguire, 1928: 19, 58, emphasis bolded in the original). Soon thereafter the Deutscher Rechts-Schutz Verein changed its name to the New York Legal Aid Society, and by 1900 only one fifth of its clients were of German descent. New York Legal Aid's mission reflected the ideology of its founders, respectable men from the German immigrant community, including Edward Salomon, a lawyer and former governor of Wisconsin from 1862-1864, and various importers and merchants. Its president from 1890 to 1916, Arthur von Briesen, gave "his unbounded energy and commitment," building the Society to be the world's premier legal services provider. He was, according to Jerold Auerbach (1976: 53-54), from "the best men."

The New York Legal Aid Society represented the deserving poor, those who "from no fault of their own" were suffering the ill effects of temporary unemployment. The Society was not a "charity" and refused to represent those whom "they felt were taking advantage of the legal system" (Maguire, 1928: 64). In 1900, its 14,000 clients came from sixty countries with a majority from eastern and southern Europe and about a quarter born in the United States. Slightly more than half had been in the United States for less than five years (*Annual Report*, 1900: 5, 9, 24). During the 1900s and 1910s special bureaus serviced seamen whom unscrupulous maritime companies, boarding houses, and other "sharpies" victimized; and women, who were mainly involved in domestic disputes. Neighborhood branches served the Lower East Side, the West Side of Manhattan, and Harlem (Maguire, 1928). In 1917, New York Legal Aid Society served 44,600 clients, forty percent of whom were native-born, and another twenty percent who had lived in the U.S. for at least five years. It was not until the mid-1950s that it would counsel a greater number (*Annual Report*, 1917: 44-45; Tweed, 1954: 39, 88).

In Chicago, the Protective Agency for Women and Children (founded in 1886) and the Bureau of Justice (founded in 1888), provided legal assistance to those who could not otherwise afford private attorneys. Chicago Woman's Club members initiated the Protective Agency and staffed it, and members of the Ethical Culture Society founded the Bureau of Justice. Both groups combined social work with direct services to walk-in clients. In addition, the organizations, which merged into the Legal Aid Society in 1905, took on reform activities such as drafting legislation that regulated wage assignments, loan-shark-like lending, and exploitative business practices. When the Illinois Supreme Court ruled some of that legislation unconstitutional, the Legal Aid Society pressured the *Chicago Tribune* to refuse advertising from offending businesses. In conjunction with the Chicago Commerce Association, it formed a wage loan society to undercut usurious lenders. For its first ten years or so, Chicago Legal Aid championed law reform, but like other legal aid groups, it shunned the taint of radicalism. The Justice Bureau had suffered from negative publicity when leaders of its founding organization, the Ethical Culture Society, backed calls for amnesty for the Haymarket martyrs, a group of immigrant anarchists blamed for and eventually executed for their alleged role in a bombing at a political rally in support of the eight-hour day (Katz, 1982: 15, 37).

The legal profession itself made its first foray into legal aid only in 1900. The Boston Legal Aid Society was founded and directed by members of the city's insular legal elite. They included judges, academics, "treatise writers," and leaders of corporate firms. Four out of five of its lawyer directors were Harvard Law School graduates, and a majority were members of the organized bar at a time when less than two percent of lawyers nationwide belonged to the American Bar Association. Its original directors viewed it, like Chicago's Legal Aid Society, as the legal services arm of local charities (Grossberg, 1978a: 21-22). Boston also served the "deserving poor," who were not, as the Society reminded its patrons, "deadbeats, derelicts, fools, and ne'er-do-wells." Instead, as Smith characterized them, they were "self-respecting, self-supporting persons. As nearly as one group can, they represent the common people" (quoted in Grossberg, 1978b: 15).

Funding Legal Aid

The legal aid movement remained private and placed the responsibility for financing legal services on the bar and private philanthropy rather than on the public. Local bar groups largely shirked their fiscal duties, and financing fell primarily to private citizens not in the profession. In New York, for example, by 1900 Legal Aid, whose directors had come from the cream of the German immigrant community, increasingly drew its board from the city's philanthropic and legal elite. The N.Y. Society's leadership operated out of a genuine concern for the plight of the deserving poor, a desire to thwart labor-backed radicalism, and an upper-class sense of noblesse oblige. Fund-raising became part of New York's social scene with gala events featuring operatic performances at Carnegie Hall and sumptuous meals at the city's best venues. In a practice that continues to this day in the nonprofit world, it recruited honorary officers who lent the organization their prominent names and a homeopathic dose of their considerable wealth. Its "letterhead" boasted names such as Elihu Root, Theodore Roosevelt, Mrs. Arthur Dodge, and Andrew Carnegie. The Society raised most of its donations from wealthy individuals (Mrs. Russell Sage, the Rockefellers) and supplemented that amount from subscriptions purchased by large-firm lawyers. It adamantly rejected government financing: President Von Briesen threatened to resign if a $25,000 municipal fund created for its own use were accepted, fearing the slippery slope that could only end in "socialized law." Von Briesen reported in the 1911 *Annual Report* that government funding would lead to political interference and "be distasteful to many of our best citizens" (*Annual Report*, 1902: 8; 1911: 11; see Maguire, 1928: 257-58). All the while, it ran annual deficits more years than not.

Funding for the Boston Society, likewise, came mainly from private citizens and not from the profession. From 1915 to 1925 less than a third (thirty-one percent) of funding came from attorneys. It had to "advertise, plead, and cajole alongside other agencies clamoring for the pocketbooks of philanthropic Bostonians." As a result, the Boston Society was reluctant to make claims against prominent businessmen who might support the Society. Those clients who could afford to pay something were charged fees of between 50¢ and $1 and ten percent of any awards (Grossberg, 1978b: 14-16).

Chicago's Legal Aid Society received funding via personal solicitations from local social, business, and civic elites, but these charitable donations proved inadequate to the growth in demand. In 1914, a year of financial depression, the number of cases it handled peaked at 16,121. The number of paid staff – attorneys and others, including caseworkers – reached thirty. Its financial difficulties were such that it cut its staff in half the following year, cut back hours, and reduced its caseload so that in its last year before incorporating into United Charities it served only 9,361 clients.

To overcome funding shortfalls, Chicago Legal Aid attempted to expand its revenue sources. When it later amalgamated into the United Charities of Chicago in 1919, Legal Aid received funding through professionally organized charity appeals. Three years after amalgamation, United Charities reached an agreement with the Chicago Bar Association (CBA) that the CBA would provide half of its funding. In exchange, the CBA's Legal Aid Committee would participate in general policy implementation (Gariepy, 1926: 34, 37, 38).

Not all legal aid organizations were averse to government funding, but those that accepted public revenues were in a minority. The number of publicly funded organizations reached its pre-Legal Services peak in the1920s, when there were a dozen such civil legal aid and public defender offices. Of the twelve that existed in 1932, only five remained in 1962. Many publicly funded organizations, including such prominent agencies as the Philadelphia Bureau, which in the 1920s was the largest municipal legal aid organization in the world, lost public support and failed during the Depression. New York Legal Aid Society shrank in size during the 1930s from lack of funds. The severity of the depression undoubtedly challenged the generosity and perhaps the wherewithal of its donors, but this organization did survive (Grossberg, 1997: 329; Acheson, 1926: 161).

Types of Cases

New York Legal Aid Society's caseload, with some important exceptions, was typical of the kinds of legal problems that poor residents of large cities encountered. Clients came with complaints of withheld wages, uncollected debts, employment agency fraud, defrauding by attorneys, failure of banks to pay deposits, lost baggage and insurance claims, various consumer swindles, and other commercial disputes. The Society represented wage earners exclusively, and only those whom no other attorneys would represent. It turned down accident cases, shied away from divorce cases, and, for most of this period, avoided criminal defense (Schmitt, 1912: 41, 9; Maguire, 1928: 76-104).

Chicago legal aid attorneys served a similar clientele and offered counsel for the same type of cases. Virtually all its cases involved civil matters. In its early years, the largest category of cases involved wage claims, where clients were plaintiffs. Over time, however, and especially after Legal Aid became a subordinate part of United Charities, it represented clients as defendants against retailers' claims for debt and in intra-class disputes, mostly in domestic relations (Katz, 1982: 40). So many of its cases involved abandonment – or as it gently put it, "domestic infelicity" – that it had to station a worker at the Court of Domestic Relations. Yet, like New York Legal Aid, it was reluctant to take on divorce cases, refusing to provide a lawyer unless a "social necessity" arose. Under United Charities' aegis, all divorce cases had to be approved by district supervisors rather than the senior attorney. Exceptions to the rule that all cases be civil were made for United Charities clients or family members of clients appearing in police court. The Legal Aid Bureau did not ration services by restricting the hours available for intake, but the number of clients fell for several years after United Charities took over the organization. Cases were dropped because the Bureau reclassified some client inquiries as social work problems. In other instances, Jewish clients, at the request of the

Jewish Social Service Bureau, were sent there, and still others avoided visiting the Bureau offices out of a fear of being tainted with charity (Gariepy, 1926: 35, 40).

Unlike many legal aid organizations during the Progressive Era, Boston provided appellate services. It did so to secure equal legal representation to the poor. As important, it pursued appeals because they clarified the law as it applied to the poor. In keeping with the Progressive Era ideal of legal rationality and granting access to the courts rather than zealous advocacy, Smith declared, "it is not of chief interest whether the legal aid organization win or lose their appeals; the prime consideration is that our common law system should have a fair chance to work itself out by having those issues fairly argued, not from one but from both points of view" (quoted in Grossberg, 1978b: 17).

Advocacy and the Courts

Legal aid attorneys felt the need to balance efficiency, justice, and their commitment to a professional ethic of service to the poor. In general, though, rather than being the zealous advocates that those who paid for their legal services expected, they rarely practiced aggressive lawyering. In civil cases, New York Legal Aid attorneys urged their clients to follow Abraham Lincoln's advice:

> Discourage litigation. Persuade your neighbor to compromise whenever you can. Point out to them how the nominal winner is often the real loser – in fees, expenses, and waste of time (quoted in Davis, 1993: 10).

Attorneys faced several barriers to zealous advocacy. Heavy caseloads prevented them from devoting the time necessary to pursue all available options. More important, the organizations' deep ambivalence toward their clients discouraged litigation. Attorneys were concerned that their clients were the victims of sharpies, con men, and unscrupulous employers, but they also lamented their willingness to engage in litigious behavior to settle scores or use the legal system to gain undeserved advantage. Progressive Era literature about legal aid was replete with examples of clients, especially immigrants, who through their ignorance and naïveté fell prey to various schemes, frauds, and malefactors. Legal aid societies helped those who seemed particularly helpless and pitiful: (1) a young girl who supported her mother by running errands and was cheated by her employer, (2) the dimwitted "Jack Tars" (sailors) who were taken in by a "Doctor" at an "Anatomical Museum" who convinced them to the tune of twenty-five dollars apiece that they had but a few weeks to live unless they entered into "treatment," and (3) the "poor assistant to a physician" who "bought" a home lot on a Staten Island golf course (Watkins, 1906: 45).

There was always the problem of sifting out the genuinely aggrieved from those who wanted to game the system for other ends. But heavy caseloads made policing the clientele difficult. The problem of determining which claims were just was complicated by the alleged propensity of some groups – Jews mostly, but also blacks – to litigate for its own sake. Attorney-in-charge of the East Side Branch of New York Legal Aid Society, Arthur G. H. Lester, wrote in 1902:

> [T]here is a strong litigious instinct in the residents of this section, caused, for one thing, by the great ease with which they can invoke the law in this country as compared with their homes abroad. This pleasure in litigating is the rule not the exception. Thirty per cent of the clients for whom we have collected money have stated to me, when their money was paid over, that they sought satisfaction more than remuneration (*Annual Report*, 1902: 32).

The extent to which legal aid organizations and their attorneys would advocate for clients depended on how they interpreted their role in protecting the interests of society. They were officers of the court interested in the efficient operation of the legal system. Reginald Heber Smith, whose experience directing Boston Legal Aid led him to write the legal aid movement's manifesto and policy guide, *Justice and the Poor* (1919), argued that the system's injustices resulted from structural defects in the court system. In addition to a lack of affordable counsel, the poor faced interminable delays and onerous court fees. Legal aid organizations had two responsibilities: to keep cases out of the courts and, when possible, to streamline court procedures.

Legal aid organizations had commitments to client service, but they carried them out in accordance with an ideological framework that emphasized individual responsibility and conformity to wage labor and the political system. While Progressive reformers strove to create courts that were a "true laboratory of progressive democracy, flexible instruments of public welfare and social governance" (Willrich, 2003: xxvi), legal aid organizations were largely absent from those experiments. On the whole they supported conservative values of social order rather than engaging in the "sociological jurisprudence" that Pound and other legal reformers urged. In New York, in the limited amount of criminal defense work that the Legal Aid Society undertook, they worked closely with the police, often helping them gain confessions of guilt from their clients (Tweed, 1954: 28). Boston, Chicago, and New York Societies did their part to bolster middle-class heteronormativity by discouraging divorce, and, in the various domestic relations courts, they sought to enforce financial obligations on wage-earning husbands (Igra, 2000). During a time of national labor agitation and a growth in political movements on the Left, leaders of the legal aid movement such as Arthur Von Briesen and Reginald Heber Smith cautioned that their organizations should be supported as bulwarks against anarchism and communism (*Annual Report*, 1893, 1895, 1903; Smith, 1919: 10-12, 182).

The degree to which legal aid societies engaged in law reform or mobilized public pressure to attack the problems of poverty differed in time and across organizations. Commentators, especially lawyers writing since the advent of the Legal Services Program, have been mostly dismissive of the legal aid movement's attempts to tackle either the worst manifestations or the root causes of poverty. In a spirited defense of the early years of Legal Services, Alan Houseman, a founder and director of Michigan Legal Services, claimed that "legal aid societies did not identify problems of the poor that could be addressed with legal action. Indeed, the common concerns and needs of the poor were largely irrelevant to legal aid societies. The purpose, rather, was individual service to clients who happened to be indigent." (Houseman, 1995: 1671, 1684; see also Davis, 1993; Johnson, 1974; in contrast, see Grossberg, 1997; Pious, 1971.)[2]

It is understandable that early Legal Services leaders such as Houseman and Johnson would contrast Legal Services' advocacy to the supposedly deficient efforts of the legal aid societies. Yet in their haste to defend Legal Services they conflate different organizations and confuse a cultural critique of Progressive era reformers with the structural constraints that the founders of the poverty bar faced.

New York Legal Aid Society pursued means outside of the courts to ameliorate the burdens the poor faced, but its reform activities often placed the onus of overcoming poverty on the poor themselves. To "protect" clients from loan sharks, it lobbied for the passage of a law that mandated a copy of an assignment of wages be filed with employers. The embarrassment that workers would experience from having to pay back usurious loans was supposed to curb them from doing business with disreputable creditors. Von Briesen wrote in the Society's *Annual Report*: "He knows that it is apt to go hard with him if his employer discovers that he has been assigning his wages, and the requirement that knowledge of the assignment be brought home to the employer before it can be valid has had a very salutary effect" (*Annual Report*, 1905; 37). The legislation's "salutary effect," though, was most likely its ability to stigmatize poverty.

Chicago's Legal Aid, on the other hand, had a reputation for more aggressive reform efforts. Its founding organizations were dedicated to charitable service and social reform – recall that founding members from the Ethical Culture Society suffered criticism for backing the Haymarket

---

[2] In fairness to Houseman, he does consider the lack of resources that plagued the early legal aid movement.

martyrs. Presidents of the Bureau of Justice and the Legal Aid Society were prominent social reformers, and the social distance between attorneys who worked at the Society and its leadership remained relatively close through the 1910s. Frank Tobey was active in New England abolitionist circles, and Rudolph Matz, who hailed from a family well known in Chicago's philanthropic community, made a reputation for himself representing the Society for the Prevention of Smoke in litigation against various factories. Staff attorneys of the Protective Society served on its board and joined with other board members in the ranks of prominent local attorneys (Katz, 1982: 34, 36).

Chicago Legal Aid Society's commitment to law reform and its championing of its clients' class interests waned by the 1920s, though. In 1919, Legal Aid became the Legal Aid Bureau of the United Charities of Chicago. While New York's and Boston's legal aid organizations had abjured the charge that they provided charity, in Chicago it became a subordinate department of the Windy City's premier charity-social work organization. United Charities, like other social work organizations, embraced the profession's turn to casework, which emphasized the individual psychological pathologies of the poor. It was, in social reformer A.J. Muste's words, that "social work had gone psychiatric in a world which had gone industrial" (quoted in Patterson, 1994: 26; on casework, see Katz, 1996: 170-72).

Even before Chicago Legal Aid had become subsumed under United Charities, it backed away from its reformist zeal. Matz, who served as president of Legal Aid Society from 1908 to 1917, had generally supported legislative reform activities, but over that period he increasingly backed efforts to pass permissive statutes that encouraged free market solutions to the problems of loan sharking and other consumer abuses, rather than prohibitive laws that regulated what businesses could do. This approach was in keeping with an orientation toward procedural justice that saw its fulfillment in the idea that "equal justice" was equivalent to access to one's day in court. Others in the legal aid movement, including activists associated with settlement houses in Chicago, urged support for public campaigns for law reform. At the 1916 national legal aid convention, Matz supported Reginald Heber Smith, the Harvard Law graduate and leader of Boston Legal Aid, in his push to put the National Alliance of Legal Aid Societies on record as favoring equal access. Writing in the Chicago Legal Aid Society's *Annual Report* for 1916, Matz explained the organization's apolitical approach:

> To my mind it is a mistake for the Legal Aid Society to attempt preventative legislation except in an incidental way.... The minute we begin to do that, the minute that becomes the primary object of the Society in the eyes of the public, we are going to be known as reformers who "have a mission," or we

are going to be considered "visionary" (quoted in Katz, 1982: 37-38).

The Expanding Scope of Legal Aid

In 1916 there were legal aid organizations in 4 cities employing 62 full-time and 113 part-time lawyers who handled 117,201 cases. Those organizations spent $181,408. Almost a decade later in 1925 and nearly fifty years after the founding of the Deutscher Rechts-Schutz Verein, following the ABA's organizational commitment to legal aid, there were fifty-seven legal aid organizations in the United States, all but nine privately supported and controlled. They had in the previous year represented over 120,000 clients. Brownell estimates that in 1947 there were 67 organizations providing civil and criminal representation to 242,000 clients. Given the growth in population and urbanization, the doubling of clients represented a marginal increase in the percentage of poor receiving legal services. Assuming that each year one in one-hundred people residing in the U.S. required legal services that they could not afford, he estimated that in 1916, during the first flourishing of legal aid organizations, fifty-one percent of the poor in areas with legal aid societies and needing aid received it. In 1947, the number rose to fifty-five percent (Clarke, 1926: 54; Brownell, 1951: 36-37; Abel, 1985; 442).

The Role of Indigent Criminal Defense

America has a long history of *pro bono* defense, constitutional guarantees of the right to counsel, and formal mechanisms to assign lawyers. Yet indigent criminal defendants have infrequently received adequate legal representation. The right to assistance of counsel requires three components: the right to retain counsel, to have counsel assigned for those who cannot afford it, and to be effectively represented or to have zealous advocacy (Note, 1971). The struggle for the right to assistance of counsel has had to proceed on all three fronts.

The right to an attorney in criminal trials was a revolutionary feature of the American legal system in that it ran counter to the theory and practice of common law. English common law prohibited lawyers for defendants in criminal proceedings, although in some of the colonies as early as the 1730s lawyers began appearing on behalf of the accused. It was also revolutionary in the sense that its codification in the Bill of Rights resulted from the American experience in opposing British rule. The Declaration of Independence, among its other charges, enumerated a list of complaints against the king that he acted arbitrarily and with deceit to undermine an American system of jurisprudence: he abolished laws, denied trial by jury, dissolved jurisdictional boundaries, and shipped defendants to distant courts. In this context in the post-independence

period, the Bill of Rights guaranteed the right to counsel in federal criminal cases.

In the early days of the Republic, most state constitutions recognized
the right of counsel for criminal defendants. New Hampshire was the first
state to assign counsel for capital cases, and, in 1795, New Jersey enacted
legislation to assign counsel for all indigent defendants (Association of the
Bar of the City of New York and National Legal Aid and Defender Association, 1959: 41-42; Friedman, 1993: 57). New York, like other states, formally recognized the right to counsel in criminal cases, and an 1881 amendment to criminal procedure law provided that defendants facing serious
charges who requested an attorney would be appointed one on a *pro bono*
basis. Yet the state allocated no funds for indigent defendants, relying on
private attorneys to represent the poor without compensation. The idea
was that *pro bono* work was an "incident of the profession" (McConville
and Mirsky, 1989: 1).

The organized bar, and particularly the legal aid movement, were reluctant advocates for criminal defense for the poor. Sectors of the bar
supported the right of the poor to an attorney in criminal cases, and the
1908 ABA *Canons of Professional Ethics* urged lawyers to take seriously
judicial appointments for indigent prisoners. But the *Canons* were aspirational, and less than a third of the states had adopted them by 1940. Few
members of the ABA at the time practiced criminal law, and the legal aid
movement that they led largely shunned criminal defense and the lawyers
who represented criminal lawyers. There was greater sentiment for the
need for indigent criminal defense among leading jurists and the academi-
cally inclined in associations such as the American Law Institute. In 1930,
it drafted a Model Code that called on trial judges to appoint lawyers at
arraignment for those accused of felonies who needed but could not afford
them (Maute, 2002: 111; Katkin, 2005: 460-61). These lawyers, too, had
few social or professional ties to the practicing criminal defense bar, nor
had they much direct experience in the criminal courts. As a result, their
proposal to appoint counsel for poor felony defendants effectively assigned
the bar's responsibility to those often least capable of providing zealous
advocacy, that is, to the inexperienced, poorly trained, or those lacking
ambition or skill whose propinquity to the hapless accused was inversely
proportional to their own success in the profession.

Legal aid societies noted that assigned counsel often used their court-
imposed obligation as an opportunity to extract a fee from the accused.
Writing in 1897, New York Legal Aid Society Attorney-in-Chief Robert
Goeller observed:

> As a rule these [assigned] attorneys try to get from the pris-
> oner or his friends a fee. If unsuccessful in this attempt they
> pay little attention to the case, make little, if any, preparation,

> often not appearing in Court at the trial. (quoted in Maguire,
> 1928: 261-62)[3]

This was not a problem solely associated with early twentieth century representation, either. As late as the 1950s the assigned-counsel system served over half the U.S. population and was utilized in both urban and rural areas. Federal Judge Edward J. Dinnock recounted the system in New York City at that time:

> When I came to the Bar in New York, a row of seedy charac-
> ters, hardly distinguishable from the prisoners used to sit on
> the front bench in the Court of General Sessions. When an ac-
> cused person would appear before the judge for pleading and
> state that he had no money to pay counsel, the judge would
> announce "I will appoint Mr. X to represent you" and the first
> of the row of seedy characters would engage the accused in
> earnest conference in the back of the courtroom. The confer-
> ence would ostensibly concern the facts of the case but, in re-
> ality, was a searching inquiry rather similar to an examina-
> tion in proceedings supplementary to execution, designed to
> disclose any assets possessed by the accused or his relatives
> or friends. The percentage of guilty pleas was much higher in
> the cases where the search proved fruitless (cited in Special
> Committee, 1959: 120).

Lest one believe that the problem has disappeared with Constitutional guarantees to representation in criminal cases, a sobering report by North Carolina's Common Sense Foundation concludes otherwise. It found that in 2002, thirty-five or one in six of the state's death row inmates had an appointed attorney who had been disbarred, suspended, or otherwise disciplined by the state (Burtman, 2002).

Yet at the time, legal aid societies shunned criminal defense. New York Legal Aid Society had no explicit policy against representing criminal defendants, but in attempting to conserve funds and, one suspects, out of a preference for aiding the deserving poor, it generally did not do so. There was concern for "impecunious Germans who had fallen into the hands of the police through ignorance of the laws here, through recklessness or misguidance" and "poor innocent Germans ... kept for weeks and months in prison." Systematic attempts to provide criminal defense were thwarted by an inability to raise funds. The Society hired for a brief time a criminal

---

[3] Complaints against the lower echelons of the bar by legal aid attorneys should be taken with several grains of salt. They had institutional and often personal biases against private practitioners who served the poor. While many, undoubtedly, were "shysters," much of the established bar's animus was directed at their immigrant status, ethnicity, and class background. For a more balanced view of their role, see Auerbach (1976); Bergstrom (1992); Anthes (2000).

attorney in 1906, and in 1909 it attempted to raise $10,000 to open a Criminal Branch but gave up on the effort when it could procure only $1,000 in pledges. In 1913 and 1914, it took on twenty-five criminal cases each year (Maguire, 1928: 17, 267-68; *Annual Reports*, 1913, 1914).

While those who could afford private criminal defense expected tireless and zealous advocacy, legal aid organizations delivered criminal representation, like its civil counterpart, that aspired to balance a need for a smoothly functioning court system, social control of the "dangerous classes," and justice for the wrongly accused. When in 1910 the Manhattan District Attorney assigned a deputy to the Essex Street Police Court, New York Legal Aid recalled its attorney to its main office so as not to duplicate efforts (*Annual Report*, 1910: 11). It expected its attorneys to attend to the moral compass of their clients, "to strive for something better than merely to 'beat the case,' whatever the means employed or whatever the guilt of the defendant." Attorneys whose clients were guilty but refused to confess and plead their guilt were encouraged to ask to be relieved of their assignment (Voluntary Defenders Committee, 1917). Despite an inability to raise funds for criminal defense from the bar, the Association of the Bar of the City of New York and other lawyers objected to a public defender office on the grounds that the need for indigent criminal defense "should be met not by the creation of one public office to contest with another, the one representing the state and the other the individual" (Voluntary Defenders Committee, 1917).

Regardless of the objections voiced in New York and other mostly East Coast cities, where 'old money" and entrenched philanthropic elites held sway, public defender organizations had their advocates.[4] Locales with strong populist traditions or politically powerful labor movements were fertile grounds for public defender offices. In other cases, mayors or state legislators lobbied for them (Goldman, 1919: 87-98). Oklahoma was the first jurisdiction to create a "public defender" when it provided the Commissioner of Charities with an official whose duty was to "institute, prosecute, or defend any suit or action in any court on behalf of any minors, orphans, defectives, dependents, and delinquents." The office was abolished in 1914, but that same year Los Angeles set up a public defender office and hired its staff through civil service examinations. Brownell found that in the late 1940s there were twenty-nine public defender offices nationwide. More than a decade later that number grew to eighty jurisdictions with public defender agencies (Association of the Bar of the City of New York and National Legal Aid and Defender Association, 1959: 44; Brownell, 1951: 35; Smith, 1919: 117).

---

4 On the reluctance of "old money" philanthropic elites to support government-run social services, see Katz (1996: 127).

The Evolving Right to a Criminal Defense

The right to retain criminal defense was guaranteed by the Sixth Amendment, but it was not enforceable in the states until the 1960s. As far back as 1833, the Supreme Court ruled in *Barron v. Baltimore*, 32 U.S. 243, that none of the privileges and immunities guaranteed in the first eight amendments to the Constitution were enforceable against the states. As a result, the right to counsel in criminal cases applied only to U.S. citizens in federal courts (Albert-Goldberg and Hartman, 1983: 98). It was up to the states themselves to apply, or not, the principle of representation in their courts. Many states guaranteed the right to legal counsel in criminal cases, but it was not until the mid-1950s that all states required that counsel be appointed in at least some criminal cases. A number of states, either through statute or case law, restricted the right to an attorney only to capital cases or those that could result in a sentence of life imprisonment (Katkin, 2005: 461-64).

The federal courts showed greater respect for the rights of poor criminal defendants than the states. In the case of *Downer v. Dunaway*, 53 F.2d 586 (5th Cir. 1931), John Downer, a black man, was accused of raping a white woman in a small Georgia town. While awaiting arraignment in the local jail, a crowd of over a thousand attempted to seize and lynch him. Through a clever ruse and under cover of darkness, a contingent of National Guardsmen spirited him out of town. Hoping to quell the citizenry's passions, town leaders promised a speedy trial. The trial judge appointed three attorneys to defend Downer – a move guaranteeing that no single lawyer would face the prospect that he alone would oppose local white sentiments. Despite having three lawyers, three more than many poor black defendants received, Downer's attorneys provided less than zealous advocacy: they neither moved for a change of venue nor asked for a continuance. Instead, without leaving the courthouse, they prepared for his capital trial in less than two hours (Emanuel, 1996: 229). The Fifth Circuit Court of Appeals ordered a retrial, stating:

> It goes without saying that an accused who is unable by reason of poverty to employ counsel is entitled to be defended in all his rights as full and to the same extent as is an accused who is able to employ his own counsel to represent him. (*Downer v. Dunaway*, 53 F.2d 586, 589 (5th Cir. 1931).)

The issue before the Court was not assignment of counsel; Downer, in fact, had three appointed attorneys, and even as early as the 1930s virtually all states recognized the right to counsel in capital cases either in their constitutions or in statutes. The issue was the *quality* of representation, an issue to which the courts and public interest attorneys would repeatedly return. Before the issue of effective counsel could be codified in law, though, it had to have a constitutional basis. *Downer* proved to be an important turning point because it raised the substantive issue of zealous advocacy. It would be up to *Powell v. Alabama*, 287 U.S. 45 (1932), to begin addressing the problem of due process.

The issue of due process rested on the Fourteenth Amendment (1868), which states that "no state shall ... deprive any person of life, liberty, or property, without due process of law." Due process is not justice but a prerequisite to justice, a guarantee to a fair trial. As Justice Felix Frankfurter wrote in *Joint Anti-Fascist Refugee Committee v. McGrath*, 341 U.S. 123 (1951), it is a "profound attitude of fairness between man and man, and more particularly between individual and government.... Due process is not a mechanical instrument. It is not a yardstick. It is a delicate process of adjustment inescapably involving the exercise of judgment by those whom the constitution entrusted with the unfolding of the process" (quoted in McIntyre, 1987: 18).

In *Powell v. Alabama*, nine young blacks – they ranged in age from 13 to 21 – were accused of raping two white women in the rural town of Scottsboro, Alabama. The Scottsboro case was an international *cause célèbre*. The defendants were undoubtedly innocent, but they had little hope of receiving a fair trial. Indeed, but for the presence of the state militia, they faced an inevitable lynching. The Alabama Constitution required counsel be appointed for indigents in capital cases, and the trial judge assigned two attorneys – one appointed the morning of the trial was from Tennessee and attempted to decline appointment due to his unfamiliarity with state criminal law. The defense counsel did not cross-examine witnesses, present its own witnesses, except the defendants, nor present opening or closing arguments. The U.S. Supreme Court, in an appeal argued by NAACP lawyers, among others, held that "given the circumstances" – a capital offense, the hostile environment, the status of the defendants as "young, ignorant and illiterate" – and a crime "regarded with especial horror in the community where they were to be tried," the right to be heard would be ' of little avail if it did not comprehend the right to be heard by counsel.... The failure of the trial court to make an effective appointment of counsel was a denial of due process within the meaning of the Fourteenth Amendment" (287 U.S. 45 (1932)). Six years later, in *Johnson v. Zerbst*, 304 U.S. 458 (1938), the Supreme Court ruled that indigent defendants charged with a felony in federal courts had a Sixth Amendment right to appointed counsel.

What was important in the cases following *Powell v. Alabama* was the idea that "special circumstances" required the assistance of counsel. Those special circumstances would always apply in capital trials, but they might not always occur in other cases. Ten years later, in *Betts v. Brady*, 316 U.S. 455 (1942), the Supreme Court found that Smith Betts, who had been charged with robbery in a Maryland state court and whose trial judge refused him an appointed attorney, could not claim special circumstances and did not warrant an appointed lawyer. It denied the automatic right to have an attorney appointed but recognized that "fundamental fairness" was a goal by which a trial should be judged. The Court stated that "asserted denial [of due process] is to be tested by an appraisal of the totality of facts in a given case. That which may, in one setting, constitute a denial of fundamental fairness, shocking to the universal sense of justice, may, in other circumstances, and in light of other considerations, fall short of such denial." From 1950 until the Court ruled in *Gideon v. Wainwright*, 372 U.S. 335 (1963), however, the Court invariably ruled in favor of defendants who claimed due process had been denied as a result of failure to appoint counsel (McIntyre, 1987: 20).

In 1963, the Supreme Court in a unanimous decision overturned the robbery conviction of Clarence Earl Gideon, a white man in his early fifties whom the journalist Anthony Lewis (1964: 5-6) characterized as "a perfectly harmless human being, rather likeable, but one tossed aside by life." The Panama City, Florida police had arrested Gideon for breaking into a pool hall from which coins from a juke box and cigarette machine had been pilfered and some beer and wine had been stolen. The presiding judge denied his request for an attorney, and after a trial in which Gideon presented his defense – he called eight witnesses – the jury found him guilty. The judge sentenced Gideon to the maximum sentence, five years in prison.

Gideon faced no special circumstances: he was mentally sound; he experienced no particular bias during the trial; and the proof and charges against him were not especially complicated. Furthermore, for a man without legal training, he did a credible job. His case presented a perfect challenge to *Betts* and the assumption that a layperson could receive a fair trial. According to Abe Fortas, who acted as his lawyer before the Supreme Court and later became a justice of the same court, Gideon "did very well for a layman, he acted like a lawyer. But it was a pitiful effort really. He may have committed this crime, but it was never proved by the prosecution. A lawyer – not a great lawyer, just an ordinary, competent lawyer – could have made ashes of the case" (quoted in Lewis, 1964: 65). The justices concurred, ruling that the quality of his defense was inadequate; in fact, the Court found it an "obvious truth" that a defendant "cannot be assured of a fair trial unless counsel is provided for him."

> Lawyers to prosecute are everywhere deemed essential to protect the public's interest in an orderly society. Similarly, there are few defendants charged with crimes, few indeed, who fail to hire the best lawyers they can get to prepare and present their defense. That government hires lawyers to

prosecute and defendants who have the money hire lawyers to defend are the strongest indications of the widespread belief that lawyers in criminal courts are necessities, not luxuries. The right of one charged with crime to counsel may not be deemed fundamental and essential in some countries, but it is in ours. (*Gideon v. Wainwright*, 372 U.S. 335 (1963), quoted in McIntyre, 1987: 21.)

The outcome of *Gideon* was immensely important but hardly surprising; the Court appointed Fortas to defend Gideon undoubtedly knowing that he would challenge *Betts*. It was not a contentious issue among prosecutors, either. Twenty-three state attorneys general signed an *amicus* brief supporting Gideon with only Alabama and North Carolina siding with Florida (Walker, 1990: 252). On the same day that the Court ruled in *Gideon*, it also held in *Douglas v. California*, 372 U.S. 353 (1963), that states were required, if defendants requested, to appoint counsel on the first appeal following conviction. In 1972, *Argersinger v. Hamlin*, 407 U.S. 25, resulted in the high court ruling that absent a knowing and intelligent waiver, a misdemeanant may not be imprisoned unless represented by counsel.

The Court's decisions leading up to and including *Gideon* and *Argersinger* guaranteed the right to counsel for anyone facing imprisonment who could not afford an attorney. Other Supreme Court rulings extended effective representation for the criminally accused. In 1961, in *Mapp v. Ohio*, 367 U.S. 643, the Court extended the exclusionary rule, which bars the use of illegally obtained evidence, to the states, reasoning that the Fourth Amendment afforded protection against unreasonable search and seizure.

Post-*Gideon*, the Court has adopted a "critical stage" test in determining a right to counsel. While the Sixth Amendment asserted the right to counsel in "criminal prosecutions," what was generally understood by that term was the right to counsel when a defendant appeared in court. *Escobedo v. Illinois*, 378 U.S. 478 (1964), in which the Court held that defendants in custody had a right to consult with their attorneys, even before they were indicted, raised the question: When does the right to counsel begin?

The Supreme Court began to answer that question in *Miranda v. Arizona*, 384 U.S. 436 (1966). Ernesto Miranda was convicted in the state court of kidnapping and rape, and the Arizona Supreme Court upheld the conviction. Shortly after his arrest the police placed him in interrogation without advising him that he had the right to have an attorney present. After two hours he issued a confession, to which he later objected when prosecutors entered it into evidence in court. Writing for the 5 to 4 majority, Chief Justice Earl Warren, who began his career as a prosecutor, asserted that an accused's right to remain silent and have an attorney began at the time of "custodial interrogation," i.e., when a person is under arrest and being interrogated. During oral arguments, Warren remarked, "I didn't know we could arrest people in this country for investigation. Wouldn't you say it was accusatory when a man was locked in jail?" (quoted in Schwartz, 1993: 280-81). In *United States v. Wade*, 388 U.S. 218 (1967), the Court ruled that there existed critical stages at which the "law enforcement machinery involved critical confrontations of the accused" (quoted in Note, 1971: 5). At those stages the right to counsel was necessary to protect the integrity of the adversary system itself.

The expansion of the right to counsel and strengthening of due process in criminal trials was part of a larger Due Process revolution. It went beyond criminal law and extended the Fourteenth Amendment's concept of equal protection to strike down the legal edifices of such disparate areas of American life as school segregation (*Brown v. Board of Education of Topeka, Kansas*, 347 U.S. 483 (1954)), poll taxes (*Harper v. Virginia Board of Election Commissioners*, 383 U.S. 663 (1966)), and minimum-time residency requirements for welfare (*Shapiro v. Thompson*, 394 U.S. 618 (1969)). (See generally Bussiere, 1997.)

As we will see, the vast expansion of individual rights that public interest lawyers advocated for and the Warren Court upheld expanded the opportunities for public interest lawyers to use the law in the civil as well as criminal realms. The settling of the right to counsel spurred the states to institutionalize and expand public defender offices, and the series of cases that refined the right to effective counsel forced public defenders and their organizations to grapple with how they could best engage in zealous advocacy (Walker, 1990: 252).

3

THE ORIGINS OF THE LEGAL SERVICES CORPORATION

In the 1960s, the impetus for federally funded legal services for the poor came not from extant legal aid organizations or leaders of the bar – recall that lawyers were laggards in supporting the original legal aid societies, as well – but from a variety of actors outside of or at the margins of the legal profession, who took advantage of its service ideal. Several of the early forays into providing legal services outside of the Legal Aid model originated from private foundations, especially the Ford Foundation. Federal agencies, and even the remnants of the settlement house movement, were also involved. They provided early financing, ideas, political support, and inspiration to those who would lead the efforts to create what eventually became the Legal Services Corporation (LSC).

The origins of Legal Services are best located in three demonstration projects that challenged the legal aid model for delivering services to the poor. Although they were each different, their founders consciously designed them to move beyond the model that Reginald Heber Smith championed of insuring the poor "their day in court." Each, in its own way, saw legal aid for the poor not as its goal but as a means to eliminating poverty. They also saw delivering legal services as a necessary but insufficient means for achieving the goal.

New Haven, Connecticut: Community Progress, Inc. (CPI)

The first of the three projects began in New Haven on January 2, 1963, in two small neighborhood offices under the auspices of Community Progress, Inc. (CPI), a nonprofit funded by the Ford Foundation to carry out its "Gray Areas" program. The project lasted but seven weeks, undone by a conflict between CPI's holistic approach to combating poverty and the founding attorneys' commitment to professional autonomy and zealous advocacy.

Ford's commitment to providing legal services in its Gray Areas program had grown out of efforts to start up law school clinics and bolster public defender offices. Foundation executive William Pincus had pioneered those areas and extended the idea of representing the poor into the realm of civil law. He encouraged Paul Ylvisaker, who headed the Foundation's Law and Governance department and initiated the Gray Areas program, to include civil legal services in the program, but there were no plans to undertake criminal defense, which would be left to local public defender offices.

When in late 1962 the Ford Foundation decided to push forward with its anti-poverty program, it chose New Haven. Its "dynamic, progressive" mayor had undertaken an ambitious program of urban renewal. And the city was home to Yale University, which provided the program with intellectual resources and the social prestige that the Foundation gravitated toward. Ylvisaker met in New Haven with a group of social planners, lawyers, and local politicians and activists. Among them were Edgar and Jean Cahn. Edgar, who held a Ph.D. in political science and at the time was attending Yale Law School, had attracted attention because of a paper he had written about social-service delivery systems. Jean, his wife, had recently graduated from Yale Law School and would become one of CPI's two attorneys.

Ylvisaker had a vision of a radically different anti-poverty program, which consisted of decentralized offices located in poor neighborhoods. CPI would combine social services, consumer education, health care, and legal aid. Teams of social workers and lawyers would, according to the CPI's funding proposal, "diagnose, refer, and coordinate" the legal problems of the poor. While it hardly embraced impact litigation or considered its mandate political lawyering, it could not avoid the systemic concerns of its neighbors and so worked closely with local black groups and undertook several civil rights cases. It was a model that ran counter to most legal aid organizations, which concentrated their facilities in a single downtown location, rejected holistic attempts to overcome poverty, and refused political issues. As a result, CPI's legal services had no connection with New Haven Legal Aid Society (Johnson, 1974: 22).

In an ironic twist, CPI fell victim to exactly the sort of political interference that legal aid societies had predicted would accompany public funding. The parents of an accused rapist asked Jean Cahn to become involved in their son's defense. The case involved a young black man and a young white woman. CPI management had directed Cahn to remain in the background, serving as a sort of advisory co-counsel to the local public defender; but when her co-counsel withdrew from the case, she felt she had no choice but to offer her client a thorough defense. Cahn asserted in the local papers her client's claim that the woman had consented to sexual advances. And "it was not long before irate New Havenites, stung by the accusation that one of their young white girls may have submitted to a Negro, shifted their anger from the accused rapist to his defender, Jean Cahn, and her employer, Community Progress, Inc." (Johnson, 1974: 23). Not having anticipated the conflict between Cahn's professional ethics and the political constraints that CPI faced, Ford's first experiment in providing legal services to the poor ended abruptly.[1]

New York City: Mobilization for Youth (MFY)

The Ford Foundation did not give up easily. Its next foray into legal services for the poor involved Mobilization for Youth (MFY), located in the Lower East Side neighborhood of New York City. MFY had its origins in the desires of leaders of the settlement house movement and city officials to control growing gang violence. In the summer of 1956, five days of escalating gang fighting between black and Puerto Rican youths threatened to spread beyond the Lower East Side and engulf the city in warfare. A cease-fire negotiated by the Henry Street Settlement (HSS) and the City Youth Board, dubbed the "Truce of '56" made national news.

The attention this urban diplomacy brought to the settlement houses gave hope to the neighborhood charities that they might gain a reprieve from their otherwise declining financial fortunes. It also encouraged them in ambitious plans that they might play a crucial role in combating the poverty and social disintegration that the charitable reformers saw about them. As a result, the Henry Street Settlement took the lead in putting together a coalition of neighborhood social service agencies, mostly operating under the umbrella of the Lower East Side Neighborhood Association (LENA) and city agencies, that over several years would become MFY. HSS officially settled on launching MFY in a meeting of its board in June 1957 when board member and businessman J.M. Kaplan pledged the support of his foundation to the effort. Four and a half years later, a different set of actors with an expanded mission to fight poverty would finally put MFY into action (Helfgot, 1981: 19). It would be an organizational model for a radical version of the War on Poverty as well as a prototype of the activist neighborhood law office that many in the legal services movement hoped to build.

The settlement house movement, and in particular the Henry Street Settlement, was a center of activity for New York's philanthropic elite, "a political front for aspiring Democratic, Fusion, and Reform Party politicians, and the chief broker of private social-welfare resources" in lower Manhattan (Raynor, 1999: 212). It hoped to secure funding to expand its "Pre-Delinquent Gang Project." To traditional after-school programs and remedial education efforts, the Pre-Delinquent Gang Project added psychological testing to identify 8–12 year olds in danger of becoming delin-

---

[1] Earl Johnson, Jr. (1974: 23) is curiously and uncharacteristically unenlightening in assigning responsibility for the closing of CPI's legal office. In a classically evasive use of the passive voice, he writes, "New Haven's neighborhood law offices were ordered to suspend operations."

quents and then sequestered them from the larger population of young people enrolled in the settlement house after-school programs. Despite assiduously courting members of Congress and calling on its social networks in the foundation world, it failed to secure National Institute for Mental Health or Ford Foundation funding.

Although funding for the HSS/MFY initial proposal failed, sympathetic gatekeepers for NIMH, notably Russell Sage Foundation sociologist Leonard S. Cottrell, Jr., persuaded the MFY board to push for a change in strategy. Instead of treating the problem of delinquency as a psychological problem rooted in dysfunctional minority individuals, Cottrell advocated for a more community-centered approach to delinquency. He argued in a manner heavily influenced by Émile Durkheim that existing neighborhood institutions were not effectively communicating with each other or with neighborhood residents. He stressed that social and educational policies needed to incorporate "community competence" – a feature, by implication, that the settlement houses were sorely lacking. Cottrell saw in the HSS a connection to local political and social elites that would be advantageous to future attempts at funding, but he felt that to secure support from NIMH a more sociological approach was needed. He introduced the HSS board to Lloyd E. Ohlin and Richard A. Cloward, two sociologists at Columbia University's School of Social Work. Ohlin had extensive ties to a network of practitioners in the field of juvenile delinquency who worked as consultants to the Ford Foundation (Raynor, 1999: 211-13).

Ohlin and Cloward were in the process of publishing *Delinquency and Opportunity: A Theory of Delinquent Gangs* (1960) when they took over the grant-writing for what would be MFY's successful application for government funding. Building on the recent work of Columbia University sociologist Robert K. Merton – Cloward was a doctoral student of Merton's – *Delinquency and Opportunity* argued that gang formation was a rational response to a lack of mainstream opportunities, opportunities that had been foreclosed because of forms of institutionalized racism that were endemic to capitalism. What they argued was a more explicitly radical formulation of Merton's thesis that urban chaos and violence resulted from disaffected residents' lack of an opportunity to participate in the dominant society. Having no legitimate means to achieve the rewards of mainstream society, delinquents sought alternative routes to these goals and were less likely to be constrained by prevalent social mores. Merton's theory centered on "the acute pressures created by the discrepancy between culturally induced goals and socially structured opportunities" (Merton, 1957: 178). It was structural inequality and racism rather than individual psychology that created the conditions favorable to juvenile delinquency, according to Ohlin and Cloward. In their redrafted MFY grant proposal they wrote:

> Where in the past attention has been focused upon the in-
> dividual delinquent, or the gang, or the parents of the de-
> linquent, or upon some other aspect of the total problem, we
> argue for an approach which seeks to alter the basic structure
> of the community. By changing the defeating conditions
> which confront the young, we expect that basic changes in
> their behavior and orientation will also occur. And we argue
> further that the immensity of the task ought not to deter us
> from mounting a major effort to achieve this end (quoted in
> Raynor, 1999: 213-14).

What the MFY board did was create a policy coalition that drew on
HSS's connections to New York City's political establishment and charitable social service elite while at the same time advancing the theoretical and
political agenda of social scientists able to procure funding from NIMH
and whose policy concerns shared some similarity with the Ford Foundation's approach to combating poverty. Ohlin's and Cloward's, but especially
Cloward's, radicalism was not shared by Pincus and Ylvisaker at Ford, but
it represented a clear break with the settlement house movement's view
that poverty resulted from individual psychological failure. Ohlin and
Cloward also shared Ford's commitment to desegregation. David Hunter
who headed the Foundation's Office of Juvenile Delinquency agreed with
Cloward and Ohlin that neighborhood institutions had to be a focus of
change, a position not shared throughout Ford (Raynor, 1999: 215).

The break with convention that MFY represented included other icon-
oclastic features. MFY planned to open storefronts throughout the Lower
East Side, bringing their services to area residents rather than relying on
clients coming to a central location such as the Henry Street Settlement
House. Opening storefronts had the practical value of "bringing law to the
people" and symbolically undermined the social distance between settlement house workers and area residents. It was a conscious reversal of the
settlement house reformers, whose Federal style architecture stood symbolically apart from the surrounding apartment buildings, which sought to
give an air of tranquility and order to the teeming slums.

Ohlin joined the Kennedy administration's Committee on Juvenile Delinquency and Child Crime (CJD), and Cloward became research director
of MFY. In June 1962, Robert Kennedy, then U.S. Attorney General, and
Mayor Robert Wagner, Jr., announced the founding of MFY and its receipt
of $13 million in grants. The bulk of the money came from New York City
and the NIMH, but a three-year federal community action project demonstration grant from CJD showed support from President Kennedy, and a
sizeable contribution from Ford demonstrated public-private sector
collaboration (*New York Herald Tribune*, September 6, 1964).

Legal services were not originally a part of the MFY anti-poverty plan.
MFY set out to provide a congeries of social services, not much different

than those delivered by traditional charitable agencies, but in encouraging clients to seek out MFY's assistance and press for solutions to particular problems, clients became constituents of often contentious politics. In a process that Daniel Patrick Moynihan (1969; see also Helfgot, 1974) would characterize as the "professionalization of reform" and through pressure from client families, MFY created a demand for intervention with the police, with welfare agencies, and in the courts. MFY's place would be to provide expertise. It contracted with the Vera Foundation, a New York City organization devoted to research and criminal justice reform, to draft a proposal for a program of legal services. The Vera Foundation recommended a program of direct legal services, legal education for lay persons on staff and in the community, and a program to encourage social change through legal research and policy lobbying. In November 1962, less than a year after the CPI aborted its program of neighborhood legal services in New Haven, MFY initiated its own program to provide lawyers for the poor. With a $50,000 CJD grant to run until the summer of 1964, it hired Edward Sparer, a young labor lawyer, to direct the program (Johnson, 1974: 23-24).

Originally, Vera proposed using law students and training community members to provide legal advice while all litigation would be referred to New York Legal Aid Society. Sparer immediately challenged the Vera Foundation's orientation, arguing that rather than relying on a traditional legal aid approach of piecemeal direct legal services, resources should be used for research and litigation to change the institutional structures that create and sustain poverty. In a memorandum dated January 20, 1964, George Brager, MFY program director, concurred that "the major objective of the Legal Unit is to affect social policy and administrative practices rather than to supply legal help to clients in an unplanful [sic] way." He went on to say, "There is nothing in the perspective of the Legal Unit which presumes that cases will be accepted indiscriminately as a result of [the] legal aid function. I know of no ethical stance which does not permit an individual lawyer or organization to choose its clients." Sparer saw MFY as an NAACP-like law office that would choose its cases to effect social change: "...ultimately, it is hoped that the poor will come to look upon the law as a tool which they can use on their own behalf to vindicate their rights and their interests – in the same way that law is used by other segments of the population" (quoted in Davis, 1993: 29, 31).

In its first full year of operation, MFY's four attorneys handled 350 housing cases, 60 workers' compensation actions, 50 consumer credit matters, and 200 criminal cases. Additionally, they worked on developing students' right to counsel in school suspensions, a brief for use in consumer fraud cases, and a plan for attacking problems in the provision of public benefits. According to Davis (1993: 31, emphasis added),

The MFY Legal Unit's work was characterized by activism and aggressive advocacy. As one attorney explained, MFY lawyers believed that their client was *more important than their professionalism*; they would violate court etiquette and the bounds of professional good taste by, for example, interrupting opposing counsel or following a judge into chambers to argue a case if it might mean a better result for their client.

MFY's stance toward zealous advocacy contrasted to Legal Aid's measured professionalism, but client demand, as the first-year caseload data suggest, prevented attorneys from embracing Sparer's vision of the Legal Unit's role as a NAACP-like law office. Four lawyers handling 660 cases left little time for developing impact litigation, especially if those lawyers were undertaking "activism and aggressive advocacy." At the same time, the political impact of MFY's litigation was not lost on City Hall.

MFY Legal Unit's caseload included suing the city's welfare department, which endangered city funding. In a preview of the political limits to legal autonomy that Legal Services would face throughout its existence, and that Legal Aid leaders had consistently cautioned against, New York City objected to funding litigation against itself and demanded an investigation of MFY's legal activities. In order to placate the city, MFY's Committee on Direct Operations prepared to review the Legal Unit's case-handling procedures, but Sparer refused to submit to review, arguing that "supervision and censure by nonlawyers would violate the confidential relationship between MFY lawyers and their clients." He contended that politically sensitive litigation demanded independence on the part of MFY. He appealed to the Legal Unit's Faculty Advisory Committee chair and Columbia University Law School professor Marvin Frankel, who would later become a federal appellate court judge. Frankel backed Sparer, arguing that MFY board attempts to interfere with the Legal Unit violated the relationship between a lawyer and client which was protected by the Canon of Legal Ethics. The board then brought the dispute before New York City District Justice Florence Kelley, who was the granddaughter of the social reformer Florence Kelley and was formerly in charge of New York Legal Aid Society's Juvenile Courts division. Judge Kelley upheld Frankel's argument that the city was free to curtail funding but also held that once it committed funding it could not exercise control over lawyers at the agency (Davis, 1993: 31–32; Johnson, 1974: 25).

Once again the issue of lawyers' autonomy asserted itself in how poverty lawyers would practice. Holistic approaches to combating poverty that combined social work, educational reform, and community empowerment had considerable cachet among charitable reformers, foundation policy entrepreneurs, and city officials. All of these groups hoped that by treating the manifold symptoms and causes of social chaos, and often not distinguishing between the two, they could eradicate poverty. They ran up against two problems when they attempted to include lawyers in their endeavors: the prerogatives of the legal profession and the relations of power between the state and their poor clients. The prerogative that poverty lawyers asserted in creating the poverty bar during the 1960s was autonomy. That autonomy meant different things to different lawyers in different settings. For Jean Cahn it meant the duty to provide zealous advocacy for her individual client regardless of how it would affect the political reception of CPI in New Haven. For Sparer and the Legal Unit at MFY, it meant that they could pursue a legal and political strategy against city welfare agencies. The insistence on lawyers' autonomy from the control of non-legal actors derives from the primacy of their singular commitment to their clients (Freedman, 1975; Luban, 1988). The crusading lawyers of the early Legal Services movement laid claims to the centrality of autonomy because they could use it to deflect demands for political subservience to power and protect organizational assets and goals. In so doing they were laying the foundation for separate legal services' organizations that could work against the state within the liberal political order (Halliday and Karpic, 1997).

Washington, D.C.: Neighborhood Legal Services Project

A third program to provide legal services for the poor, in Washington, D.C. in late 1963, shared similar funders, personnel, and objectives to those of the CPI and MFY experiments.[2] An initial proposal came from a D.C. group, Washington Action for Youth (WAY), which the President's Committee on Juvenile Delinquency sponsored. Like MFY, WAY had as its mission combating juvenile delinquency. WAY's proposal duplicated MFY's in purpose and structure, but before the Ford Foundation or the President's Committee could act on it, Ford decided to expand its work in Washington and incorporate it in a more ambitious Gray Areas program in the Cardozo neighborhood of northwest Washington. To signal a change in the level of complexity and seriousness with which it intended to tackle the District of Columbia's poverty, the Ford Foundation subsumed the work of WAY under the aegis of the United Planning Organization (UPO). UPO set up a program of neighborhood offices, planning councils, and advisory groups, and in May 1964, proposed adding neighborhood legal services to the mix. An attorney and special assistant to the Director of UPO, William Grinker, took charge of the legal services program and hired criminal defense attorney and deputy director of the Public Defender Office in the District, Gary Bellow, as a consultant. Bellow met Edgar and Jean Cahn,

---

[2] I draw here on Earl Johnson's definitive account in *Justice and Reform* (1975: 27-32).

who had moved to Washington, when he was drafting the funding proposal.

The Cahns conveyed to Bellow two important points from the New Haven CPI experiment: legal services should be decentralized in neighborhood offices and lawyers had to be autonomous from UPO. At the time, the Cahns were working on an article for the *Yale Law Journal* that would come out in the summer of 1964, "The War on Poverty: A Civilian Perspective." They noted in the article that the "War on Poverty" was more than a military metaphor for a social policy to alleviate poverty. The martial metaphor became an orientation, in fact, a *modus operandi*. A war on poverty called for a top-down battle plan, an all-out assault dictated by a general command. It was the approach that CPI took in New Haven. The model could be efficient, but that efficiency came at the cost of democracy and, ultimately, effectiveness. Donors and experts directed the war's "comprehensive strategy" to the end of fulfilling the needs of organizational incumbents – funders, board members, and staff – rather than recipients.

> The disturbing defect of CPI, viewed as a military service operation, lies in its record of enervating existing leadership, failing to develop potential leadership, undercutting incipient protest, and manipulating local organizations so that they become mere instruments of the comprehensive strategy. A service-oriented program not only neglects to provide for and instill the civilian perspective; it is likely to be subversive of that perspective, particularly because of the donor-donee relationships which are established. All too easily such relationships become a means of perpetuating dependency rather than terminating it. A service program fills a need, but experts, not recipients, designate the need... (Cahn and Cahn, 1964: 1321).

As an alternative to the military approach, the Cahns offered a "civilian perspective." Unlike the military campaign that the war on poverty metaphor evokes, the civilian perspective calls for a bottom-up promotion of "neighborhood dissent and criticism." Organizations should have structures that encourage the poor to express their independence, power, and grievances. In addition, the civilian perspective emphasized the dignity of the individual and the importance of non-material factors. "[T]he elimination of poverty" should "be understood as comprehending spiritual as well as physical subsistence and as involving the assurance of civic as well as economic self-sufficiency" (Cahn and Cahn, 1964: 1331).

Bellow followed MFY's example in decentralizing services, representing neighborhood organizations, educating laypersons, both staff and residents, in their legal rights, and pushing for a proactive legal strategy. In a move that potentially contradicted the need for the autonomy of lawyers, he retained MFY's emphasis on teamwork with other professions.

UPO Director Grinker and Bellow hoped to avoid the political pressures that afflicted CPI by creating a counterweight to possible non-legal meddling. They decided to seek support from the local bar, specifically a group of federal judges organized in the Judicial Council. They turned to the Judicial Council because it was an alternative to the conservative D.C. bar association, and the committee the Council appointed contained some of the District's most influential and liberal lawyers. These lawyers, Howard Law School professor Patricia Harris, Covington and Burling senior partner Howard Westwood, and Kenneth Pye, associate dean of Georgetown Law School, would later play roles in establishing the Legal Services Program. In the meantime, though, they rejected UPO's proposal for being overly sociological in its language and for bypassing the existing legal aid organization. Bellow rewrote the proposal replacing the sociological jargon with arguments from the legal profession, and Westwood, one of the few committee members with a connection to the D.C. Legal Aid Society, urged bypassing the traditional provider. He reasoned:

> If the characters with the money wanted some new organization that would make them feel as though they were discovering a new world, that was okay with me. I knew damned well there was no new world.... If, to get the dough, we had to have an organization separate from the old, limping society, so what? (quoted in Johnson, 1975: 29).

On the second go-round, the UPO proposal garnered unanimous support, and in November 1964, the Ford Foundation and the President's Committee funded three neighborhood offices and fourteen lawyers to staff the Neighborhood Legal Services Project (NLSP). To ensure autonomy for the lawyers in the Project, a separate board of local lawyers charged with policy and administrative oversight served as directors.

Bellow held a vision of combating poverty that shared CPI's – and the earlier Henry Street Settlement's – "holistic" approach to treating clients as being enmeshed in a web of debilitating problems. He rejected Sparer's advice to pursue strategic litigation and intended to work with UPO staff to address poor families' complex of problems through interdisciplinary teams. Some UPO officials saw the addition of lawyers to the organization as a way to get clients to use the organization's other social service providers. They surmised that clients used social workers and psychologists with reluctance because clients did not want to admit that they suffered an illness or weakness. Those same clients, on the other hand, willingly consulted with lawyers because lawyers solved legal "problems," to which they attached no shame.

Yet despite Bellow's intentions, the press of legal work, client demands, and the separate knowledge concerns of lawyers made integrating the law and social work nearly impossible. Caseload was high: within five months of operation NLSP was counseling 445 clients a month, a yearly rate of 5,000. Clients remained reluctant to accept social service assistance, and whether purposefully or not, NLSP veered in the direction of strategic litigation. It devoted its legal efforts primarily toward addressing clients' economic problems: consumer credit, housing problems, welfare and veterans benefits, juvenile delinquency, and a limited number of criminal defense cases. It referred all domestic relations cases to the D.C. Legal Aid Society. It devoted energy and resources to training, offered over fifty hours of instruction to staff attorneys, and produced more than a thousand pages of written material on legal strategies and tactics in the areas of consumer, tenant, and welfare law. With the aid of twenty law students it researched legal theories that might affect the economic plight of its clients.

The Establishment of the Legal Services Program and the War on Poverty

In his first State of the Union address in January 1964, President Lyndon Johnson declared "an unconditional war on poverty in America. [We] shall not rest until that war is won." Later in the month, he proposed the Economic Opportunities Bill of 1964, and throughout the spring, Johnson campaigned before labor, business, religious, and civil rights leaders for a series of anti-poverty programs. He took his campaign to the public as well. By August 1964, Congress passed the bill. The bill had been based on the Task Force on Manpower Conservation Report; the Task Force had been set up by Kennedy just weeks after the August 1963 March on Washington for Jobs and Freedom that Martin Luther King, Jr., A. Phillip Randolph, and Bayard Rustin had organized. The War on Poverty was but one aspect of Johnson's Great Society (Piven and Cloward, 1977: 270).

The Great Society was the most ambitious federal program since the New Deal. It would bring about the legislative dismantling of segregation, the establishment of Medicare and Medicaid, programs advancing bilingual education. For the first time in U.S. history, it would provide significant federal funding for public education. It put in place the Endangered Species and Wilderness Acts. Also included were consumer acts such as the Motor Vehicle Safety Act and Child Safety Act, the National Endowment for the Arts and the Humanities, and the Corporation for Public Broadcasting.

The most significant and controversial initiative of the Great Society was the War on Poverty. Johnson launched the Great Society and entered the War on Poverty with significant popular support. Outside of the white South, the civil rights agenda enjoyed popular backing, and he was able to build on the Kennedy administration's New Frontier initiatives. His 1964 landslide victory over Goldwater and congressional elections that delivered a 68-32 margin in the Senate and a 295-140 margin in the House of Representatives to the Democrats gave him an extraordinary mandate and the ability to overcome recalcitrant conservatives of both parties (Brinkley, 1991; Unger, 1996: 104).

In the summer of 1964, Edgar and Jean Cahn formed the Advisory Panel on Legal Services to explore adding legal services to the Office of Economic Opportunity (OEO) programs. At the time, Edgar Cahn was serving as Sargent Shriver's special assistant. Johnson had appointed former Peace Corps Director Shriver to head his task force on poverty in February, and Shriver, at Jean and Edgar Cahn's insistence, had come to the conclusion that legal services belonged in the anti-poverty program. The Advisory Panel consisted of a close-knit group, mostly friends of the Cahns who wanted to provide legal services to the poor but also wanted to challenge the prevailing ways of delivering those services. The guiding document was the Cahns' own law review article, "The War on Poverty: A Civilian Perspective" (Houseman, 1995; Johnson, 1975: 39).

The Cahns and Gary Bellow knew from their experience in Neighborhood Legal Services that no legal program as ambitious as what they planned for the War on Poverty could hope to see the light of day without the backing of the organized bar. Their plan faced two additional hurdles. It challenged the "military perspective" of OEO personnel who were conducting the War on Poverty, and it intended to bypass the traditional legal aid organizations that for three-quarters of a century had the sole "franchise" for delivering legal services to the poor. They knew they needed political allies in high places; neutralizing bar opposition would be insufficient.

The Economic Opportunity Act created a series of Community Action Programs (CAPs) that bypassed state and local governments and instituted the skeleton of a new urban machine, which would initiate a "direct relationship between the national government and the ghettoes." The federal government in creating the CAPs established organizations that employed social workers, other professionals, and "community workers" – "close kin," according to Piven and Cloward, "to the old ward workers," who received and doled out patronage.

The Cahns' critique of the OEO top-down approach zeroed in on the programs' potential for self-serving action. As an alternative, they offered a more radical method of empowering the poor that claimed lawyers as neutral bearers of client interests. The Community Action Agencies (CAAs, the groups that carried out the CAPs) were competing over finite funds, and many gave low priority to lawyers, who would insist on independence from CAA control and might take positions at odds with CAA goals (Piven and Cloward, 1971: 261, 288; Houseman and Perle, 2003: 7). In fact, OEO officials who administered the CAAs retaliated against Legal Service projects by refusing to request increased appropriations from Congress (Pious, 1971). Jean Cahn's experiences in New Haven further drove home the idea that lawyers had to maintain independence from those outside of the legal profession. CAAs could not be relied upon should lawyers want to engage in advocacy that threatened their interests.

Early in the process of planning for a legal services program, the Task Force debated how much local bar associations should be involved in setting up individual programs. The Cahns and Abram Chayes, a State Department counsel and early proponent of turning neighborhood legal service projects into a national program, supported local bar involvement to head off political challenges legal services lawyers might encounter. Gary Bellow and Adam Walinsky, a speechwriter and advisor to Robert Kennedy, initially opposed local bar involvement because they were wary of the undue influence of conservative lawyers whose main loyalties were to local elites, a problem they identified with legal aid organizations. Moreover, they feared Southern bar associations would sabotage civil rights cases or other meaningful legal work. Their positions would evolve but not before the ABA entered the program planning and political maneuvering that would lead to Congressional approval of Legal Services.

In 1963, when the Cahns first began laying out their "Civilian Perspective" article, and during the first half of 1964 when the Task Force was meeting, no one had considered inviting the ABA into the process. It was Lowell Beck, an assistant director of the ABA's Washington, D.C. office, who approached Edgar Cahn about reports he had read in the *Washington Post* about a newly conceived neighborhood law office program. While he was favorably impressed with Cahn's plans for a nationwide legal services program, the ABA leadership treated the possible program with caution. Their caution was confirmed when a Health, Education, and Welfare-sponsored conference on the experiences of early legal services programs in New Haven, New York, and Boston failed to invite ABA representatives. In fact, only by pulling strings could the chair of the ABA Standing Committee on Lawyer Referral William McAlpin, and National Legal Aid and Defender Association (NLADA) executive secretary Junius Allison, secure an invitation.

What they heard the first day of the conference intrigued McAlpin and alienated Allison. A series of speeches attacked the legacy of the legal aid movement from three angles. (1) An attorney from MFY seized on a decade-old claim by Harrison Tweed, former president of both the New York Legal Aid Society and City Bar, that applicants to N.Y. Legal Aid had not increased in forty years. Resultant unmet needs were due to "alienation and self-selection" on the part of the Society and called for "new organizational forms." (2) The private attorney who presided over the board of CPI's successor organization in New Haven excoriated legal aid societies for lacking "any capability of dealing creatively with the problems of the deprived citizens at the core of the city," and claimed that "an illusion of service for these clients has taken the place of constructive social therapy." (3) A young woman attorney formerly with the established Washington firm of Covington and Burling criticized legal aid societies for excessive timidity before the barratry rules. She charged that, in eschewing all forms of advertising, the D.C. Legal Aid Society waited for clients who knew they needed a lawyer, knew there was a legal aid organization, were able to overcome their distrust of lawyers, and had the wherewithal to make their way to the legal aid office. Later that same afternoon, Edgar Cahn upped the ante with the ABA and NLADA representatives by announcing that OEO had decided to inaugurate a national civil legal services program (Johnson, 1975: 43-47).

Junius Allison reacted as one might expect: he dismissed the conference criticisms as coming from neophytes and academics. He remarked that it was an insult to the legal aid movement to hold a conference on legal services without recognizing the accomplishments of the nation's 246 existing legal aid societies. He put the matter of a new legal services program on NLADA's December Executive Committee meeting agenda. There, he expressed concern at the hostile attitude of conference participants and speculated that OEO might freeze existing legal aid organizations out of the program. At this meeting Edward Carr, director of the New York Legal Aid Society, voiced the fear that OEO would create competing organizations that would discourage existing private sources from continuing to fund the legal aid societies. In a scenario that was to prove prescient, if self-serving, Carr feared the poor would be abandoned were the federal government to cut back on its support for the program. The NLADA Executive Committee issued a statement condemning the still to be formulated OEO plan. In so doing, it managed to eliminate itself from any future role in influencing OEO's plans (Johnson, 1975: 47-49).

By the end of June 1966, the OEO had funded 130 legal service projects, and along with funding for training programs and legal research support, OEO had spent $20 million. In 1968, OEO funded 260 programs in every state but North Dakota where the governor vetoed all applications. By the end of 1972, the LSP budget had increased more than threefold to $71.5 million (Houseman, 1995: 1680-81).

To further the goal of law reform, OEO funded "back-up centers." They were research, policy, and litigation programs that specialized in a substantive area of law such as housing or welfare or served a particular social group, for example Indians or the elderly. After leaving MFY, Edward Sparer started the first program, the Center for Social Welfare Policy and

Law (CSWPL),[3] at the Columbia University School of Social Work – the Law School would have no part of the program – with initial funding from the Stern Family Fund and Ford Foundation. These centers engaged in litigation and lobbying that was intended to have national effects. They also provided training and support for local LSP projects (Davis, 1993: 35-6; Houseman, 1995: 1682).

Opposition to Legal Services

After bar leaders had gained control over the LSP structure and the grant-making process, they set out to enlist legal aid societies in the program. They promoted the program to the various local groups, many of which resisted the requests for proposals.

> A "sales campaign" was necessary due to the reluctance of the societies to rely on public funding for their activities. Some of the bar groups suspected dark plots to promote confrontation or civil rights litigation in local communities, and opposed the projects on ideological grounds. Some bar groups feared that projects would take away business from the local practitioners (Pious, 1971: 374).

National bar leaders were instrumental in overcoming local opposition to LSP. Opposition was particularly strong in California, New Mexico, North Carolina, Oregon, and Tennessee. By June of 1966, though, local opposition subsided considerably; local bar groups sponsored more than seventy applications, supported the efforts of another forty-two local groups, and only opposed six (Pious, 1971: 374).

In June 1966, Clinton Bamberger, Jr., resigned as Director of LSP to run for Attorney General in Maryland. With the support of national bar leaders, Deputy Director Earl Johnson took over as acting, then permanent, Director. Johnson actively encouraged Legal Services projects to move away from the old legal aid model. He stressed three criteria for evaluating the local projects: engagement in law reform and appellate work, community education, and, finally, representation of the poor on the governing board. His hope was that law reform and appellate advocacy would lighten the case load of attorneys and alleviate the plight of the poor by addressing the problems that sent clients to lawyers in the first place. With an eye on potential opposition from the right, Johnson minimized ideological ele-

---

3 It was at CSWPL that Sparer set out the legal strategy for a constitutional "right to live." While that quest ultimately failed, CSWPL-supported litigation succeeded in overturning some of the most noxious features of the welfare system by eliminating residency laws, "man in the house" rules that disqualified mothers who cohabited with men, and midnight raids to check up on recipients. CSWPL was instrumental in the establishment of due process protections and a right to adequate benefits (Davis, 1993: 35-6; Diller, 1995: 1415).

ments of Legal Services and emphasized its compatibility with existing legal institutions. In a *University of Miami Law Review* article, he and his deputy director for research, Gerald Caplan, wrote:

> In the broadest sense, the program is neither liberal nor conservative. It has elements of both, and should have an appeal which cuts across traditional lines of political philosophy and party politics. ... It utilizes existing institutions, existing law, professional personnel. It represents change within the system (quoted in Pious, 1971: 378).

According to Pious, the early LSP local governing boards were under the direction of lawyers. In June of 1967, lawyers comprised fifty-five percent of local governing boards with representatives of the poor making up another third. Bar leaders prevented community action agency officials and lawyers who were interested in applying the Cahns' "civilian perspective" from controlling boards. Most boards were made up largely of lawyers, plus a substantial minority (though often a majority) of state or local bar association members. Local and state judges were on boards to gain support for projects, and members who were civic leaders reflected the policies set by professional bars (Pious 1971: 375). A third of board members represented the poor but were not necessarily poor themselves.

While bar leaders put the brakes on activist control and "maximum feasible participation" by the poor, they also insulated the program from Congressional interference. National ABA leaders lobbied Republicans to prevent LSP from becoming a partisan issue: compared to other OEO programs, Congressional oversight was "negligible." When in 1967 California Republican Senator George Murphy introduced an amendment to prohibit LSP projects from suing local, state, or federal agencies, bar leaders rallied to push its defeat. The same year, amendments to change the operations of the Program failed to pass with two exceptions: a requirement that LSP officials consult with local and state bar officials before approving any final grants and a prohibition on the representation of indigents on felony charges. Bar leaders were supportive of LSP requests for budget increases, but their opposition to CAP involvement meant that CAP officials had little incentive to request higher funding (Pious, 1971: 375-77).

In November 1965, the NLADA convention revised its Standards for legal aid organizations, calling on them to include law reform, appellate work, and community education. Two years later at its convention, delegates voted to endorse tenant rent withholding, reform of the welfare system through litigation, and suits against government agencies. According to Pious:

> By 1967 neither the NLADA nor the ABA were as traditional or insular as they once had been. They accepted reluctantly

and then enthusiastically the law reform and appellate advocacy approaches of the projects. The change in attitude on the
part of bar leaders was evolutionary and incremental rather
than revolutionary and radical, but nevertheless it resulted in
support for these goals in Congress when they were threatened by amendments (Pious, 1971: 379).

Despite the ABA's general support for the program, organizations applying for grant approval had to design their projects to pass muster with
state and local bars and state judiciaries. Pious contends that "only the few
projects whose boards were not dominated by local and state bar delegations could be innovative" (Pious, 1971: 381). State judiciaries, which had
to approve the incorporation of the organizations that sponsored LSP
projects, looked askance at projects that engaged in group representation
and community advocacy. In New York, a justice of the Court of Appeals
(New York State's "Supreme Court"), Charles Breitel, rejected the nonprofit application of an LSP-aspiring organization. He insisted that a
majority of its board consist of attorneys and cautioned it to reject representation of "political factions or organizations of social and economic
protest, however worthy" (cited in Pious, 1971: 382). In May 1967 in
Philadelphia six months after Justice Breitel delivered his opinion, Judge
Raymond Alexander came to the opposite conclusion in approving a
charter for the Community Legal Services Program in Philadelphia:

> Are the poor to be denied a lawyer's advocacy and left without
> his peculiar assistance in forums beyond the judicial and in
> the cases whose ends encompass social and economic as well
> as legal justice? Surely this is a narrow view of the law.... No
> acceptable jurisprudence can fail to recognize that "legal"
> rights have an intimate relation to social and economic justice,
> nor that these ends are legitimately sought in the judicial
> forum (cited in Pious, 1971: 383).

Private interests also had an effect on what projects would be proposed
and what final shape they would take. Agribusiness applied considerable
pressure on state governors and federal legislators to curtail rural Legal
Services Program projects, most notoriously in the case of California Rural
Legal Assistance but also South Florida Migrant Legal Services. Congressional representatives were likely to insert themselves into the process
when projects threatened to represent the poor too zealously. Members of
Kentucky's and Missouri's delegations succeeded in placing requirements
that grantees have state and local bar consultations before final approval.
California's delegation, as we saw, came close to preventing LSP projects
from suing government agencies. And a Florida Congressman, angered by
LSP's representation of alleged rioters (Johnson, 1999; Pious, 1971),

introduced an amendment to the LSP statute that prevented the representation of felons in criminal court.

Political controls were not overtly exercised because they were infrequently required. Through nature or design, lawyers shied away from controversial projects. The grant-approval process encouraged legal aid society and local bar sponsorship, and neither of those groups was inclined to undertake thoroughgoing challenges to the status quo. As Alan Houseman, a founder of Michigan Legal Services suggests, "[T]he problem was not that aggressive applicants were turned down; the problem was that aggressive applicants did not apply because they did not exist at the local level" (Houseman, 1995: 1680).

There were examples of LSP projects that conformed to the vision of the pioneers of neighborhood legal services. In these projects, innovative legal strategies were applied on behalf of the poor, including challenges to powerful vested interests. These were exceptional, though: they had boards insulated from local bar pressures (such as one project whose governing board was comprised entirely of law school professors), or they successfully took advantage of national LSP support. Johnson and Caplan pushed for innovative strategies involving law reform, appellate advocacy, and legal education for local groups, but they could not force projects to take up those strategies. Instead, they designed programs that provided resources to make such work easier. They funded a National Training Institute, instituted the Reginald Heber Smith fellowships, "Reggies," to recruit top-ranking graduates from elite law schools into programs that pursued law reform and impact litigation, provided law school scholarships for minority students, and conducted research on poverty law through law schools and a National Clearinghouse. Johnson and Caplan left in the summer of 1968, and their successor Burt Griffin, a former director of Cleveland Legal Aid, changed their law reform and appellate emphasis to individual client services and community economic development (Pious, 1972: 386).

Conclusion

From the vantage of the post-1996 restrictions on the Legal Services Corporation,[4] the early years of the Legal Services Program seem like a

---

4 In 1996, Congress passed legislation that imposed restrictions on legal programs that receive any funding from the Legal Services Corporation. Those restrictions included prohibitions on: class action suits, including the filing of amicus briefs; accepting attorney fees, even when they are statutorily approved or court ordered; representation of prisoners in civil matters, even in litigation unrelated to incarceration; representation of many classes of immigrants, especially the undocumented; litigation related to abortions or representation of public housing tenants in evictions related to drug crimes; and outreach efforts and offers of representation to victims whose rights may have been violated (Abel and Udell, 2002: 877-

golden era when idealistic lawyers were unrestrained by the meddling of conservative politicians. But as the story of the LSC shows, political constraints always figured in Legal Services projects. As we shall see in later chapters, however, changes under President Ronald Reagan laid the groundwork for the substantial restrictions imposed by the Republican majority in Congress in 1996 and for the most part acceded to by the Clinton administration and the organized bar.

79). Some of those restrictions have been subsequently ruled unconstitutional in the lower courts in *Dobbins v. LSC* and *Velasquez v. LSC*.

4

FORCED TO THE COURTS: THE NAACP, THE ACLU, AND POLITICAL MOBILIZATION LAWYERING

The NAACP Legal Defense Fund (LDF or the Fund) and the ACLU are perhaps the best known legal advocacy organizations in the United States, and the NAACP[1] and ACLU are perhaps the best know non-electoral political groups. The American Civil Liberties Union has long come to the aid of victims of government repression and proudly claimed that it has but one client, the Constitution. The National Association for the Advancement of Colored People is the oldest and largest civil rights group in the nation. Both, from their beginnings, have expended considerable resources addressing constituent concerns in the courts, and for those reasons alone they would be of interest to anyone studying the intersection of politics and the legal system. In addition to their defense of individuals unjustly accused or denied legal rights, they have also changed the shape of the law through the use of litigation.

This chapter, and the next, present case studies of two organizations founded within a decade of one another that came from similar political milieux, whose founders were often from the same social background and in a number of cases were the same people. The NAACP and the ACLU started as political organizations concerned with unpopular people and causes. Neither organization was founded by lawyers, nor was their primary focus shaping a legal strategy to effect change. But various political, financial, and organizational factors – some structural, some contingent, some that were shared and some that were different – forced them to the courts. By the 1920s it was clear to the leaders of the ACLU and the NAACP that use of the courts would be strategic to their organizational existence.

Changing political and cultural contexts over their first four decades contributed to the role these organizations played in major judicial change and in the role lawyers and lawyering played in these organizations. By the 1930s, both the NAACP and the ACLU took on the organizational shape and primary strategies that marked their successful and visible use of the

---

[1] As I will detail in this chapter, the National Association for the Advancement of Colored People (NAACP) in 1940 created the NAACP Legal Defense and Education Fund, Inc. (LDF or the Fund) to conduct its legal work under a separate organizational framework. Through the 1940s and into the 1950s, the LDF operated much as a "wholly-owned subsidiary" of the NAACP. Throughout this chapter, as far as is practicable, I differentiate the two entities.

courts in the 1950s, 1960s, and 1970s. In many ways they confirm sociologist Arthur Stinchcombe's observation (1965: 143-44) that organizations' founding moments correlate highly with their culture and social structure.

The National Association for the Advancement of Colored People (NAACP)

The National Association for the Advancement of Colored People was the organizational outcome of the Niagara Movement, a group of prominent black Americans, who in 1905 came together to protest discrimination, and white allies such as Southern social reformer William English Walling and New York social workers Mary White Ovington and Henry Moskowitz. Holding their inaugural meeting at the Henry Street Settlement on New York's Lower East Side in 1909, forty activists set in motion the founding of the NAACP. The Association was not a legal services organization nor was it comprised of many lawyers. Its first members were black and white social reformers, journalists, anti-lynching activists, and suffragists who sought to mobilize political pressure and use the courts to advance the civil and political rights of nonwhite Americans. Its charter issued two years later stated its aims and how they might be achieved:

> To promote equality of rights and to eradicate caste or race prejudice among the citizens of the United States: to advance the interest of colored citizens; to secure for them impartial suffrage; and to increase their opportunities for securing justice in the courts, education for the children, employment according to their ability and complete equality before law (quoted in Bush, 1999: 78).

The nature of its leadership, once removed from broad-based constituencies (at its founding in 1909, the NAACP had only one black person, W.E.B. DuBois, in its inner circle), pushed it in the direction of publicity and legal tactics. In the face of increasing racial violence and entrenched discrimination, however, it gravitated more toward activism. The NAACP provided a vehicle in which a small, emerging black middle class and its white allies could address deep-rooted racism. By 1911, the NAACP had twenty-four chapters, and the following year the number climbed to fifty. In 1919, there were 300 branches with 155 in the South. Its growth resulted from the work of a black field staff including James Weldon Johnson who would assume its top administrative staff position, Secretary, in 1921. By then the Association claimed 88,000 members (Meier and Rudwick, 1976: 129; Bush, 1999: 78-79, 81).

The combination of representing a largely disenfranchised constituency that had not organized itself politically or economically, and having a mission – representing legally oppressed citizens – that went to the heart of the legal system, forced the NAACP into the courts. Within three months of its founding, it opened its first branch in Chicago, and one of its first actions was to file a petition for pardon in South Carolina on behalf of a sharecropper sentenced to death. Between 1913 and 1927, it argued five cases before the U.S. Supreme Court, including *Buchanan v. Warley*, 245 U.S. 60 (1917), which held that ordinances requiring residential segregation were violations of the Fourteenth Amendment, and *Moore v. Dempsey*, 261 U.S. 86 (1923), which found that the presence of an armed white mob interfered with the defendants' trial and amounted to a denial of due process guaranteed by the Fourteenth Amendment. *Moore* also marked the beginning of a long process of stricter scrutiny by the Supreme Court in state criminal trials (Tushnet, 1987: 1; Cortner, 1988).

The NAACP's legal work was initially done in an ad hoc fashion and relied on white volunteer attorneys. Those attorneys were highly respected and prominent members of the national bar, including Moorefield Storey, a president of the Association and former president of the ABA, and Louis Marshall, the "tireless attorney for Jewish rights organizations." Storey or Marshall represented NAACP clients in all five cases that it brought before the Supreme Court between 1913 and 1927. They were both wealthy and served without remuneration. In general, while the NAACP paid local counsel, both black and white, financial remuneration could scarcely have been a significant motivating factor for the prominent white lawyers, since the NAACP seldom paid their usual fees. White lawyers retained by the NAACP, even in local cases, were from the leading law schools. Like many of the supporters of the early legal aid movement, they embraced their *pro bono* legal work as an obligation to the legal profession. They saw themselves as protectors of the disadvantaged, but also (and perhaps this is why they, like colleagues in the ACLU, gravitated toward political lawyering) they saw upholding the service ideal as upholding the Constitution. They were, according to historians August Meier and Elliott Rudwick, "essentially conservative men, characterized either by a degree of aristocratic noblesse oblige toward blacks or by a conservative's concern with due process, law and order, and the protection of an individual's constitutional rights and property" (Meier and Rudwick, 1976: 132, 133-34).

It was not until 1920 that the work of the Association's National Legal Committee came under the (joint) supervision of a black member of the organization, assistant secretary Walter White, who was not an attorney. The major constraint on the involvement of black attorneys in NAACP work was their abysmally small numbers. It meant that even in local cases white lawyers represented the organization in the courts. Cases pursued by branches in northern and border states were litigated by a few black lawyers, but they often associated themselves with white counsel. Local branches in the South relied mostly on white attorneys. In 1900 there were 728 black lawyers in the U.S., approximately two thirds of one percent of attorneys nationwide. In 1930, the percentage increased to 0.8. The paltry numbers of black lawyers was even smaller in the South. In 1910, when ninety percent of black Americans lived below the Mason-Dixon Line, more than fifty percent of black lawyers resided in the North and West. In 1910, Georgia had eighteen attorneys, South Carolina seventeen, and Mississippi twenty-one. The full implementation of Jim Crow laws devastated the ranks of black lawyers. By 1940 Georgia had eight lawyers, South Carolina five, and Mississippi three. To practice in the South, and often in the North, black attorneys had to associate themselves with white lawyers in important cases (Meier and Rudwick, 1976: 130-31; Abel, 1989: 280).

The largest source of black attorneys then, and well into the 1960s, was Howard University Law School. It opened in 1868 with a two-year program that primarily served government clerks and had no admission requirements. In 1877 the District of Columbia set in place a requirement for three years of training, and in 1879 Congress in its appropriation refused to fund professional schools at Howard. The school continued to train lawyers, but many had to leave Washington to set up practice in their home communities. The NAACP's reliance on white attorneys was to change, though. In the 1920s, a group of African American lawyers studied constitutional law at Harvard Law School under the tutelage of Felix Frankfurter, a professor at the school before he was appointed to the Supreme Court. These attorneys provided the human and social capital that was to train and equip a generation of black civil rights lawyers. The key institutional setting in which they carried out this work was Howard University Law School. The political context underlying this development involved race riots in cities large and small, in the North and South; the continuation of lynching; and a Supreme Court hostile to racial equality (Meier and Rudwick, 1976: 129-30, 142; Stevens, 1983: 81-82).

The legal codification of segregation in the South under Jim Crow law represented the low point of state-sponsored racism. For more than half a century the legality of black inferiority would be encapsulated in *Plessy v. Ferguson*, 163 U.S. 537 (1896), with its anodyne-sounding doctrine of "separate but equal." The social and extra-legal support for the separate but equal doctrine rested upon the physical subjugation of blacks. From 1917 to 1923 there were race riots in Chicago, East St. Louis, Illinois, Omaha, Tulsa, and Rosewood, Florida. The call for the founding meeting of the NAACP came in response to the horror of a race riot in Abraham Lincoln's hometown, Springfield, Illinois. Even more than the dread of race riots that seemed to occur out of thin air, the constant threat of lynching served to remind blacks of their subjugated position. Between 1880 and 1930, white Southern lynch mobs executed 3,320 blacks and 723 whites. There had been a long history of lynching as part of America's "frontier justice," and lynching had typically involved whites killing whites, but in the late 1880s a wave of lynching swept the South and the proportion of black victims rose from sixty-eight to ninety-one percent of the national total. By 1930, ninety-five percent of lynchings occurred in the South.

Much could be said about the ritualized brutality and holiday-making aspects of lynching for whites, its connection to the "Southern rape complex," and its use as a guarantor of cheap black labor. Above all, however, the impunity with which whites could torture and kill African Americans, and their vehement defense of the right to do so, brought home the inhumanity perpetrated against blacks. From its beginning the NAACP made anti-lynching legislation a principal political objective. Despite its considerable efforts, it was unsuccessful in outlawing the extra-judicial murder of blacks: the United States never made lynching a federal crime, and it was not until 1946 that there was a successful federal prosecution of a lyncher for a civil rights violation (Fairclough, 2001: 23-25; see Cash, 1941).

The American Civil Liberties Union (ACLU)

The ACLU's initial trajectory was similar to the NAACP's. It too began representing a constituency that confronted a hostile majority. Facing government repression from the executive branch, it was forced into the courts. The American Civil Liberties Union had its origins in 1916 when a "small group of social workers, journalists and other genteel pacifists" formed the American Union Against Militarism (AUAM). A young social worker – not an attorney – with roots that went back to the Mayflower, Roger Baldwin, was the driving force of the organization.

The AUAM's socially and politically well-connected leadership, which included such Progressive Era reformers as Crystal and Max Eastman, Lillian Wald of the Henry Street Settlement House, and social work reformer Paul Kellogg, had hoped to pressure the Wilson administration to keep the United States out of the war. (They had especially good connections in the War Department.) When the U.S. entered World War I in April 1917, the AUAM altered its mission, putting a strain on the group's leadership. Baldwin led a militant group within the AUAM, the Bureau for Conscientious Objectors (BCO), and he, with Crystal Eastman precipitated a factional split, which created the National Civil Liberties Bureau within the organization. The Bureau took up publicity and lobbying campaigns to protest censorship, and maintained contacts during and after the war with radicals in the labor movement such as the leadership of the Industrial Workers of the World (IWW).

The Founding Context

The context within which the ACLU's predecessor organizations formed and dissolved provided motivations and opportunities for politically engaged lawyering. In the first place, the debate to enter the war had split the nation, but the decision to defeat the German "autocracy" united the government. The all-out effort to mobilize required coordination in industry, commerce, and the military; it also required the creation of a loyal and patriotic citizenry. To create that unity of purpose the government would brook no dissent. Throughout much of the Midwest and in every large city, there was the problem of the so-called "hyphenated Americans," mostly first- and second-generation German-Americans but also other recent immigrant groups with ties to the German allies. Their loyalty remained in question, and as a social group they overlapped with a second group of potential fifth columnists: socialists and labor radicals.

Wilson left no doubt where he stood in enforcing patriotism: "Woe be to the man or group of men that seeks to stand in our way." Congress passed a passel of legislation to fine or jail anyone who attempted to undermine the war effort – in reality, any criticism of the Wilson administration: the Alien Act, the Alien Enemies Act, the Espionage Act, the Sedition Act, the Selective Service Act, and the Trading with the Enemy Act. Federal courts in Chicago, Kansas City, and Sacramento convicted and jailed over two hundred members of the IWW. Eugene V. Debs was condemned to prison for ten years, and Victor Berger, Milwaukee socialist and later mayor, was sentenced to a twenty-year term (Goldman, 1955: 196; McGeer, 2003: 289).

Pacifism was one form of dissent that particularly challenged the tolerance of the war's boosters in and out of government. Former President Theodore Roosevelt attacked pacifists as "a whole raft of sexless creatures." He warned that "the Hun within our gates is the worst of the foes of our own household.... Whether he is pro-German or poses as a pacifist ... matters little." He advocated the disenfranchisement and internment of disloyal native-born Americans. The American Protective League, a private vigilante group with U.S. Justice Department sponsorship, rounded up 20,000 suspected draft dodgers in New York City. Despite the government crackdown on dissent and private vigilantism, the combination of a large population of German-Americans, a politically radicalized sector of the working class – Morris Hillquit ran for Mayor in New York on a platform of opposition to the war and gained one in five votes in the fall of 1917 – and a healthy bohemian culture produced a political milieu in New York in which AUAM activists could comfortably operate (Walker, 1990: 15).

Wartime fever affected the legal community, even that portion that served the least fortunate. In 1916, Arthur von Briesen, the long-time president of the New York Legal Aid Society, resigned his position, citing difficulties raising funds in an atmosphere in which his identification with the German-American community proved a detriment. A few months before Von Briesen's resignation, Elihu Root, who served as an Honorary Vice President of New York Legal Aid Society and was perhaps the period's preeminent lawyer-statesman, attacked New York's immigrant lawyers for lacking loyalty to American institutions (*New York Times*, January 19, 1916; February 25, 1916). That same intolerance and suppressing of dissent motivated a group who were to become a backbone of support for the National Civil Liberties Bureau (NCLB): well-heeled lawyers of a not particularly radical bent who nonetheless "idealized the Constitution and were outraged by the violations of free speech and due process" (Walker, 1990: 21). Among them was noted jurist and Harvard Law School professor Zechariah Chaffee. These lawyers joined social workers who saw free speech as an extension of social reform, and Protestant clergymen and lay activists such as Norman Thomas who were inspired by the ideas of the social gospel, to form the political core of the NCLB (Walker, 1990: 23).

One of the three legal counsel to the Bureau, Albert DeSilver, came from a wealthy background, considered himself a pro-war patriot, but also insisted, "my law-abiding neck gets very warm under its law-abiding collar these days at the extraordinary violations of fundamental laws which are being put over" (quoted in Walker, 1990: 21). He is reported to have used his war bonds to post bail for defendants in free speech cases. DeSilver was just the type of supporter that Roger Baldwin and Crystal Eastman had hope to attract. Besides the financial resources and legal knowledge he could bring to the organization, he represented the sort of political leverage that Bureau leadership hoped could be used in Washington. Anti-war progressives had based their opposition in part on the deleterious effects the war would have on American democracy and social progress. Baldwin expected that a pro-War supporter of civil liberties with impeccably patrician bona fides would be just the type to convince Progressives in the Wilson administration of the folly of war. The mindset of NCLB figures such as Baldwin had a parallel among some in the NAACP who thought that personally lobbying those in the highest reaches of the government would bring some relief for black Americans. It was tough going: it took six years of intensive lobbying before Woodrow Wilson would condemn lynching. FDR would eventually condemn it, too, but neither pushed for legislation to outlaw it.

Baldwin's personal connections failed him, but the Bureau would not be deterred. It determined, instead, to sway *public* opinion by agitating through public forums and in the press, and by issuing a continuous stream of pamphlets and memos. But this course was blocked as well. Postal Service seizures of NCLB pamphlets such as *War's Heretics* and *The Truth About the IWW*, despite initial assurances to Baldwin from the government that they did not pose a threat of sedition, led the NCLB to seek relief through the courts. The long delays that accompanied litigation moved Baldwin to appeal to public opinion, but attempts to set up public meetings were stymied when auditorium managers refused to rent their halls. Baldwin's efforts had an effect on elite opinion. Zechariah Chafee credited an NCLB pamphlet with influencing his thinking on the First Amendment; his writings, in turn, influenced Supreme Court Justice Oliver Wendell Holmes, Jr.'s dissent in the 1919 case *Abrams v. United States*, 250 U.S. 616, in which he famously wrote: "Government may regulate speech that produces or is intended to produce a clear and imminent danger."

The NCLB's political commitment to pacifism encouraged it to seek legal solutions. Without a mass constituency it could mobilize, or in whose name it could speak, it decided to oppose the war by serving individuals facing induction. Its three attorneys, DeSilver, Walter Nelles, and Harry Weinberger, faced daunting demands. They had not only to pursue litigation in defense of the organization's agitation against censorship and government repression, but they were also swamped with requests for legal advice from draft-age men. Lacking the resources of direct service legal providers such as the legal aid societies – in New York, to the contrary, the Legal Aid Society advised young men to enlist – they passed on much of the work to sympathetic lawyers. By the fall of 1917, cooperating attorneys were handling up to 125 conscientious objector cases a week. From its beginning the NCLB created a supply of lawyers able and eager to engage in civil liberties work. Building networks of sympathetic lawyers was not always easy, although it was possible in New York and a few other urban settings.

Maintaining a sufficient supply of cooperating attorneys would be a challenge for the ACLU throughout its history. The NAACP would face an even more daunting task when it had to call on black lawyers in the Deep, and not-so-Deep, South: as late as 1956 Delaware had only one black lawyer; between 1937 and 1947 Alabama had one black lawyer, as well; in 1950, Virginia had three black attorneys, all in Richmond; and Georgia had a dozen such lawyers, all in Atlanta, and only one who did civil rights work (Walker, 1990: 23-24; Greenberg, 2004: 38).

The American Civil Liberties Union Becomes Official

In 1920, the Bureau changed its name to the American Civil Liberties Union in order to signal its move beyond issues of pacifism. It joined the NAACP (1909), the Anti-Defamation League (1913), and the American Jewish Congress (1916) on the rather sparse national landscape of civil rights groups. Its founding could not have come at a less auspicious time. The heady days of Progressive Era reform had come to a standstill. Reaction seemed everywhere. The reform movements associated with the political ferment of the preceding two decades had mostly run their course. The Socialist Party and the IWW had been devastated by government repression. The Supreme Court in *Abrams* (1919), *Schenck*, 249 U.S. 47

(1919), and *Debs*, 249 U.S. 211 (1919), had just rejected all First Amendment claims. That same year, the labor movement suffered defeats in nationwide walkouts in steel and coal, and the Justice Department initiated the Palmer Raids. As the ACLU was being formed, Congress was debating the passage of a peacetime sedition law. Even so, Baldwin would bring to the ACLU charismatic leadership, deep-seated moralism, and an ascetic devotion to the causes he took up. He also had the ability to infect others with his enthusiasm. The repressive atmosphere that had accompanied wartime mobilization put the issue of civil liberties on the agenda for a fraction of political and social reformers. It offered a target for activists and lawyers interested in broad legal and political reform (Walker, 1990: 47).

The government's push to criminalize dissent during and after the war, notably in the free speech fights and Palmer Raids, forced the ACLU into litigation. Yet the group was not a "lawyers' organization." Despite its lack of organic ties to the working class, it concentrated its efforts on aiding the labor movement. It was a passionate cause for Baldwin: "I champion civil liberty as the best of the nonviolent means of building the power on which workers' rule must be based. If I aid reactionaries to get free speech now and then, if I go outside the class-struggle to fight against censorship, it is only because those liberties help to create a more hospitable atmosphere for working class liberties" (quoted in Tushnet, 1987: 4).

Over time Baldwin's passion for "workers' rule" may have subsided, but the affinity that civil libertarians had for labor during the 1920s, and radicalism more generally during the twentieth century, was an expression of distrust of the state. When American capitalists regularly appealed to the courts and law enforcement authorities at all levels of government to suppress labor's ability to combine, reformers sympathetic to unions and working people challenged the state on principle, taking up civil liberties as a cause. The labor movement itself championed the cause of civil liberties. In the 1910s, the IWW had launched free speech fights in almost every locale it was organizing and experienced success in Fresno, Kansas City, Sioux City, and Des Moines. That historical legacy and hope for radical social change led ACLU activists to embrace the left wing of the labor movement. A strike in 1923 by dockworkers in the Los Angeles port of San Pedro led to the organization of the group's first permanent affiliate, the Southern California ACLU (Goldstein, 1978: 86, 93; Rabin, 1976: 210-11; Walker, 1990: 47-48).

ACLU Attorneys and the Legal Landscape

The ACLU's legal staff was small. Most of the attorneys who worked on its cases during Baldwin's tenure volunteered their professional services. Members of the board recruited highly skilled and experienced litigators through personal contacts. Even as late as 1960, the ACLU had a staff of only five permanent lawyers, two in New York and one each in Chicago, Los Angeles, and San Francisco. Like the NAACP, it relied on a geographically dispersed corps of activists and lawyers. According to the ACLU's 1921 *Annual Report*, the organization claimed 1000 "correspondents" and 800 cooperating attorneys. These figures were exaggerated but still represented an indication of support for the ACLU's aims among the political and social elite, as well as in a "rank and file" of less prominent status (Walker, 1990: 52).

Arthur Garfield Hays was among the former. A prestigious corporate and entertainment attorney who "made millions representing Wall Street brokers and bankers," Hays identified with the underdog. He got his start as a civil liberties lawyer when he was briefly jailed advocating for Pennsylvania coalminers' right to assemble. In 1923, Hays became the ACLU's general counsel, where he upheld a commitment to the First Amendment that would make him one of the Union's chief "free speech absolutists." Some of his important civil liberties work included defending Sacco and Vanzetti, co-counsel with Clarence Darrow in the Scopes trial, and defending the Scottsboro case. He appeared in Berlin in 1933 on behalf of Bulgarian Communist leader Georgi Dmitrov, whom the Nazis had accused of burning down the Reichstag. As a principled proponent of free speech he did not shy from controversy. Speaking before a Communist Party rally, he decried the inability of the bourgeoisie to get a fair trial in the USSR, and at a convention of the American Law Students Association convention he defended the free speech rights of Nazi sympathizers in the German American Bund (*New York Times*, February 26, 1939: 12; December 15, 1954: 31; Rabin, 1976: 211; Walker, 1990: 53).

Other prominent attorneys in the ACLU's early leadership included General Counsel Walter Nelles, who later became a Yale Law School professor, and Walter Pollak, a New York corporate law attorney. They had a strictly legal approach to civil liberties that they thought should take precedence over political and educational activities, a strategy they pushed the organization to pursue. Nelles and Pollak argued the ACLU's first case before the U.S. Supreme Court, in *Gitlow v. New York*, 268 U.S. 652 (1925). The Justices affirmed the constitutionality of Communist Party founder Benjamin Gitlow's conviction under New York State's 1902 Criminal Anarchy Act for his pamphlet, *The Left-Wing Manifesto*, which urged "proletarian revolution and the communist reconstruction of society." Two years later, Nelles and Pollak appeared before the high court in a similar case, *Whitney v. California*, 274 U.S. 357 (1927). Again, the Supreme Court decisively upheld the states' right to suppress speech.

Nelles and Pollak, however, saw the two decisions in an optimistic light. In *Gitlow*, the conservative Justice Edward Stanford wrote in the majority opinion that "freedom of speech and of the press – which are protected by the First Amendment from abridgement from Congress – are among the fundamental personal rights and 'liberties' protected by the due process clause of the Fourteenth Amendment from impairment by the states," the first time the court had articulated that doctrine. In *Whitney*, the Justices unanimously sustained Charlotte Anita Whitney's conviction for sedition. What gave hope to civil libertarians was Justice Louis Brandeis' concurring opinion, joined by Holmes. In it, Brandeis wrote some of the most famous lines in First Amendment jurisprudence:

> To courageous, self-reliant men, with confidence in the power of free and fearless reasoning applied through the processes of popular government, no danger flowing from speech can be deemed clear and present, unless the incidence of the evil apprehended is so imminent that it may befall before there is opportunity for full discussion. If there be time to expose through discussion the falsehood and fallacies, to avert the evil by the processes of education, the remedy to be applied is more speech, not enforced silence. (*Whitney v. California*, 274 U.S. 357 (1927).)

Brandeis reconceptualized Holmes' earlier "clear and present danger" test that would restrict free speech whenever it represented such a threat. Brandeis' formulation, to which Holmes signed on, emphasized that proximity and danger were crucial elements in deciding the limits to free speech (Walker, 1990: 79-80).

Organizational Advances and Political Weaknesses

The ACLU experienced mixed results in the 1920s in the field of civil liberties. It made organizational gains and positively affected constitutional law, although those gains would not be realized until later. Its push to become a national organization would open up the possibilities for influencing the course of constitutional law but also reveal the limitations of Baldwin's personality-driven and New York-centered model. Its expansion beyond New York with the founding of the Southern California branch in 1923, and its participation in headline grabbing trials such as the Sacco and Vanzetti and Scopes trials, brought national exposure and financial reward.

Baldwin's charismatic leadership kept the organization alive during the politically dismal 1920s. Through his travels, speaking, and writing, he increased the organization's visibility, raised funds, and recruited prominent liberals to its board. He brought together and offered an organizational home for the nation's leading legal experts in civil liberties. Walter Pollak, who would distinguish himself as a Supreme Court litigator, wrote briefs that influenced the extension of civil rights law. Felix Frankfurter served as the organization's expert on labor injunctions, before his appointment to the Court in 1939. Arthur Garfield Hays set the legal tone for and was a leading advocate for the ACLU's absolutist position on free speech, and Morris Ernst pioneered the fight against censorship in the arts.

Baldwin took control of day-to-day operations and subjected his staff to authoritarian and often petty interference. He rewrote the material drafted by his publicity directors – in one five-year period during the 1940s, the ACLU had twenty-five publicity directors – and upbraided subordinates for lack of zeal. He expected monk-like devotion and paid low wages, even paying himself not much more than a subsistence salary. For most of the 1920s and 1930s Baldwin earned less than $2,500 per year; in 1940 his salary rose to $3,600. In 1921, he relented to his staff's request for Columbus Day off only when they threatened to strike. When Baldwin led the ACLU, it never ran a deficit. He told Dwight MacDonald that he "ran it the way a family operates – spent only as much as came in each year." According to MacDonald, Baldwin never sought large donations and tried to limit them to a maximum of $1,000. His lack of financial aggressiveness, however, did not prevent the organization from accepting Albert DeSilver's largesse. Until his death in an accident in 1924, general counsel DeSilver donated $1,000 to $1,500 every month, sometimes accounting for half the organization's yearly budget of $20,000 (MacDonald, 1953b: 30; Walker, 1990: 66-70).

In its first year the ACLU had a budget of $20,000 and a thousand members. Ten years later, it had grown to $25,000 and 2,500 members who paid a two-dollar fee. The remainder of its income came mostly from wealthy supporters, many of whom were Quakers. DeSilver's widow continued to support the organization through much of the 1920s. Members received a monthly bulletin and elected the National Committee but otherwise had no voice in the organization. They were members much like one could be a member of the National Geographic Society. New York had the largest concentration of members with San Francisco, Los Angeles, Chicago, Boston, and Philadelphia also having large local groups. Members could be active in local affiliates, especially outside of New York, where Baldwin exercised political and organizational control of the Union by controlling its Board of Directors and National Committees. The National Committee, a letterhead committee of supporters, in 1920 included such left-wing and liberal political luminaries as Jane Addams, Helen Keller, Felix Frankfurter, Morris Hillquit, and Norman Thomas. Later it included well-known gadflies and figures from the arts and consisted of sixty members from throughout the country; they exercised nominal authority over all policy matters, meeting once a year to elect a Board of Directors. The election was pro forma. The Board of Directors was recruited by

Baldwin with some consultation from the National Committee and heads of the affiliates. It convened every other week at the Hotel Martinique in midtown Manhattan; as a result members had to be from the New York area. The Board meetings were exciting social and political affairs and involved discussion and debate of the most pressing current civil liberties issues. In his autobiography, playwright Elmer Rice noted that "nothing in my civic life meant more to me than my thirty-year membership on the board of the ACLU": "week after week, year after year," ACLU meetings gave him "a panoramic revelation of America's political and economic life." While he cherished the social aspects of the Union, he, like many of the other celebrity members, also devoted considerable energy to the organization, specifically its anticensorship committee. As part of the National Council of Freedom from Censorship Committee, Rice engaged in debates, went on speaking tours, wrote pamphlets, and conducted extensive correspondence with both supporters and antagonists in various campaigns against censorship (Rice, 1963: 346-47; MacDonald, 1953b; Walker, 1990: 67).

The ACLU's strength in gaining publicity on the national stage and, at times, moving the courts in a more civil liberties direction, however, proved incapable of fundamentally affecting the nation's rightward drift. As a political force, the ACLU had limited influence outside of the corridors of urban liberalism. For instance, it succeeded in forcing New York City's Board of Education to open up its school buildings for public lectures (the Board had a policy that required all speakers to "be loyal to American Institutions"). When, however, in 1923 the Ku Klux Klan took over the Akron, Ohio school board and tried to fire Catholic teachers, the Union, lacking a membership base or local attorneys, was forced to observe affairs from a distance. Even the Scopes trial that brought so much attention to the organization was not the result of the ACLU's ties to the community. It came to defend Tennessee biology teacher John Scopes because it solicited him as a defendant. The trial was a media coup and fundraising bonanza for the national organization and gave Clarence Darrow tremendous attention. Scopes lost the trial and was only saved from paying the $500 fine by a judicial mistake. The trial proved to be but a skirmish in the cultural war that has yet to end. It occasioned no end to the ridicule of the "backwardness" of rural America and, as a result, led the near majority of states that had passed anti-evolution laws to rescind them or let them lie dormant. Yet, at the same time, the teaching of evolution in high school science nationwide stopped until the early 1960s when the alarm over the Soviet Union's launching of "Sputnik" forced the country to rethink its approach to science education (Larson, 2006; Walker, 1990: 75-76).

The ACLU was one of the few predominantly white organizations with a national presence that took a stand against racism in the 1920s. It worked closely with the NAACP, offering a seat on its executive board to an official of the civil rights group. It effected a division of labor in which the NAACP would litigate cases involving blacks' rights. With few contacts in the South's hostile political climate, the ACLU was mostly restricted to publicizing civil liberties issues and repeatedly condemned racist violence, especially that of the KKK, which during the 1920s was ascendant in many parts of the U.S. In 1931, it published a comprehensive report, *Black Justice*, which detailed violations of blacks' rights (Walker, 1990: 60, 62).

Funding Social Change: The Garland Fund

In the 1920s the NAACP received funding from the American Fund for Public Service, popularly known as the Garland Fund after its benefactor Charles Garland. Charles Garland, whose father was a railroad promoter, received a bequest of $1,000,000, and being a Tolstoyan anarchist, he did not feel entitled to the money. He decided that the money should go to supporting social change. Roger Baldwin, along with Norman Thomas and liberal University of Chicago English professor Robert Morss Lovett, assisted him in setting up the Fund. Its board of directors included (1) Scott Nearing, a dissident academic twice fired for his antiwar views during World War I and a "back to the land" advocate, (2) Rabbi Judah Magnes, a prominent liberal, (3) William Z. Foster, a leader of the Communist Party, and (4) James Weldon Johnson, secretary (executive director) of the NAACP. Elizabeth Gurley Flynn, before she was a Communist Party member, worked on staff. The Fund's endowment consisted of stock in the First National Bank of New York, which did so well that with the endowment doubling during the 1920s, it appeared that trustees of the Fund might be stymied in spending it down.

From 1925 to 1929, the NAACP received $31,500 from the Garland Fund for litigation and legal defense efforts. The Association needed these funds because membership dues could not support its areas of legal work, which included: (1) the defense of Ossian Sweet, a Detroit doctor charged with murder after defending himself against a mob attack on his home in a white neighborhood, (2) challenges to racially restrictive zoning and covenants, and (3) ongoing challenges to Texas' white primary. The Garland Fund also granted the NAACP magazine *Crisis* $5,000 to investigate school funding in the South. The investigation found wide disparities undermining claims of separate but equal.

The Garland Fund brought to the surface a debate in the NAACP between those who advocated a position of "economic instrumentalism" (including Ralph Bunche and W.E.B. Du Bois) that saw the courts as reflecting the interests of the ruling class and those who accepted a theory of "autonomous legalism" that saw the norms of political fairness embodied in the Constitution as being only occasionally effective. Practically, the debate concerned whether the Fund should encourage an anti-discrimination campaign or a labor-organizing drive – Baldwin backed the latter. The Fund's Committee on Negro Work (which consisted of James Weldon Johnson of the NAACP, Morris Ernst of the NAACP Legal Committee and ACLU, and Lewis Gannett of the ACLU) decided, with the backing of $100,000, "to finance a large-scale, widespread, dramatic campaign to give the Southern Negro his constitutional rights, his civil and political equality, and therewith a self-consciousness and self-respect which would inevitably tend to effect a revolution in the economic life of this country" (quoting Committee on Negro Work in Tushnet, 1987: 7).

The NAACP would bring this about by supporting lawsuits by taxpayers in seven Deep South states to equalize expenditures between white and black students. These suits, prefiguring a tactic that would be taken up by the welfare rights movement and supporting attorneys in the 1960s, would raise the costs of dual school systems so high that they would bring about an end to segregated schools. They would serve as a positive example to blacks throughout the South to bring similar legal action. Suits in localities would be appealed, won, and thus be binding on larger jurisdictions, and they would "focus as nothing else will public attention north and south on the vicious discrimination in the apportionment of public school funds" (quoting letter of Morris Ernst to Walter White, in Tushnet, 1987: 14; see Piven and Cloward, 1966).

Alas, with the stock market crash the funds had almost disappeared by 1935. The NAACP saw hardly any of the money promised it, but it conducted the study (referred to as the Margold Report after its author Nathan Margold, a Felix Frankfurter protégé who worked for the NAACP for a year and then went on to become a prominent government attorney during the New Deal) that became the blueprint for the legal strategy that led to *Brown v. Board of Education* (MacDonald, 1953a: 53; Tushnet, 1987: 2-3, 6-7).

NAACP: Black Attorneys Move to the Fore

In 1929, Louis Marshall and Moorefield Storey both died within a few months. While the passing, in Walter White's words, of "our greatest legal assets," was a blow to the Association's legal team, it also opened the way for a new generation of lawyers to enter the fray. In litigating, the NAACP often retained white lawyers to gain expertise or community support, but it also had to retain black lawyers to maintain its relations with the black community and show support to them. In 1931, the National Bar Association, the ABA's black counterpart, at its annual convention condemned "the untrustworthy and sinister practices" of black preachers and doctors who sent other blacks to white lawyers. They also criticized unnamed legal defense organizations for not employing black attorneys. Delegates voted to send their resolution to both the NAACP and to the Communist Party-supported International Labor Defense. Black lawyers and other professionals in cities such as Chicago and Houston pushed for more black involvement in the Association's litigation, but there were countervailing pressures from sympathetic whites and black civic leaders that bi-racial counsel was important. This was hardly a mere symbolic issue. Charles Hamilton Houston (Dean of Howard University Law School, later to become NAACP special counsel) pointed out in his report to Dean Roscoe Pound of Harvard Law School that, especially in Border States such as Maryland and in the District of Columbia, "certain judges will not give a Negro lawyer an impartial hearing where opposing counsel is white" (Houston, 1928; Meier and Rudwick, 1976: 146, 148-49).

Increasing pressure from black lawyers, with support from activists in NAACP branches, to take on major responsibilities for the Association's legal strategy coincided with the development of a stratum of talented and well-trained African American lawyers. These included graduates of Harvard and other elite schools who were trained in constitutional law and graduates of Howard's upgraded and newly-accredited law school.

As previously noted, in the 1920s a group of black law students studied constitutional law with Felix Frankfurter at Harvard. The preeminent members of this "small but growing elite of brilliant young black men" were Jesse Heslip of Toledo, president from 1931 to 1933 of the National Bar Association, and William H. Hastie and Charles Hamilton Houston, both of whom served on the *Harvard Law Review*. They would be the mentors of the nation's first generation of civil rights lawyers, but the institutional anchor in which they would carry out their leadership was the considerably less elite Howard University.

In 1922, Howard University demanded a high school diploma for admission. A year later the school made important changes that would affect the supply of civil rights lawyers. It began a requirement of at least two years of college and added a day school. The law school appointed three full-time professors with the promise of paying salaries of $1,500 ($16,370 in 2006 dollars), if the school could afford it. The library reached 1,000 volumes – the American Association of Law Schools (AALS) requirement for membership. As of 1928 approximately 1,000 lawyers had graduated from Southern black schools, 700 of them from Howard. That same year, the part-time program was extended to four years. In 1930-31, the ABA bestowed accreditation on Howard, which was elected to the AALS in 1931. Students found meeting the school's standards for admission difficult, and enrollment declined. In the 1923-24 school year, the school had 135 students. By 1926-27, it had 82 (Stevens, 1983: 196).

Charles Hamilton Houston became dean of Howard University Law School in 1929. He had studied under Frankfurter at Harvard and graduated in the top five percent of his class in 1922. He stayed on at Harvard to earn a doctor of juridical science and later traveled to Europe on a scholarship, where he earned a doctor of civil law at the University of Madrid. He noted that the black attorney was highly confined in his practice to

> only a few, very definite stereotyped situations: the errant spouse, the parent abandoning the children, administration of small estates comprised of a little money in the bank life insurance policies, and the family residence, and petty criminal offences. As long as the cases run true to type he makes a fairly brave showing. But shunted ever so little off the beaten path, he becomes befuddled (quoted in Meier and Rudwick, 1976: 131).

Recognizing the limits under which most black lawyers would operate, he nevertheless aspired to make Howard more rigorous so as to give blacks the tools they needed to make a difference. Houston believed the law was a tool for social change and that lawyers were obligated to use it to achieve justice. Accordingly, he commented, "a lawyer's either a social engineer or he's a parasite on society" (quoted in Fairclough, 2001: 198; Greenberg, 2004: 4-5).

The NAACP appointed Houston to part-time counsel in 1934 and in 1935 to special counsel, making him the first black to occupy that post. In *Hollins v. State of Oklahoma*, 295 U.S. 394 (1935), he and an all-black team of attorneys successfully argued before the Supreme Court to have the death sentence of a black man accused of rape overturned on the grounds that blacks were excluded from the jury. This was the first prominent case of the NAACP to include all-black counsel and one of the first times all-black counsel appeared before the U.S. Supreme Court. In 1936 the NAACP hired Thurgood Marshall as an assistant special counsel at the urging of Houston, who was consumed by his attempts to gain Lloyd Gaines, *Missouri ex rel. Gaines v. Canada*, 305 U.S. 337 (1938), admittance to the University of Missouri Law School. Two years later Marshall was promoted to special counsel (Meier and Rudwick, 1976: 151, 155).

Marshall's apprenticeship for the position of America's most important black lawyer was much different from that of his predecessor. Marshall had graduated from the North's only black men's college, Lincoln University, in 1930 and then graduated first in his class from Howard University Law School in 1933. He did not extend his education by gaining a doctorate at an Ivy League university or travel on scholarship to study in Europe. He started his own practice after graduating and worked with the local NAACP branch in Baltimore. In fact, he spent little of it in courtrooms. When he assumed the position as assistant special counsel, he devoted most of his time to traveling through Maryland's twenty-three counties, organizing African American teachers to demand equal pay with their white counterparts. He took with him the simple message that there was no justice in paying white janitors $960 a year and black elementary-school teachers $621. He tried to convince white school officials of the injustice and urged black teachers to act. Organizing teachers was important because they fit into the plans for attacking segregation in education that the Margold Report had laid out. It was also crucial to success because of the social role teachers played in the black community, especially in the South. First of all, there were lots of black teachers, and, second, they occupied leadership positions, often the best educated and constantly in contact with all segments of the community. Between the time he was hired and became special counsel in 1938, Marshall won nine equal-pay agreements from Maryland county school boards (Kluger, 1976: 214-15; Greenberg, 2004: 29-30).

A change was occurring in the NAACP that would give it greater depth in the black community and put its legal work in the center of the coming civil rights movement. In 1930, the organization had a reputation for elitism. It was perceived in the black community as populated by businessmen and professionals, members of the "self-appointed Negro Upper class." When the Association recruited black lawyers to its Legal Committee in the early 1930s it did so, according to Tushnet "to stimulate membership activity in its branches, to demonstrate the advance of the race into areas previously dominated by whites, and to respond to pressure by black lawyers seeking recognition for their own achievements." These efforts did little to build popular support for the NAACP among the mass of blacks. Going directly to teachers, and through them to black parents, brought the NAACP closer to its constituency and addressed the aspirations of teachers for economic advancement and status recognition and the community's desire for educational equity. In addition, black workers, especially mail carriers and other federal civil service employees who enjoyed some job protection and status, became more politically confident and asserted leadership in local branches. Southern cities like New Orleans had NAACP branches under the control of black workers, and in Northern cities like Detroit where blacks had a toehold in private sector unions, workers vied for leadership of the Association. With a changing leadership and local branch activism spurred in part by the actions of people like Thurgood Marshall, the NAACP continued growing and asserting itself as the leading voice of black America (Kluger, 1976: 214; Tushnet, 1987: 29; Fairclough, 2001: 183-84).

In March 1939, Marshall decided to forgo the county-by-county negotiations over equal pay. Instead, he took the case to the U.S. District Court: in *Mills v. Board of Education of Anne Arundel County*, 30 F. Supp. 245 (1939), Judge W. Calvin Chestnut ruled that the discriminatory pay policy that held in much of Maryland "violated the supreme law of the land." The county chose not to appeal the case and henceforth, along with the Supreme Court victory in *Gaines* (1938), the NAACP embarked on a strategy of suing in the federal courts, a plan whose success would be realized in *Brown v. Board of Education* (1954). It was a move that at the time made perfect sense; given the small NAACP legal staff and a dearth of attorneys in the South who could try cases in local courts, litigating in federal courts promised to make law that would be binding on the nation. It also meant that a more efficient division of labor could be effected. Lawyers after all were hired for their legal expertise, not for their organizing talent. But it was a move that threatened the organic ties between attorneys and clients (Kluger, 1976: 215).

Making Expertise Count/ACLU

In the 1930s the ACLU deepened its commitment to a legal strategy for change and broadened its political mandate. In 1929 it appointed Arthur Garfield Hays and Morris Ernst as general co-counsel, signaling a decisive shift in its priorities and providing the legal expertise that would allow it to become the leading activist voice of constitutional law. Hays and Ernst jointly held the positions of general counsel through the mid-1950s. Besides planning the Union's legal strategy and arguing in the courts, they supervised the New York office's two staff attorneys who in turn supervised the volunteer cooperating attorneys.

Baldwin proposed in early 1929 to expand the ACLU's program. He wanted renewed attention paid to the struggle for Negro rights. He also proposed launching a major campaign on behalf of Native Americans and expected the organization to take up a vigorous defense of immigrants in naturalization and deportation hearings. In keeping with its roots in the peace and workers movements, the ACLU decided to mount a political offensive against mandatory military training in schools and to continue to support organized labor. It sought to have a role in shaping public policy with its legal and policy expertise. Two points should be emphasized here: timing, and the manner in which the ACLU sought to expand its political program. Baldwin and the ACLU were the champions of underdogs and lost causes. He wanted the organization to advocate politically for blacks, Indians, immigrants, workers and at the same time to oppose militarism. Once again, the ACLU's timing was all wrong. None of these groups enjoyed much social cachet in America, nor was there much of a reason to expect that the ACLU's position with regard to mandatory military training would be popular. Prohibition created an oppositional culture, but it was more libertine than liberal. To advocate on behalf of blacks, Native Americans, and immigrants, it would have to mobilize not only its paltry membership but its resources of legal and educational expertise and its social capital.

Two early 1930s cases were indicative of the way in which Baldwin was able to use his personal connections and organizational resources to increase the profile of the ACLU. These were the investigation of police brutality and the lobbying for the passage of the Norris-LaGuardia Act to abolish labor injunctions. In both cases, he entered on the side of unpopular social groups, accused criminals and labor and pushed an agenda of liberal reform. In this way he used expertise, personal connections, and political pressure on opinion-shapers in the media and legislatures to effect change. In 1929, Herbert Hoover established the Wickersham Commission to investigate American criminal justice. It was the first federal study to look at the system as a whole, but is mostly remembered for its report on police brutality. Baldwin successfully lobbied the Commission to hire Walter Pollak, Zechariah Chaffee, who had conducted a similar study for the ACLU in Boston, and Carl Stern. These volunteer attorneys associated closely with the ACLU to write the report. It attracted national attention, documenting the pervasive use of the "third degree – the inflicting of pain, physical or mental, to extract confessions or statements," including keeping suspects "standing for hours ... deprived of food or sleep" or the shining of bright lights directly in the face. The report, entitled *Lawlessness in Law Enforcement* (1931), aided the movement for professionalization of law enforcement by creating a constituency for change outside of the policing community. It also recommended that the police be held accountable to the law through formal procedures.

Likewise, when organized labor was at its nadir, the ACLU challenged one of the greatest impediments to labor's ability to organize effectively, the labor injunction, which essentially made picketing illegal. In 1930 Baldwin organized a group of experts and political notables, the National Committee on Labor Injunctions, to publicize the deleterious effects of the courts on labor's right to organize. The same year, ACLU volunteer attorneys Felix Frankfurter and Nathan Greene published *The Labor Injunction*. Frankfurter went on to help draft the Norris-LaGuardia Act (1932), which restricted the use of injunctions against labor unions and marked the beginning of a series of New Deal laws that increased the voice and power of American workers (Walker, 1999: 87-88).

Finally, it chose to fight censorship in books, plays, movies, and radio, and gained an important victory in *United States v. Dennett*, 39 F.2d 564 (2d Cir. 1930), when it successfully appealed the obscenity conviction of Mary Ware Dennett for the publication of *The Sex Side of Life*, a primer on sexuality for adolescents. Dennett was a long-time member of the ACLU and had been the secretary of the National American Women's Suffrage Association. The pamphlet, originally published in 1918 in the *Medical Review of Reviews*, had by the late 1920s sold over 35,000 copies. She had among her allies notable liberals such as John Dewey and conservative figures like the publisher Roy Howard and Mrs. Marshall Field. A defense committee raised both consciousness and funds. After the federal Second Circuit Court of Appeals overturned her conviction, an excess of $1,265 was turned over to the ACLU.

The ACLU enjoyed success in its fight against censorship because it was hardly on the side of the underdog. The Dennett case marked a watershed in public attitudes toward sexuality and changing gender roles. Fifteen years earlier, issues of sex education and birth control had been the province of radicals such as Emma Goldman, Elizabeth Gurley Flynn, and Margaret Sanger. Censorship of material that dealt explicitly with sex gained prominent and relatively widespread opposition. It also gained adherents to the ACLU. Four years later, ACLU general counsel Morris Ernst won another landmark case, *United States v. One Book Entitled Ulysses*, 72 F.2d 705 (2d Cir. 1934), that overturned the Customs Service's ban on James Joyce's *Ulysses* (Walker, 1990: 84-7).

Groundbreaking cases in defense of the First Amendment vindicated the ACLU's earlier efforts in the Supreme Court. In *Stromberg v. California*, 283 U.S. 359 (1931), an appeal the ACLU argued with the help of the Communist Party-backed International Labor Defense, the Supreme Court overturned the conviction of Communist Party member Yetta Stromberg for displaying "a red flag, banner or badge ... as a sign, symbol, or emblem of opposition to organized government." It held contrary to *Schenk* (1919), and in accordance with Holmes' dissent in *Abrams* (1919), that the maintenance of the opportunity for free political discussion ... is a fundamental principle of our constitutional system." A second case before the Supreme Court, *Near v. Minnesota*, 283 U.S. 697 (1931), addressed freedom of the press. *The Saturday Press* expressed the anti-Catholic, anti-Semitic, anti-black, and anti-labor opinions of its publisher Jay Near. Minnesota authorities closed down the publication under a 1925 public nuisance abatement law after it had charged the mayor, police chief, and county attorney with corruption and nonfeasance. The Court ruled the law unconstitutional, holding that "the liberty of the press and of speech is within the liberties safeguarded by the due process clause of the Fourteenth Amendment from invasion by state action." The ruling affirmed for the first time the freedom of the press against prior restraint and vindicated arguments that Walter Pollak had made earlier in *Gitlow* (1925).

In the 1930s the ACLU's ties to the labor movement remained strong. Board members, including perennial Socialist Party presidential candidate Norman Thomas, still spent much of their political energy on union organizing, and the radicalism associated with the fledgling Committee for Industrial Organization (CIC) resonated among leftists of all classes. Across the Hudson from its headquarters the ACLU became involved in a protracted struggle for the right to organize that would bring in much favorable publicity and expand the space in which free speech could take place. Jersey City mayor Frank "Boss" Hague had run the city in an autocratic manner since he was first elected in 1917. Promising the local business community that Jersey City would remain a safe place for its investments, Boss Hague kept the town free from labor organizing by banning CIO leaflets, denying meeting space for the ACLU and Socialist Party, harassing pickets, and breaking up open-air gatherings. His tactics and the labor movement response resembled the battle over free speech that the IWW had waged in the 1910s. The ACLU became involved when Board member Corliss Lamont, Harvard-trained lawyer and son of the Chairman of J.P. Morgan, , was arrested for picketing in 1934. Over the next four years in coalition with the CIO and the Communist and Socialist Parties, the ACLU mounted a campaign of publicity that attracted national attention and civil disobedience that occasioned hundreds of arrests. Boss Hague had declared, "we hear about constitutional rights, free speech and free press, but every time I hear these words, I say to myself, 'that man is a Red, that man is a Communist.'" He had his police physically evict Norman Thomas from the city and threatened Arthur Garfield Hays for public speaking (Walker, 1999: 110).

Late in 1937, when the CIO decided to launch another organizing campaign, Morris Ernst decided to shift legal tactics. Instead of inviting arrests, he decided to seek an immediate injunction against Hague's systematic denial of First Amendment rights. District Court Judge William Clark granted the injunction and ordered Hague to cease the illegal harassment of the CIO and ACLU's activities. The Supreme Court upheld the injunction, in *Hague v. Committee for Industrial Organization*, 307 U.S. 496 (1939). The Court broke ground in First Amendment jurisprudence when it ruled that the streets and parks were public forums in which free speech could not "in the guise of regulation, be abridged or denied."

> Wherever the title of streets and parks may rest, they have immemorially been held in trust for the use of the public and, time out of mind, have been used for purposes of assembly, communicating thoughts between citizens, and discussing public questions. Such use of the streets and public places has, from ancient times, been a part of the privileges, immunities, rights, and liberties of citizens. (*Hague*, 307 U.S. 496, 515 (1939).)

Beyond its victories in the courts, the ACLU expanded its affiliates to Cleveland, Philadelphia, San Francisco, Seattle, and St. Louis. State chapters were opened in Indiana, Iowa, and Texas between 1935 and 1939. While decisions affecting the national character and legal strategy of the organization were made by Baldwin in New York, local affiliates had autonomy to undertake campaigns at their home bases. The Chicago Civil

Liberties Committee regularly opposed the police department's film censorship board, and it also engaged in local civil rights organizing as the first predominantly white group to advocate for a state antidiscrimination law. The St. Louis affiliate had an extensive series of subcommittees tackling many areas of civil liberties concern: academic freedom, freedom of the press, labor, federal legislation, and conscientious objection to the draft (Walker, 1999: 118-19).

The spread of ACLU affiliates and influence was the result of a dialectic of victory and repression, of political mobilization from below and government response. The defeat of Boss Hague occurred in a context of massive CIO organizing and popular electoral support for the Left nationally and locally (Zeiger, 1995: ch. 5). Likewise, the advances made against censorship reflected changing roles for women, expanded ideas of appropriate sexuality, and spread of education (Goode, 1963; Veysey, 1965). The policies that the Union had championed in the 1920s were established, if unevenly, in law and policy. Roger Baldwin's social connections to those in the corridors of power were beginning to be translated into influence. Eleanor Roosevelt headlined the Chicago ACLU convention in 1939. Attorney General Frank Murphy addressed the ACLU's national Conference on Civil Liberties in the Present Emergency. The President declared a Bill of Rights Day, and Chicago and New York designated Bill of Rights weeks. The Baltimore ABA Bill of Rights Committee asserted that the Bill of Rights "has long since ceased to be news. It is an accepted and integral part of everyday and ordinary use" (Walker, 1999: 134).

These expansions in civil liberties brought about a backlash. The growth of the labor movement and the political Left produced a surge of anti-radicalism mostly in the guise of anticommunism. In 1938, the U.S. House created a Special Committee on Un-American Activities (HUAC). Popularly known as the Dies Committee, after its chairman Martin Dies, Jr. (D-TX), its original mandate was to investigate the Ku Klux Klan and right-wing German-American movements, but it quickly turned its attention to left-wing movements and American Communist Party influence, in particular in the CIO, New Deal agencies, and Hollywood. Ironically, a number of key witnesses before the Committee, among them Luis Budenz, Benjamin Gitlow, and J.B. Matthews, were former employees or clients of the ACLU. When the Red Scare came to New York's City College it targeted not only leftist professors and students primarily associated with the Communist Party but also free-thinking radicals such as British philosopher Bertrand Russell, to whom City College offered a position and then rescinded it after Protestant and Catholic clergy protested his appointment. The Catholic dioceses attacked him as a "professor of paganism," and the state legislature censured him as an "advocate of barnyard morality." Mayor Fiorello LaGuardia quietly deleted Russell's position from the

City College budget, but not so quietly that it prevented the ACLU and the American Association of University Professors (AAUP) from suing. Judge McGeehan ruled against the ACLU and AAUP declaring that the appointment was "an insult to the people of the City of New York" and "in direct violation of the public health, safety, and the morals of the people." The Court of Appeals refused to consider the case (Belfrage, 1973; Schrecker, 1986; Walker, 1999: 120-21, 124-25).

The Public Interest Bar Consolidates

The Great Depression encouraged movements for social change throughout the country, and the legal profession was affected by and responded to the social and economic turmoil as well. Structurally and ideologically committed to stability – the basis of the legal system relied on rationally-derived rules intended to deliver predictable results – the profession experienced turmoil. The country experienced an economic collapse not seen since the nineteenth century. Detroit labor lawyer Maurice Sugar recalled that in the midst of one of the world's largest concentrations of industrial wealth, "literal starvation had been the lot of some, garbage cans and dumps the source of food for many.... Repossessions, evictions, bankruptcies, foreclosures had become the order of the day. Everywhere was suffering, misery, despair" (quoted in Babson, 1999: 55).

The economic hardship affected the profession unevenly. In New York City seventeen percent of firm lawyers earned as little as $2,000 a year, but more than a third of solo practitioners earned less. In 1933, the median income of lawyers in Manhattan was below $3,000; nearly half the members of the metropolitan bar earned less than the minimum subsistence level for American families. In 1934, 1,500 lawyers in NYC declared they were the equivalent of paupers to qualify for work relief. Jewish lawyers, who at every level of income below $5,000 exceeded their proportion to the general population of lawyers, were particularly hard hit. They were overrepresented among solo practitioners, they were excluded from established Gentile law firms, and they depended on a preponderantly Jewish clientele.

During the thirties the profession came under renewed criticism and self-criticism, especially for its ties to the business community. Columbia University professor Adolph A. Berle accused the profession of being "virtually an intellectual jobber and contractor in business matters." Harvard law professor Calvert Magruder implored the profession to "cease to take its ethics, its economics, and its political ideals from the banker." The National Lawyers Guild in its founding manifesto attacked the ABA, whose "concern for liberty has been secondary to its concern for property" (Auerbach, 1976: 159, 162, 199).

The profession was experiencing a sense of collective role strain in trying to reconcile its commitment to stability with the loss of social legitimacy that accompanied the turmoil of the 1930s. An overall response was the growth of political lawyering that went beyond the organizational and political boundaries of the NAACP and the ACLU. The first manifestation of this broadening trend was the movement of elite lawyers and ethnic minority lawyers trained at elite law schools into government service. Political and ideological changes during the New Deal motivated a cadre of law professors and students eager to enter the field of public interest law. The growth of regulatory agencies during the New Deal required lawyers to staff the activist agencies. Demand for lawyers in the federal government created one of the few growth areas of employment in the profession. Work increased for established lawyers willing to staff federal bureaucracies, but their lure was greater for recent law graduates and professors, who came to accept that public service had an important role in legal education. Law schools met the demand for government lawyers by creating administrative law courses in first-year curriculums. Walter Gellhorn, an ACLU board member and Columbia University Law School professor, devoted his class in clinical practice to civil liberties and civil rights cases referred to him by the ACLU, NAACP, and American Jewish Congress. Yale set up a program structured like contemporary clinics in which second-year students worked in federal agencies under the mentorship of senior lawyers or policy makers and met with other students and government officials to discuss issues "along the frontiers of public law" (Brown, 1948: 134-55; Irons, 1982; Stevens, 1983: 160; Abel, 1989: 280).

Lawyers *qua* lawyers began to organize. A small group of left-leaning lawyers, including Morris Ernst, Jerome Frank, Karl Llewellyn, and labor lawyer and supporter of Irish nationalism, Frank Walsh, met in New York in late 1936 to discuss forming a "democratic, socially-conscious, lawyers' guild." Early in 1937 the National Lawyers Guild was founded as a racially inclusive alternative to the American Bar Association – the ABA would not lift its ban against black members until 1943 – and in reaction to the profession's close identification with corporate interests (Auerbach, 1976: 198-200).

Attorneys joined the National Lawyers Guild for a variety of reasons. Some wanted to rally lawyers to the New Deal; others, especially Karl Llewellyn, wanted it to advocate for, and perhaps provide, low cost legal services; and others were upset by the ABA's racism and obeisance to commercial values. The Guild was, in Jerold Auerbach's words,

> an always incongruous, usually tenuous, alliance of liberal lawyers with strong ties to the professional establishment, radical attorneys with equally strong commitments to the political Left, law teachers who were dismayed by the commer-

cial tone of the organized bar, and low-status urban practitioners from ethnic minority groups who were frustrated in
their quest for professional success (Auerbach, 1976: 200).

Many joined because they felt the need for a counterweight to political
lawyering on the Right. The ABA's hegemonic role as the institutional
spokesman for the elite of the profession surely stuck in the craw of many a
radical attorney, but it generally played out that role in the manner of an
"apolitical" guarantor of the general interests of the bar and so tended to
take partisan political sides infrequently. The same could not be said for
the National Lawyers Committee, the legal arm of the American Liberty
League, a group of "disaffected businessmen" on the Right. In opposing
Roosevelt's liberalism, this group claimed to welcome all classes of people
but was led by northern industrialists, notably executives of Du Pont and
General Motors, and anti-New Deal Democrats. It dismissed the New Deal
as a Rooseveltian road to socialism and based its opposition on the principle of personal liberty and "foster[ing] the right to work, earn, save and
acquire property." The National Lawyers Committee took out newspaper
and radio ads offering free legal advice to anyone willing to oppose New
Deal legislation in the courts. Its greatest legal moment was in its unsuccessful challenge to the Wagner Act before the Supreme Court, but with
virtually nothing to show from its efforts, it ran out of steam. By encouraging small property owners to litigate against government involvement in
the economy it was a harbinger of the business-funded "freedom-based
public interest law movement" of the late twentieth century (Rudolph,
1950; Leuchtenburg, 1963: 92; Shamir, 1995: 92; Hillbink, 2002: 83; Edwards, 2004).

More traditional sectors of the bar increased their involvement in public interest pursuits. The American Bar Association established its Committee on the Bill of Rights in 1938, and in 1939 U.S. Attorney General
Frank Murphy created the Civil Liberties Unit, which would later become
the Civil Rights Division of the Justice Department. With American entry
into the war, pressure for lawyers to engage in public service also increased
(Brown, 1948: 38-39; Stevens, 1983: 180, 199; Walker, 1999: 111, 113).

5

POLITICAL MOBILIZATION LAWYERING:
POLITICS, HISTORY, AND ORGANIZATIONAL CULTURE

This chapter continues the case study of the previous chapter. In it I present a roughly chronological narrative of the NAACP-LDF and ACLU from the late-1940s to the mid-1970s to highlight the interaction of politics, historical context, and organizational culture on the choices the two organizations made to carry out their missions.

In retrospect, the long campaign to desegregate schools that had its legal culmination in *Brown v. Board of Education*, 347 U.S. 483 (1954), seems like the brilliant application of legal expertise. Historical accounts such as Tushnet's (1987), and autobiographical versions such as Jack Greenberg's (2004), emphasize legal tactics, oratorical skills, and competing arguments. According to Greenberg, the eventual successor to Thurgood Marshall at the NAACP Legal Defense Fund, the early graduate and professional school cases that LDF brought against segregated schools in the South "were litigation campaign law making cases *par excellence*." They provided little relief of major importance, although the few students who received advanced degrees undoubtedly benefited. The importance of these cases was in long-term law making (Wasby, 1984: 89).

The difficulty that attends such narratives of litigation-inspired social change is that the reaction to the narratives both overcredits the specialized knowledge and political acumen of lawyers for their "groundbreaking" feats, and blames the same lawyers for the backlash and subsequent failings that the social change wrought. A body of literature has arisen expressing skepticism over the role legal strategies play in promoting social change and blaming lawyers for the decline in social movement activism. The arguments fall into two categories: neo-realist and structuralist critiques. Neo-realist analyses, of which Critical Legal Studies is the most influential branch (Kelman, 1987), emphasize that the law provides few resources for social movements. It offers, in Gerald Rosenberg's phrase, a "hollow hope." The gap between "law on the books" and law as it is practiced is a result of inherent judicial limitations. The courts are limited because they lack independence from other branches of government, lack any of their own power – they control neither police nor policy – and neither elites nor the general public understand or follow judicial edicts (McCann, 1986, 1994: 288-93; Rosenberg, 1991).

The structuralist critique builds on neo-realist skepticism of the power of the courts but goes further and argues that the organizational costs of litigation subtract from the ability of social movements to effect change. Litigation is expensive, and resource-poor social movements can ill-afford the costs (both financial and psychological) of going to court and possibly losing. Litigation, the argument charges, diverts activists from more productive tasks such as recruiting and mobilizing constituent groups. It gives undue authority to attorneys, who in pursuing litigation put restrictions on the activities of clients, essentially discouraging them from other forms of protest and pressure. Finally, litigation purportedly moves struggles that are concerned with system-wide injustice into individual disputes between discrete parties (Scheingold, 1974; McCann, 1986; Gordon, 2005).

A major aim of this study has been to explore the political context and connections in which public interest lawyering proceeded. To see how litigation and political organizing have affected one another, it is useful to examine what happened on the ground. The following narrative of one case that led to *Brown* illustrates how the structuralist critique underestimates the way in which going to court could be a rallying point for movement activists. It also imagines a greater repertoire of social movement strategies and tactics than may exist. Finally, it emphasizes the costs in money and activist demoralization of losing without the counterbalancing "profit" derived from victory.

The neo-realist critique appears to have greater efficacy in the wake of the backlash that followed *Brown*. Much of what LDF did in the courts from 1954 through the 1960s was re-litigating *Brown*. Despite its legal efforts, fifty years after the decision, school and housing segregation has returned to education and housing (Massey and Denton, 1993; Kozol, 2005; Orfield and Lee, 2007). The courts were largely powerless in the face of local executive intransigence and federal executive neglect. The dilatory tactics that Southern lawmakers and the lower courts embraced made it appear that they neither understood nor were they willing to follow the Supreme Court's rulings. On the other hand, the neo-realist critique falls short by underestimating the *symbolic* power of judicial victory in the context of grassroots organizing. The "myth of rights" has to be understood as having a counterpart in the "politics of rights" (Scheingold, 1974; McCann, 1994). The Montgomery Bus Boycott, lunch counter sit-ins, and Freedom Rides were part of a general upheaval of protest and litigation that fed off one another.

In the South of the 1940s, in an atmosphere where any challenge to, or even questioning of, the racial status quo brought the threat of financial ruin or worse, the issue of how to begin mobilizing loomed large. While much of the black population, especially in rural areas, seemed intimidated, there was an eagerness to do something. Southern branches of the

NAACP in conjunction with LDF used litigation to mobilize local blacks, but the unfolding relationship between litigation and mobilization was complicated. Instructive of the difficulties and promise of NAACP legal mobilizing is the story of *Briggs v. Elliott.*[1]

Briggs v. Elliott, 342 U.S. 350 (1952), was the first of five cases filed that the Supreme Court combined in *Brown v Board of Education*. It concerned the segregated schools of Summerton, South Carolina, and when it first reached the Supreme Court in 1952, the Court remanded the case back to the District Court. The Supreme Court avoided ruling on whether the Fourteenth Amendment guarantee of equal protection applied to elementary and secondary schools. It noted that the District Court had ruled otherwise but at the same time recognized that the segregated schools of Clarendon County, South Carolina were unequal. When conditions in the Summerton schools had not changed, lawyers for the NAACP appealed directly to the highest court. That court, noting that in the meantime a report had been issued by the school district, sent the matter back to the lower court.

The history of *Briggs* started simply enough as an idea planted in the mind of an individual. The Reverend Joseph Albert DeLaine was the son of a slave, a college educated preacher, and principal of a segregated school just outside of the town of Summerton. In the summer of 1947, J.A. DeLaine was attending an extension course at his alma mater, Allen University, in Columbia when he was called with his classmates to a talk by the Reverend James M. Hinton. Hinton was the South Carolina representative of the black-owned Pilgrim Health and Life Insurance Company and the president of the state chapter of the NAACP. Hinton was an inspiring speaker, and his message was simple:

> The colored people could not rise until they got educated, and was it not powerfully clear that the whites did not want them educated? To give the Negro anything more than the most rudimentary training was to make him restless with his lot and a competitor for your job. And then who would tend the fields for no reward beyond bare subsistence? The black schools of South Carolina were a disgrace, said Hinton. In the first place, it was an ordeal to get to them because there were no buses for black children. Was there no clearer way for whites to say they did not want the Negro to rise above his present station? (Kluger, 1976: 13).

Hinton had a proposal and a request. The South Carolina NAACP would bring suit against the state of South Carolina for failing to provide

---

[1] This narrative, unless otherwise noted, is based on *Simple Justice*, Richard Kluger's (1976) comprehensive history of *Brown v. Board of Education.*

buses. What Hinton wanted was a plaintiff. It was no mean feat finding
one in South Carolina. According to DeLaine, Hinton declared, "No teacher
or preacher in South Carolina has the courage to find a plaintiff to test the
legality of the discriminatory bus-transportation practices in this state."

Courage would be required of many people, and for good reason. But a
lawsuit required more than courage: it needed a plaintiff. The plaintiff had
to have proper legal standing, i.e., he had to be a *bona fide* taxpayer who
could claim a legitimate harm on behalf of his children. In addition, there
were practical requirements that he be reliable, committed to seeing the
suit through to the end, and of good moral character. Nothing could doom
a lawsuit quicker than having a plaintiff change his mind or give up and
leave town. Missing plaintiffs had been a problem in the NAACP's higher
education litigation. For example, in *Missouri ex rel. Gaines v. Canada*,
305 U.S. 337 (1938), Lloyd Gaines disappeared after the Court ordered
that he be admitted to the University of Missouri law school. In the meantime, the state had appropriated $200,000 to start a separate law school
for blacks at Lincoln University. As a result, when the Court remanded the
case to the state to determine whether Lincoln University met the Supreme
Court's requirement of "substantial equality," the issue of whether separate
facilities could be equal went unresolved when no plaintiff appeared
(Tushnet, 1987: 73-74).

DeLaine took up the challenge, received backing from his church
board, and went looking for a plaintiff. Levi Pearson farmed 160 acres with
his brother in the nearby town of Jordan. He had three children who
attended Scott's Branch High School nine miles from their farm. The
children could either walk the nine miles to school or take a second-hand
bus the black community had bought and which frequently broke down.
When DeLaine had earlier appealed to the white superintendent of schools
of Clarendon County for reimbursement, L.B. McCord responded that
Negroes did not pay much in taxes, and area whites could not be expected
to shoulder the burden of paying for colored transportation. Pearson had
helped pay for that bus and knew all too well the difficulties getting to
school, especially when seasonal flooding made swollen streams impassa-
ble on foot. DeLaine explained that the NAACP did not want to rile up the
local whites with the idea that there was a mass protest in the making, so
all they needed was the name of one person. Pearson understood the risks
and agreed. Now DeLaine and the NAACP had what they were looking for,
a plaintiff.

For the next step, DeLaine held a meeting in the Columbia office of
Harold R. Boulware in July 1947. Boulware had graduated in 1938 from
Howard University Law School and had practiced law in South Carolina
starting in 1940. In 1942, he served as counsel for the NAACP branches in
the state (Tushnet, 1987: 87). He was typical of the type of lawyer that

Dean Houston had described. According to Jack Greenberg, "he practiced alone, had limited experience in complex cases, and mostly handled marginal matters.

> Once I accompanied him to a judge's chamber in a divorce case. I was shocked when he took out a bottle of whiskey he had brought along and offered it to the judge as a token of good will. I was startled too, when the judge took it without a word and put it in a bottom drawer of his desk (Greenberg, 2004: 125).

At the meeting Boulware drew up a petition requesting in the name of Pearson's children that "school bus transportation be furnished, maintained, and operated out of public funds in School District Number 26 of Clarendon County, South Carolina, for use of the said children of your Petitioner and other Negro school children similarly situated." Boulware submitted the petition to the appropriate school board, county, and state authorities and, as it was ignored for eight months, filed suit on March 16, 1948 in the U.S. District Court. The complaint charged "irreparable damage "and sought a permanent injunction "forever restraining and enjoining the defendants ... from making a distinction on account of race or color" in providing free bus service for white students while denying it to blacks. Signing the document were Harold Boulware of Columbia, South Carolina, and LDF attorney Thurgood Marshall.

With the filing of the document came an added responsibility for Pearson and DeLaine. Levi Pearson became the acting president of a new branch of the NAACP and DeLaine its secretary. It was, according to Kluger, "practically speaking, an undercover operation. A more open arrangement would have been suicidal in Clarendon County."

And with the filing came the backlash. When Pearson went to plant his crop that spring of 1948, every white-owned, and they were all white-owned, store and bank denied him credit. He had enough cash set aside to purchase seed but could not afford fertilizer. So Levi and his brother took advantage of the land they owned and cut down some of its valuable timber, but the mill to which he would sell it belonged to the grammar school board chairman.

The case of *Pearson v. County Board of Education* took a turn for the worse. On June 8, 1948, the day before the case was to be heard, it was dismissed. Pearson's farm lay just on the wrong side of the line between the school district to which he paid his taxes and District No. 26 to which Scott's Branch High School belonged. The white county school officials had checked his tax records more thoroughly than had the Legal Defense Fund's lawyer. The Court held that Pearson had no legal standing.

The NAACP-LDF's legal strategy to attack inequitable school transportation was in shambles, but Pearson fared as poorly. He had borrowed money that spring from the impoverished black community to buy fertilizer only to discover that in the fall not a single white farmer would provide him with a harvester. His crop of oats, beans, and wheat sat in the fields and rotted.

Filing suit against inadequate school transportation with a single plaintiff had saved the black community the enmity of Clarendon County whites, but it also yielded no results. Pearson and DeLaine refused to concede, however. In fact, they upped the ante. In a meeting in the spring of 1949 with national NAACP-LDF legal counsel Thurgood Marshall, they decided to take on segregation as a violation of the Fourteenth Amendment. They would pursue a test case but with twenty plaintiffs. If DeLaine and his fledgling local chapter could not put together the necessary twenty, Marshall and the NAACP would just move on.

A series of meetings throughout the county had inspired Clarendon blacks to an extent none had witnessed before, but still no plaintiffs came forward. To complicate DeLaine's task the white community made it clear that they were watching events carefully. They summarily fired the principal of eighteen years at Scott's Branch High School and replaced him with a "black man without a college degree but with long experience doing the white man's bidding." Besides being compliant, the new principal proved to be incompetent and a thief who embezzled monies from school fundraising. At a meeting of three hundred angry parents DeLaine took on a more public leadership role and finally began to gather the necessary petitioners. He and other community leaders spent the rest of the summer petitioning the white officials of the county for redress.

The white officials met the challenge by ignoring it, and when that proved impossible they tried to co-opt and intimidate DeLaine at the same time. They fired him from his position as a teacher at a nearby school and offered him the job as principal at Scott's Branch (the school board had let the offending principal go). They also offered to suspend student fees that only blacks paid. When he refused to go along, the school officials appointed his wife, a teacher at the school for more than a dozen years, as acting principal. Efforts to undermine his leadership failed, and he spent the rest of the summer and fall organizing and enlisting support.

On November 11, 1949, J.A. DeLaine presented Thurgood Marshall with the twenty plaintiffs he needed. The first on the list was Harry Briggs, a Navy veteran and father of five children who had pumped gas in town for more than fourteen years but whom the owners had prevented that whole time from doing repair work. The day before Christmas, Briggs' boss gave him a carton of cigarettes and let him go. His wife lost her job of six years as a chambermaid in a local motel. One petitioner lost his job at a local garage; the driver-salesman for Esso got fired despite "never having come up a penny short in ten years on the job." Teachers were let go, and Negro farmers found they could not get their cotton ginned. Billy Fleming who ran the Fleming-DeLaine funeral home discovered that black sharecroppers could no longer use his services because their white bosses refused to pay that funeral parlor's bills. DeLaine's wife and niece lost their teaching jobs, and the Reverend found himself the object of a libel suit brought by the ex-principal whom the white county school board had dismissed the previous October. The all-white jury found DeLaine liable and awarded $2,700 in damages. In April, a notorious white bigot stomped to death a black youth for the offense of urinating on the side of the road.

The black community of Clarendon County had to sustain itself under similar circumstances for the next year. Finally, the NAACP brought to trial *Briggs v. Elliott*, so named, as Richard Kluger aptly put it, "after Harry Briggs, the former gas-station attendant they would never let become a mechanic, and Roderick W. Elliott, flinty chairman of School District No. 22 and owner of the sawmill whose pickup man would not take away the trees that Levi Pearson had cut down to pay for his urgently needed fertilizer."

The possibility of legal redress inspired J.A. Delaine and Levi Pearson, and the black community of Clarendon County; as important, it also pushed them to organize. They founded a local NAACP branch and called upon networks of solidarity. The political organizing did not prevent whites from retaliating economically and physically, but it may have lessened the extent of that retaliation, and it certainly served notice that the Negroes of Summerton, South Carolina were a force to be reckoned with. Several years later, LDF, too, would have to go to the black community for support. In June 1953, the Supreme Court ordered the *Brown* cases be reargued to address specific questions concerning original intent, the power of the Court to abolish school segregation, and how desegregation might be brought about. To do this, the LDF had to undertake new fundraising of approximately $39,000. The black press raised from its readers $14,000; the black American Teachers Association gave $5,000 (the National Education Association would not admit black Southern teachers), and the CIO contributed $2,500. The South Carolina and Virginia state conference branches of the NAACP gave between them $10,100 – this was during a period when the NAACP and the LDF were engaged in one of their frequent organizational conflicts and the Association ordered its branches to have no contact with LDF – and churches and fraternal orders raised the remaining funds. To raise such funds, staff members, including Thurgood Marshall, had to speak as many as twenty times a month before audiences all over the country (Greenberg, 2004: 192).

After the Supreme Court ruled in *Brown II*, 349 U.S. 294 (1955), that segregation be dismantled "with all deliberate speed," i.e., in no great rush, the NAACP-LDF had before it the task of enforcing the decision through subsequent litigation, and then moving on to dismantle segregation in other areas of social life. It therefore took up cases to desegregate higher education, as in *Lucy v. Adams*, 350 U.S. 1 (1955). It went to court to enjoin Governor Orval Faubus from preventing the Little Rock Nine from attending Central High School, assisted in the defense of Rosa Parks, extended *Brown*'s rejection of *Plessy* to public transportation in *Gayle v. Browder*, 352 U.S. 903 (1956), and scored a number of victories in criminal matters.

Marshall recognized that dismantling segregation would require more than the application of legal expertise, as crucial as that was to overthrowing the racial order. As early as 1951, he had requested the addition of non-lawyers to the LDF staff to educate the public and insure community support. Money also had to be raised. The NAACP board had originally organized LDF to increase the Association's income. Over time as the organizations became increasingly independent – an Internal Revenue Service investigation of LDF's independence from the NAACP in 1957 pressured the organizations to separate even more – competition over money, among other real and symbolic assets, caused relations between LDF and the NAACP to become more and more strained. The Fund's headline-grabbing successes in the courts and its nonprofit status made up for its lack of a membership from which dues could be collected. LDF turned to direct mail solicitations and the cultivation of wealthy individuals and small foundations. It received a grant of $75,000 from the Philip Murray Foundation for a campaign of education regarding desegregation and fieldwork to protect the jobs of black teachers.

The IRS investigation in 1957 encouraged LDF to end its overlapping board membership with the NAACP and cut all physical and financial ties between the two groups. Ideological commitments remained very close, especially between LDF and local NAACP branches with which most cooperating attorneys identified, but rivalries between LDF and NAACP leadership were tense and only made worse by LDF's apparent success in fund-raising. In 1959, the LDF budget had increased to $362,000 which included the Fund's first large bequest of $140,000. The money was used to hire new attorneys. In the next two years unsolicited contributions increased, but the biggest boost to finances came from direct mailings to supporters, subscribers to liberal magazines, and other supporters of liberal causes. By 1961 income was over $586,000 (Greenberg, 2004: 125, 215, 222, 313; Meltsner, 2006: 101-07).

Managing Role Strain: The ACLU in the Early 1940s

During the early 1940s, the ACLU participated in a number of cases that tested the organization's coherence and ability to cope with role conflict. In 1940, after a rancorous debate, the Board and National Committee voted to bar from leadership anyone who supported totalitarianism. As a result, they put on trial and expelled founding board member and prominent Communist Party leader Elizabeth Gurley Flynn. This action against Flynn was engineered by a coterie of influentials in the organization, co-general counsel Morris Ernst, Norman Thomas, and Rev. John Haynes Holmes. They were ideologically predisposed to anticommunism, and Thomas and Holmes were the consummate political infighters, but the decision to bring Flynn to trial reflected recurring tensions between the ACLU and the Communist Party and its various sponsored groups, for example, International Labor Defense, over issues including how best to defend the Scottsboro defendants. Purging Communists from its leadership also put a damper on criticism from Martin Dies' Committee on Un-American Activities that was proving an impediment to the sort of insider lobbying in Washington in which Baldwin still put so much faith. The decision to expel Flynn split the board – the vote to expel her was a tie broken by the meeting chair, Holmes – but it was also a case of charismatic failure. Baldwin's personality was not enough; while he backed Flynn's expulsion, he was incapable of controlling the board through his usual methods of setting meeting agendas and appealing to members' sense of personal loyalty (Belfrage, 1973: 36; Walker, 1999: 128-33).

During the war, the ACLU almost alone challenged the Roosevelt administration's attack on civil liberties. It fought Executive Order 9066, which sent over 100,000 Japanese-Americans to concentration camps by giving the Secretary of War the ability to designate military zones in the U.S., "from which any or all persons may be excluded." It lobbied for liberal conscientious objector (CO) rules before the war and took up the defense of militant COs when they challenged authorities in the Civilian Public Service camps that housed them. Finally, the ACLU opposed the Smith Act that made it illegal to "advocate, abet, advise, or teach the duty, necessity, desirability, or propriety of overthrowing or destroying any government in the United States by force or violence." In the first of the Smith Act trials twenty-nine Trotskyists who were indicted a few months before the U.S. joined World War II provided their own counsel, but the ACLU handled publicity and fund-raising, and helped with the appeal.

In each of the above cases, Baldwin had to fashion a compromise between members' different ideological stances and the Union's interests. In "ordinary times" Roger Baldwin could set the national agenda through the force of his personality and by manipulating meetings and monopolizing the Union's material resources. But in having recruited a National Committee of well-known and politically sophisticated personalities – many of whom represented organizations with engaged memberships – and having created an organization of autonomous affiliates, he had on his hands a political group that had a life, in fact several lives, of its own. How the

Union should respond to government treatment of subversives created a major division in the National Committee that pitted conservatives, liberals, and radicals against the organization's traditional pacifists. Whitney North Seymour, Wall Street lawyer and future president of the prestigious City Bar Association who led the conservatives, almost instinctively deferred to the office of the President. Liberals such as Morris Ernst, Elmer Rice, and New York State Assistant Attorney General Raymond Wise owed their political allegiance to FDR and were wont to extend him the benefit of the doubt when it came to the necessity of curtailing civil liberties in a time of war.

The radicals, who were best represented by Corliss Lamont, had shown sympathies for the Soviet Union and were eager for the U.S. to join in the fight against Germany. For them, all political energies ought to be devoted to fighting fascism. In opposition were the old-line pacifists and anticommunists, such as Baldwin, Norman Thomas, and John Haynes Holmes. They saw the principal threat to liberty as the enormous concentration of power in the hands of centralized government; democracies were as susceptible to oppression as were totalitarian regimes. A majority of the board – against the wishes of Baldwin – forced through a compromise position. In what became known as the "Seymour resolution," the ACLU went on record asserting that it "will not participate – except where the fundamentals of due process are denied – in cases where, after investigation, there are grounds for a belief that the defendant is cooperating with or acting on behalf of the enemy, even though the particular charge against the defendant might otherwise be appropriate for intervention" (Walker, 1999: 123, 136-54, 157).

Complicating matters further were rivalries between the East Coast headquarters and West Coast affiliates. The Southern and Northern California affiliates were the oldest and, because of their geographical distance, had developed a sense of autonomy. They had created a more actively involved base which allowed them, for example, to intervene quickly in the political crisis that arose during the internment of Japanese-Americans. The Northern California affiliate threatened the compromises that the board had crafted when they defended Japanese-American citizens under the name of the ACLU. The local knowledge, political enthusiasm, and connections to cooperating attorneys that affiliates could muster gave the ACLU wide reach, material resources, legal and political expertise, and a constituency that complemented its efforts in the courts through education and agitation. A relatively active membership structured in somewhat autonomous affiliate branches also meant that the efficiencies that internal consistency were meant to bring about were at times difficult to achieve.

Given the organizational strain the ACLU faced in defending civil liberties in a war against fascism, the Union's decision to go to the courts in a fairly traditional way rather than encouraging protest worked to the organization's benefit. It may not have been able to survive another bruising battle à la the Flynn affair. The narrow legal arguments that ensued about Japanese-Americans as a suspect class allowed all sides in the ACLU to claim that they were adhering to principle even when the Supreme Court ruled in *Korematsu v. United States*, 323 U.S. 214 (1944), that the need to prevent espionage trumped Japanese-Americans' rights. The structuralist argument that lawyers dampen political conflict has resonance, but in this case the tendency of litigation to channel organizational energies onto a narrow field forestalled a potentially more bitter battle. In a sense the ACLU's legal team functioned as Talcott Parsons would have predicted, but with a twist. Instead of "cooling out" their client – Fred Korematsu, after all, was the actual client – they carried out a form of social control on their patrons (Parsons, 1954; see also Goffman, 1952; Lin, 2003).

The NAACP in the 1940s

In the 1940s the NAACP had ceased to be a purely middle-class organization. Its campaigns in the 1930s to organize teachers, agitate against lynchings, and defend the Scottsboro Boys were beginning to pay off. The struggle to vote became another important vehicle for inserting the organization in the black community.

Throughout its history the NAACP had agitated for the right to vote and had gone to the courts to pursue its political campaigns for voting rights. In *Guinn v. United States*, 238 U.S. 347 (1915), it filed an amicus brief in the suit that overturned Oklahoma's "grandfather clause," which had exempted white men from literacy tests if their grandfathers had voted. In 1927, the Supreme Court ruled in a Texas case, *Nixon v. Herndon*, 273 U.S. 536 (1927), argued by the NAACP, that white-only primaries were unconstitutional. In the 1930s the NAACP increased its agitation for the vote, but especially during World War II the organization pushed for public campaigns for the franchise under the slogan "A Voteless People is a Hopeless People." The campaign for the vote paralleled an explosive growth in membership. In 1940 the Association had 50,000 members in 350 branches. In the mid-1940s it had between 350,000 and 400,000 members. Black servicemen joined the NAACP in droves during World War II (Fairclough, 2001: 183-84, 192, 196-97; Berg, 2002: 54; Greenberg, 2004: 13).

The NAACP Legal Defense and Educational Fund, Inc.

On March 20, 1940, the NAACP created the NAACP Legal Defense and Educational Fund, Inc (LDF). The NAACP was a political organization, and while non-partisan in the strict sense that it favored no political party and remained neutral in elections, it was involved in lobbying and propaganda, making it ineligible for tax-exempt status. Lacking tax exemption, the Association forfeited the donations that many well-meaning, and well-off, individuals might otherwise make. With the hope of reaping the benefits that tax exemption ought to confer, the NAACP board created a charitable organization to perform the Association's non-lobbying and non-propaganda activities. The board members of LDF were also all on the NAACP board, and, like the NAACP board, it was interracial. Unlike the NAACP board, LDF's board was not democratically elected but depended on the parent group's direction. In practice, though, operation of the LDF was handed over to Thurgood Marshall, the chief counsel.

The organizational separation was meant to be a legal fiction. Pressure, however, from the Internal Revenue Service to make the separation real, in combination with diverging organizational interests, had the consequence over time of putting the two organizations in competition for funds, prestige, and control over their respective political directions. The LDF's first budget in 1941 was for $13,910. In 1945, it was almost $76,000, and by 1950, the organization raised $145,000. It was able to raise such funds, according to Jack Greenberg, because it was enormously successful in court and enjoyed the services of a "great fund-raiser," Harold Oram. Through his work raising funds for Spanish Civil War refugees and for National Sharecroppers Week and his founding of the International Rescue Committee, an organization founded initially to aid refugees from Nazi Germany, he brought to LDF a list of 50,000 people disposed to donate to liberal causes. In 1949, LDF had a staff of eight, five of whom were attorneys. A starting assistant attorney earned $3,200 ($25,892 in 2006 dollars) (Greenberg, 2004: 17-20, 28).

Organizational Growth in the 1950s: The ACLU

In 1950, Roger Baldwin retired from the ACLU after thirty years as its executive director. After three decades as the nation's most important voice for civil liberties, the Union seemed at an organizational impasse. Its budget that year was $82,000, its membership 9,000 nationwide,[2] and its inner circle of board members was increasingly at odds over issues concerning the rights of Communists. A special Committee on Planning Policy convened in 1948 and chaired by Columbia University Law School professor Walter Gellhorn suggested the organization downplay its litigation strategy and emphasize public education. It recommended that the Union

---

[2] Compare to the NAACP's membership, which a conservative estimate put at 150,000 in 1949. In a more generous estimate, Greenberg estimates membership in 1947 at 369,000 (Greenberg, 2004: 13; McLeod, 2005).

give priority to civil rights and to the battle against censorship. The Committee report rejected the idea of increasing membership because "the ACLU cannot itself become a mass organization, with membership in the hundreds of thousands, or even a moderately large organization with, say, fifty thousand." The ACLU, it concluded, had "nothing to give its members in the form of services, tangible rewards, or prestige" (quoted in Walker, 1999: 204). Issued before the board had "elevated" Baldwin to the position of "ambassador," the report reflected the pessimism of an organization overly reliant on a leader of declining charisma and insufficiently modernized (Jacobs, 1977).

Baldwin's identification with and his unstinting devotion to the cause of civil liberties served the ACLU well when it was a lonely voice in the wilderness, but his autocratic rule and penurious monasticism held the Union back from meeting the challenges of the time. In addition to his increasing inability to politically direct the organization, his day-to-day management proved untenable. Staff turnover was high and morale low. One former employee of Baldwin's remarked, "Worthy-cause organizations are always lousy employers, but of all the do-gooders I've worked for, Baldwin was by far the worst." According to Dwight MacDonald:

> Baldwin's idea was that the staff, like himself, should be willing to accept bad wages in a good cause. By 1940, however, this notion had become archaic. Doing good was by then a profession, and the "cause" worker was no longer an idealistic eccentric but a normal, and therefore normally paid, part of the social mechanism. Morally impressive though it was, Baldwin's refusal to accept more than thirty-six hundred dollars a year meant that most of the other executives' salaries had to be scaled down from there ... Nor was it better in the humbler jobs. Baldwin held stenographers' salaries down so firmly that only the most moderately skilled would take a job at the Union, with the result that he and his executives often found it simpler to type their own letters (1953b: 30).

When the ACLU tried to hire a replacement for Baldwin, its first choice turned down the $7,200 (approximately $59,000 in 2006 dollars) offer as insufficient. The task was made even more difficult by the ACLU's attempt to remain respectable in the political mainstream. Gellhorn's Committee on Policy Planning advised that "other things being equal ... the ACLU director should not be one whose interest in civil liberties might be mistakenly ascribed to his being a member of an oppressed minority group" (quoted in Walker, 1999: 206). In other words, no Jews, women, blacks or other minorities need apply.

The board hired Patrick Murphy Malin, a Quaker and economics professor at Swarthmore College who happened to be married to one of the Philadelphia Biddles. He received a salary of $13,500 and his top aides around $7,000 per year. Stenographer salaries rose from $37.50 a week to sixty dollars. Malin lacked Baldwin's charisma, identification with civil liberties and speaking and writing talents, but he made up for those deficits as a superb administrator and more important as an astute organizational entrepreneur.

Malin immediately increased membership by hiring a national field director and creating staffed, autonomous, affiliate offices in New York, Philadelphia, and Cleveland. These were in addition to the staffed affiliates in Boston, Chicago, San Francisco, and Los Angeles. The board gave affiliates for the first time an official role in setting policy, as well. By 1954 there were active affiliates in sixteen states – Ohio had nine, Connecticut and Colorado two apiece. In the next two years the Union gained a foothold in the South with affiliates organized in Miami, Kentucky, and New Orleans. Evidence of their autonomy might be adduced from the outspoken dissent of several local affiliates from the national ACLU's strident anticommunism.

Membership increased even more dramatically. Perhaps because he had a fresh eye, or perhaps because with Baldwin gone the membership felt free to express itself more clearly, Malin found on his first annual membership tour that there was a strong concern for the cold war's effects on civil liberties, a demand for a campaign against censorship and for a strict separation of church and state, and a commitment to civil rights. By 1955 membership had more than tripled to 30,000 and at the end of the decade doubled again to 60,000. In 1974, membership passed 275,000 in 375 local chapters in forty-nine states. Five-thousand volunteer lawyers worked with a full-time staff of thirty-four attorneys in nineteen local offices and twenty-five lawyers in three ACLU national offices (MacDonald, 1953b: 31; Rabin, 1976: 211; Meltsner, 2006: 157).

In the late 1940s and throughout most of the 1950s, the U.S. Supreme Court reversed what seemed to be a loosening of restrictions on subversive and unpopular speech. In *Dennis v. United States*, 341 U.S. 494 (1951), the Court ruled that the conviction of Eugene Dennis and ten other leaders of the Communist Party was constitutional. The Communist leaders' conspiracy presented a "clear and present danger" according to Chief Justice Vinson's majority opinion, even if the conspiracy was not imminent. In addition, Judge Harold Medina put a further chill on the right to dissent when during the original trial he cited each of the defendants' attorneys for contempt and sentenced them to prison terms. In the wake of the Court's ruling the government indicted another 145 "second-tier" leaders of the Party. Many of the second-tier defendants found securing legal counsel impossible, even though they had the fees to pay for representation. It was in large part through the efforts of local ACLU affiliates that that the local bar would supply lawyers to the defendants. It was not until 1957 that the

Court reversed its anticommunist course. In *Yates v. United States*, 354 U.S. 298 (1957), the Supreme Court overturned the convictions of the second-tier Party leaders, drawing a distinction between the statement of an idea and the advocacy that an action be undertaken. In *Watkins v. United States*, 354 U.S. 178 (1957), the Court held that John Watkins, a UAW official and former Communist Party member, did not have to "name names." HUAC, the court ruled, had "no congressional power to expose for the sake of exposure." These rulings proved a belated vindication of the litigation strategy the ACLU had pursued since its inception, but the left wing of the bar paid a heavy price during the decade. In addition to the jailing of the Communist Party's lawyers that resulted from the Smith Act trials, Attorney General Herbert Brownell in a speech at the 1953 ABA convention threatened the National Lawyers Guild with placement on the list of "subversive organizations." Within days of Brownell's speech the Guild lost half its membership, and by 1955 its ranks had dwindled to 500 from a membership of 4,000 at its founding (Rabinowitz, 1987-88; Walker, 1999: 187-88, 242-43).

Despite the repression of the Cold War, the ACLU, acting alone and with other legal groups, created a new body of law that extended civil rights and freedom from censorship. It also strengthened the separation of church and state and the provisions of due process. The Union filed *amicus curiae* briefs in *Brown* and all the other major civil rights cases of the period. It continued in the tradition of the Wickersham Report by publishing an exposé of police misconduct, *Secret Detention by the Chicago Police*, that influenced the Supreme Court ruling in *Escobedo v. Illinois* (1961) that suspects are entitled to consult an attorney before being interrogated. A series of anti-censorship cases undermined obscenity laws. In *Burstyn v. Wilson*, 343 U.S. 495 (1952), the Supreme Court ruled that movies were a form of expression protected by the First Amendment. In San Francisco, the Northern California affiliate secured an acquittal for Lawrence Ferlinghetti at his obscenity trial for publishing Allen Ginsburg's poem *Howl*, and in 1959 the ACLU successfully argued in the Supreme Court against banning the film version of *Lady Chatterley's Lover*. The same year, the Postmaster General lost in the circuit court in his bid to ban Grove Press' unexpurgated edition of the novel (Walker, 1999: 232-35).

By the mid-1970s the ACLU was a national organization with a highly decentralized structure. Local affiliates determined their own policy priorities and had tenuous ties to the national office, which was moving away from volunteer attorneys. Staff attorneys also moved away from their previous roles as "generalists directing volunteer litigators. Instead, they became project attorneys in areas such as the rights of juveniles, women, or prisoners, abortion, or sexual privacy. These projects received their funding from private foundations. The organization also shifted gears away from a policy of filing amicus briefs toward the direct representation of clients.

> Growth in membership had provided a base from which a nationwide law reform effort could be sustained, but only on a highly diffuse, fragmented basis. On the other hand, the national office maintained its distinctly centralized character, not by continuing to rely on a small cadre of volunteers, but by building sufficiently large in-house professional staff to make the use of volunteers increasingly less attractive. At the same time, however, foundation funding of distinct projects provided the impetus for growth of a specialized group of staff professionals that had no earlier counterpart (Rabin, 1976: 213).

The NAACP in the 1950s

The 1950s was a long decade in the history of the civil rights movement. The Supreme Court's unanimous decision in *Brown v. Board of Education*, 347 U.S. 483 (1954), to overturn *Plessy v. Ferguson* (1896) and the doctrine of separate but equal made the LDF famous. Leading up to the *Brown* decision, the LDF won important rulings before the Supreme Court in (1) *McLaurin v. Oklahoma State Regents*, 339 U.S. 637 (1950), which held that the Fourteenth Amendment right of due process meant that public institutions of higher learning could not treat students differently solely because of their race, and (2) *Sweatt v. Painter*, 339 U.S. 629 (1950), which held that Texas' separate public law school was not equal in its facilities. Further, the Texas school was not equal in "intangibles," such as exposure to a range of students and the networks that they comprise – hence an unconstitutional denial of the equal protection clause of the Fourteenth Amendment. Both cases were part of LDF's strategy of building up a record that would provide precedents for their legal assault on *Plessy*. In another case that LDF argued before the Supreme Court, *Barrows v. Jackson*, 346 U.S. 249 (1953), the Justices found the Constitution prohibited states from enforcing restrictive covenants. Because the covenants were between private individuals, they were not illegal, but states could not enforce them because doing so would constitute a state action to deny an individual use of property.

NAACP-LDF Growth in the 1960s

Jack Greenberg became general counsel of the NAACP-LDF in 1961, receiving a salary of $20,000 ($131,000 in 2006 dollars), after President Kennedy had appointed Thurgood Marshall to the U.S. Court of Appeals for the Second Circuit in New York. Constance Motley received a promotion to associate counselor at a salary of $18,000. During the first half of the 1960s, the Fund's work had greatly expanded. In 1962 the Fund had twenty-nine cases before the Supreme Court, more than any other law office with the exception of the Solicitor General's. LDF staff lawyers took an active part in the defense of students who sat-in and those who participated in the freedom rides, but the small staff could not be present at a majority of the cases. Greenberg reports:

> [W]e conferred over the phone, shipped out model papers and briefs, personally attended cases that might have broader import, paid modest legal fees, and furnished some bail money. We stayed on top of cases so that as they worked their way up to the appellate courts and the Supreme Court they would present the right issues and evidence (Greenberg, 2004: 298).

This proved a burden to LDF – in conjunction with cooperating lawyers, it represented approximately 17,000 demonstrators – not only because of the vast numbers of young people sitting-in and joining the Freedom Rides but also because of the tactics that states took to harass the protesters. In 1961, when Freedom Riders were traveling into Mississippi, they faced constant arrest. Mississippi officials attempted to stanch the flow of protesters by trying each case individually and charging burdensome bail fees. Those official tactics required attorneys on the ground. LDF tried to have a staff attorney in Jackson, Mississippi at all times, but it proved difficult to assign a lawyer there when the Fund's docket was so full. Instead, it hired three local lawyers for a total of $1,200 a month.

By 1965, the LDF had 135 school desegregation cases. Responding to passage of the Equal Employment Opportunity Act, it filed nearly 1,000 employment cases with the Equal Employment Opportunity Commission in 1965 and brought sixteen lawsuits in 1966. In *Turner v. City of Memphis*, 369 U.S. 350 (1962), a case to desegregate city parks, the Supreme Court warned that the time for "all deliberate speed" had passed. LDF won cases integrating the University of Mississippi, the University of Alabama, Clemson College, and Auburn University, at which point every Southern state had some blacks in formerly all-white state universities. Fund attorneys successfully argued *McLaughlin v. Florida*, 379 U.S. 184 (1964), overturning laws prohibiting interracial "cohabitation," a ruling that led to the end of anti-miscegenation laws. In accomplishing all this work, LDF increased its lawyers from five to seventeen and its budget from $500,000 to $1.7 million (Greenberg, 2004: 316-17, 323).

With the passage of the Civil Rights Act in 1964, LDF's caseload changed. Defending civil rights activists and later trying Title VII cases required more lawyers than were necessary for the controlled and limited constitutional litigation of the *Brown* era. It undertook a major campaign to enforce Title VII employment discrimination cases that required lawyer-intensive trials involving questions of fact. As of 1970, it had twenty-eight lawyers on staff who were able to take on a large volume of cases because of an increase in cooperating attorneys who in the mid-1960s numbered about 200, mostly private practitioners with local reputations as civil rights lawyers. In addition, they were the organization's contact with the African American community.

Successful litigation increased the Fund's ability to boost its income. In *Newman v. Piggie Park*, 390 U.S. 400 (1968), the Supreme Court ruled that successful civil rights plaintiffs "should ordinarily recover an attorney's fee unless special circumstances would render such an award unjust." Counsel fees amounted to about a fifth of LDF's budget, and, according to Rabin, LDF pursued cases for the first time where a successful outcome in the immediate conflict was the principal justification for representation. An additional pressure came into play, although perhaps too much should not be made of it: Funding was always a political issue. In 1970 the Fund became embroiled in internal controversy when the staff wanted to defend anti-war activist and Communist Party leader Angela Davis for her alleged role in a deadly hostage crisis and prison escape. Greenberg overruled the staff's request as beyond the scope of the organization's work, although there was clearly a generational and ideological gap between them, as well. In the controversy that surrounded Greenberg's decision to forgo defending Davis, he reports that one reason (although not the main one) to keep LDF off the defense was that doing so would run counter to funders' expectations.

By the end of 1975, LDF had an active docket of about 200 employment discrimination cases, and its budget was just under $4.3 million. Individual giving to the Fund increased in dollar amounts and in number of donors. Greenberg notes that by the end of the 1970s, LDF litigation "had become in some ways like big law firm cases with none of the frantic excitement that characterized the movement in the early 1960s" (Greenberg, 2004: 308; see ibid., 39-95, 462; Rabin, 1976: 217-18, 222-23, 248; Meltsner, 2006: 122-24).

The decisions the ACLU and NAACP/NAACP-LDF made to pursue litigation in support of political change were shaped by their historical legacies, the political opportunities and constraints that followed from being associated with constituent organizations, and the social movements that those organizations shaped and responded to. The process of litigation and styles of lawyering they pursued affected the litigation and shaped how they fomented and aided social change. As we will see in the following chapters, new forms of public interest law, *pro bono* practice institutionalized in large firms and a separate form of public interest law I call entrepreneurial lawyering, borrowed much from direct service and political mobilization lawyering.

6

PRO BONO INSTITUTIONALIZATION
IN LARGE LAW FIRMS

Why did large private law firms become involved in providing services to the poor? This chapter shows that this move occurred in response to threats to the profession's legitimacy and autonomy. Large firms embraced a model of *pro bono* involvement that stressed a service ideal compatible with their business model. Faced with the need to recruit and retain attorneys, demands from the courts for mandatory *pro bono*, and pressure from the ABA and other bar associations to make up for cuts in government funded legal services in the 1970s, large firms began the process toward a massive shift in how pro bono services were delivered. Firms increased *pro bono* service to head off populist distrust of the profession. This was fueled by a newly established and aggressive legal press that wrote for a general audience and reported on lawyers' venality and corruption.

Moving away from the idea that *pro bono publico* was the responsibility of individual attorneys, local bar associations with the participation of large firms first created organizations to mobilize lawyers for *pro bono* service and then nurtured – sometimes prodded – these same firms to organize those services in-house. Legal Service Corporation funding for Private Attorney Involvement (PAI) provided the resources for the initial organizational attempts at encouraging private firm involvement in the field of legal aid to the poor.

In previous chapters, I have concentrated on lawyers and organizations primarily dedicated to serving the poor and disenfranchised. This chapter is, however, concerned with the provision of *pro bono* legal services by attorneys – and especially large law firms – that practice in the for-profit sector.

Pro bono publico is important for several reasons. Private sector attorneys provide a considerable amount of legal services through it. It has been a long-standing concern of the legal profession that lawyers demonstrate their commitment to equal access by performing *pro bono*, and it has functioned to some extent as a pathway to public interest careers for attorneys who chose not to or could not secure positions in the field after graduating from law school. Students who plan to enter the private bar but hope eventually to work in public interest jobs often seek *pro bono* opportunities for the experiences they provided and the networks they built. In a study Epstein (2002) conducted of law students interested in public interest careers, counselors and faculty members at elite schools advised students that, upon graduation, working at large firms and performing *pro bono* would better prepare them for positions at the most prestigious public interest organizations than other kinds of positions. Finally, public interest employers stress the importance of *pro bono* work as (1) an entrée into the field for those who have worked in the for-profit sector and (2) as a form of "cause lawyering" that can be conducted from within the corporate sector (Davis, 2001: 120).

Pro bono represents one of the largest providers of legal services to the poor and disenfranchised. In terms of the number of personnel, a greater number of practitioners come from the *pro bono* sphere than any other component of civil legal services (citing Sandefur, Cummings, 2004: 18). While many of those providers are solo practitioners or work in small firms, large firms now provide substantial amounts of free civil legal services. This has not always been the case. It is a relatively recent phenomenon that large firms, the most prestigious and resource-rich sector of the profession, have involved themselves institutionally, as firms, in the provision of *pro bono* services to the poor. In fact, as G. Edward White (1986) reminds us, there was a time when practically no elite lawyers offered their legal expertise in public service.

Some theorists, especially neo-institutionalists in economics and many *pro bono* advocates, have maintained that the institutionalization of *pro bono* in large firms can be explained by the need to apply efficient organizational fixes to problems of coordination (Williamson, 1975; Lardent, 1989; Cummings, 2004). I propose, however, that large firms support *pro bono* because of political and business concerns rather than the drive for "efficiency."

Pro Bono Before the 1970s

Pro bono publico has a long history dating back to the Roman Empire. It found expression in English common law, and has been an integral part of the American legal profession's service ideal, a defining attribute of the professions that differentiates them from businesses (Parsons, 1954: 42-43; Freidson, 2001: 122). As far back as thirteenth century England, "the 1275 First Statute of Westminster obligated serjeants, the most respected advocates of the time, to serve the poor for free, vowing not to covet profit over faithful service to the king's people." In the United States, the nineteenth century jurist and retired Pennsylvania Supreme Court Justice George Sharswood lectured students at the University of Pennsylvania Law School that the duty to work *pro bono* had "no enforcement mechanisms beyond moral compulsion and the threat of professional dishonor[,]" but if a client cannot pay, then legal services should be provided gratis (Maute, 2002: 97, 105-06).

Until the last quarter of the twentieth century, the profession's commitment to *pro bono* typically took three forms. First, the courts provided assigned counsel to some indigent criminal defendants and, less frequently, to poor defendants involved in civil proceedings. Many states guaranteed to the criminally accused the right to representation, but with the exception of capital cases, they provided no mechanism for funding counsel. Assigned counsel most frequently came from "court house regulars" who took cases from judges with whom they had personal or political relationships. They did so in the hope of procuring payment from the accused or their families.

A second, and the historically most common, way in which *pro bono* has been performed involved attorneys who provided free or reduced-fee legal services to the poor and disenfranchised or to charitable organizations in an ad hoc fashion. Referrals usually came from personal networks. The expertise of individual lawyers who resided within those networks limited the scope of *pro bono* services available. The model for individual *pro bono* services was the small-town lawyer who knew his neighbors and represented those whom he knew to be poor and deserving. The service was voluntary and an instance of personal charity. It reflected George Sharswood's admonition that "it is hoped, that the time will never come ... when a poor man with an honest cause, though without a fee, cannot obtain the services of honorable counsel, in the prosecution or defense of his rights" (citing Sharswood in Cummings, 2004: 11).

The third form arose in the last quarter of the nineteenth century when immigrant and civic groups – and not lawyers – formed legal aid societies. In 1876, German immigrants formed the Deutscher Rechts-Schutz Verein (German Legal Aid Society). Chicago saw the formation of the Protective Agency for Women and Children (founded 1886) and the Bureau of Justice (founded 1888). The profession eventually responded to the need for legal services for the poor. In 1909, the first bar-sponsored legal aid organization was founded in Columbus, Ohio. Grappling with the problems of urbanization and industrialization as they affected a population of rural migrants and immigrants, lawyers from the corporate bar and members of the philanthropic and political elite in some of the nation's largest cities built on these efforts during the Progressive Era. Through legal aid societies, they institutionalized a specific form of service based on noblesse oblige, good government, and a form of citizenship that stressed order and conformity to wage labor. The organizations all relied to some extent on the voluntary services of lawyers, although in the largest cities volunteer lawyers supplemented full-time attorneys (Maguire, 1928: 19; Brownell, 1951: 9; Grossberg, 1997; Willrich, 2003).

In the 1960s legal representation of the poor changed dramatically. U.S. Supreme Court decisions expanded the rights of representation for indigent criminal defendants and set in motion the creation of public defender agencies in most of the nation's largest cities. These publicly funded organizations, in turn, produced a large number of positions for young attorneys. For example, New York Legal Aid Society expanded the number of its lawyers defending indigents accused of crimes fourfold during the 1960s. Changes in the law that expanded the rights of accused criminals increased the demand for defense attorneys and raised the prestige of that segment of the profession. On the civil side, the Johnson administration, as part of its War on Poverty, created the Legal Services Program.

The Competition for Lawyers

During the 1960s the legal profession grew (Abel, 1989; Galanter and Palay, 1991). An influx of young lawyers, including women and minorities (Epstein, 1981), entered the previously exclusionary ranks of the large corporate law firms. Those firms offered high salaries but they found themselves in an increasingly disadvantageous position in recruiting the "best and the brightest" law school graduates (Auerbach, 1976: 278-79). Top graduates of elite law schools went to work for the Legal Services Program. Ralph Nader and his "Raiders" – young recent graduates of law schools who were driven by political zeal to move to Washington, D.C. – took low-paying jobs in organizations formed to battle the political establishment (Berman and Cahn, 1970). According to Mark Green, "in 1970, none of the thirty-nine law review editors graduating from Harvard expect[ed] to enter private practice" (citing Green in Galanter and Palay, 1991: 56).

To compete with (a) Legal Services, (b) "Nader's Raiders," (c) a growing movement of environmental groups, and (d) other experiments in alternative legal practices – and to quell the growing disenchantment of associates with the establishment, legal and otherwise – a number of large firms decided to enter the field of poverty law. They expanded support for *pro bono* and did little to discourage associates from challenging the political conservatism of the elite of the bar. For example, the prestigious firm of Piper & Marbury opened its own storefront law office to serve Baltimore's poor (Ashman, 1972). In a 1970 *Yale Law Journal* Comment, "The New Public Interest Lawyers," the author stated, "In response to agitation by associates and law students, some major commercial law firms have systematically undertaken to provide legal services to non-paying clients" (Comment, 1970: 1106-07; see also Falk, 1970: 1).

Precursors of *Pro Bono* Institutionalization

The material and cultural basis for the later and more profound institutionalization of *pro bono* in large firms was set during the 1970s. Large-firm associates in New York founded the Council of New York Law Associates in 1969, the same year that the Chicago Council of Lawyers – a similar "alternative" bar – was initiated. Its members intended it to be a meeting point for young large-firm attorneys and as a pressure group to advocate for increased opportunities for *pro bono* and public interest work. "Although it eschewed direct involvement in politics, even in the anti-war movement, which was popular among young professionals in New York City, its leadership was active in liberal political and social causes, including the anti-war movement, reflecting its reformist predilection" (Powell, 1988: 101). The prestigious Association of the Bar of the City of New York provided the New York Council with free meeting space. Undoubtedly, the Association of the Bar felt pressure from its own group of young associates, the Young Lawyers Committee (Morris, 1997; see also Powell, 1988: 162). In 1976, the Council of New York Law Associates and the Young Lawyers Committee joined forces to incorporate New York Lawyers for the Public Interest. The organization moved beyond aggregating the individual efforts of large firm associates and enlisted the support of the firms themselves, requiring them to accept *pro bono* referrals and make yearly financial contributions. Six months after its founding NYLPI had signed up nine of the city's most prestigious firms. By the end of 1979 that number had grown to thirty. By 1991, the number doubled again to fifty-seven firms and three corporate law departments (Morris, 1997: 107-08; New York Lawyers for the Public Interest, 1991: 6-7).

Pro bono referral services sprang up in other major cities. The Boston Bar Association sponsored the Volunteer Lawyers Project in 1977. The Project was one of the organizational expressions of internal challenges to Boston's elite bar by a group of young attorneys dubbed the "Young Turks." They agitated within the Association for greater inclusiveness and more transparency in internal governance. In addition, they pushed the leadership to advocate more boldly for increased legal services and take a more active role in the civil rights movement (Jones et al., 1993: 114-16, 120-21). In Los Angeles, the Beverly Hills and Los Angeles County Bar Associations formed Public Counsel in 1970; it is currently the largest *pro bono* coordinating organization in the country (Cummings, 2004: 42).

The Declining Number of Poverty Lawyers and Increases in *Pro Bono*

The extensive expansion of legal rights and the politicization of the public interest bar that occurred in the 1960s and early 1970s came with a price. Several Republican politicians, including Ronald Reagan and Spiro

Agnew, gained prominence by exploiting a growing popular concern for "law and order" and by attacking the Legal Services Program (Johnson, 1999). After his reelection Nixon appointed Howard Phillips in 1973 as acting Director of LSP. Phillips was later to gain prominence during Reagan's presidency as an important conservative activist and a preeminent proponent of "defunding the Left."

In 1982,[1] Ronald Reagan proposed the elimination of the Legal Services Corporation. Powerful conservative political actors who were "opposed to the idea of effective access for the poor to the legal system" (Kilwein, 1999: 43) backed the campaign during the 1980s, but Legal Services had powerful allies in the leadership of the bar and among Democratic congressional legislators. They were able to thwart efforts to kill the program, but throughout the 1980s funding decreased, and Congress restricted the type of work that could be performed and the clients who could be represented. A provision to the Legal Services Corporation charter that would have profound effects on the growth of *pro bono* services passed in 1981. That year legislation mandated that every LSC grantee spend the equivalent of one-eighth of its LSC funding on private attorney involvement (PAI). LSC grantees could use those funds to pay private attorneys as a form of Judicare, or (as most Legal Services organizations did) they could set up programs to recruit and train volunteer attorneys and coordinate their efforts with low income clients (Cummings, 2004: 24). Between 1980 and 1985, the number of *pro bono* programs increased from 88 to over 500 (McBurney, 2003: 1). In addition, the 1980s saw the growth of IOLTA programs, which provided funds to *pro bono* and legal services programs. These Interest on Lawyer Trust Accounts pooled small amounts of money that lawyers hold for individual clients, which if deposited individually would produce no interest. Florida initiated the nation's first IOLTA in 1981, and by 1985 they existed in thirty-five states (Abel, 1989: 133; *Legal Times*, April 4, 1983: 6).

Pressure from sectors of the bar and the courts to provide legal services to the poor with *pro bono* representation mounted in the 1980s. In some instances the judges were responding to court decisions that mandated civil representation – for example, a 1976 California Supreme Court decision, *Payne v. Superior Court*, 17 Cal. 3d 908, established the right of indigent prisoners to counsel in certain civil as well as criminal cases. State judges in El Paso County, Texas ordered attorneys to take two domestic

---

[1] At its height in Fiscal Year 1981, Legal Services Corporation employed over six-thousand lawyers, approximately one lawyer for every five-thousand poor people. Funding that year amounted to $321 million, or $1.65 *per capita* (Johnson, 1999: 32). This would be equal to $684 million in 2003 dollars. In comparison, the LSC budget for 2003 was $339 million (LSC Budget, FY 2003: http://www.lsc.gov/pressr/pr_03a.htm).

relations cases without charge per year. In other instances, attempts to require *pro bono* service were explicitly tied to cutbacks in funding for the Legal Services Corporation. In Florida, several prominent attorneys, including two past presidents of the ABA, petitioned the Florida Supreme Court to require twenty-five hours of *pro bono* service or $500 "to assist in the delivery of legal services to the poor." The court unanimously rejected the petition – as did the Florida Bar Association – but the petition lent credence to calls to shore up voluntary efforts to overcome funding cutbacks in the Legal Services Corporation (*National Law Journal*, May 30, 1982: 3). In California, a month after Florida's highest court rejected a plan for mandatory *pro bono*, a trial judge in Ventura County ordered private attorneys to defend indigents sued civilly by the district attorney's office. In Missouri a state circuit judge ordered an attorney to represent a prisoner in a medical malpractice suit. As in the Florida case, higher courts ruled that judges could not compel lawyers to represent clients on a *pro bono* basis in civil cases (*National Law Journal*, May 20, 1985). Those cases, however, signaled that sectors of the legal profession were willing to take steps to fulfill obligations to provide representation to the poor although such mandates were professionally unpopular.[2]

While the ranks of Legal Service lawyers were shrinking, the rate of growth of independent public interest organizations also slowed and could not replace the loss of Legal Service attorneys. Nan Aron, founder of the Alliance for Justice and former trial lawyer for the Equal Employment Opportunity Commission, points out that public interest law centers grew from 23 in 1969 with 50 full-time attorneys to 108 centers with 600 attorneys in 1975 to 158 groups employing 906 lawyers in 1984 (cited in Cummings, 2004: 26). Many of the public interest law centers performed the important task of law reform, but they provided few legal services for individual indigent clients.

The Ebb and Flow of Legitimacy: Large Firms and *Pro Bono*

Leaders of the bar recognized that the legal needs of the poor were largely going unmet.[3] They urged increased *pro bono* efforts, especially

---

[2] Mandatory pro bono apparently had support from the general population. According to a 1986 *National Law Journal* survey, fifty-five percent of those polled thought attorneys should be required by law to devote time to public or community service (*National Law Journal*, August 18, 1986: S2).

[3] But see Cummings (2004: 23), who, citing the Legal Services Corporation's "Serving the Civil Legal Needs of Low-Income Americans," http://www.lsc.gov/FOIA/other/exsum.pdf (2000), asserts that despite federal funding cuts, LSC's total funding has remained relatively constant. What has not remained constant is the number of attorneys employed by LSC, the ratio of attorneys to poor people, or per capita spending. In addition, the Republican-dominated Congress passed, and President Bill Clinton signed, legislation in 1996 that

from large firms. During the 1980s when the number of poverty lawyers was stagnating, the size and revenues of law firms were growing at dizzying rates. For example, the number of attorneys in the legal aid and public defender employment sector increased seven percent from 1980 to 1991. During the same period the number of lawyers nationwide grew by 49 percent and in private practice by 59 percent. Yet, as a percentage of total lawyers, those exclusively serving the poor dropped from 1.5 to 1.1 percent (Curran and Carson, 1994: 7). From 1972 to 1987, revenues of the twenty largest firms increased four-fold in constant dollars. In Galanter and Palay's (1991) sample of thirty-five large firms, firm size expanded from 124 in 1975 to 251 in 1986. In a sample of 37 medium sized firms, they found an increase in size from 44 to 89 lawyers (Galanter and Palay, 1991: 46).

This increase in law firm size might have escaped public attention had it not been for the sharp increases in starting salaries for associates. In 1967, the "going rate" for first year associates at New York's most elite firms was $10,000 (approximately $54,000 in 2003 dollars). The following year brought the first of the "Cravath shocks" when the firm of Cravath Swaine & Moore unilaterally raised entering associates salaries to $15,000. Elite New York firms followed suit, but those increases were restricted to a few dozen firms, mostly in New York. In 1986, when starting salaries had grown to $53,000, Cravath administered a second "shock." It would raise salaries to $65,000 ($106,000 in 2003 dollars). The entire compensation structure for large firms had to be adjusted upward to maintain differentials between first-year and more experienced associates. Likewise, junior partners' draws increased to keep their compensation above senior associates. Unlike the first Cravath shock, starting associate salaries increasingly spread across the entire country (Galanter and Palay, 1991: 56-57). On the front page of its business section the *New York Times* trumpeted, "At Cravath, $65,000 to Start." Two months earlier the firm had decided to supplement the pay of associates by $10,000 for each judge they had clerked for before entering the firm (*New York Times*, April 18, 1986: D1).

The seamy side of large law firms was the subject of several books with titles like *Rascals: The Selling of the Legal Profession* (Brown, 1989), *Shark Tank* (Eisler, 1990), *Skadden: Power, Money and the Rise of a Legal Empire* (Caplan, 1993), books that were aimed at the general public in the late 1980s and into the 1990s. Steven Brill, a lawyer and entrepreneur, started the *American Lawyer* magazine in 1979 and drew a large readership as it chronicled the "inside story" of law firms, including the excesses of the profession and its large firm denizens. Against this back-

---

prohibited LSC lawyers from using non-LSC funds for banned activities. Portions of that legislation have been ruled unconstitutional by the federal courts in *Dobbins v. LSC* and *Velasquez v. LSC*.

drop which offered exposure of their practices and often unwelcome publicity, large firms' involvement in *pro bono* programs grew. For example, the Association of the Bar of the City of New York (ABCNY) announced in 1984 a plan in which thirty firms and nineteen corporate counsels pledged to provide fifty hours of *pro bono* services per attorney (*National Law Journal*, May 14, 1984: 2). In 1985, the ABA reported that there existed more than four-hundred organized *pro bono* programs with 77,000 attorneys participating (*ABA Journal*, October 1985). Although increased attention in the legal press was being paid to *pro bono* efforts and programs in large firms, an ABA-sponsored survey reported that sixty-five percent of those attorneys who performed *pro bono* services worked in one- or two-person firms (*ABA Journal*, November 1985).

Pro Bono in Large Firms: Efficiency vs. Competition in the 1990s

In the 1990s, ostensibly in response to disappointing efforts to fashion *pro bono* into a full-service delivery mechanism, leaders of the bar devoted greater efforts to involving large firms in *pro bono* service. Social movement entrepreneurs such as Esther Lardent, former director of the Volunteer Lawyers Project of the Boston Bar Association and a consultant on legal matters to the Ford Foundation, praised the increased visibility and creativity of *pro bono* programs in the 1980s. Still, she bemoaned the inability of those programs to develop into effective legal services delivery systems. The argument that Lardent framed[4] was that *pro bono* programs created in the 1980s were ad hoc and local attempts to replace declining Legal Services funding. As a result, the programs gave "little thought ... to the definition of an effective *pro bono* program." The programs typically measured success by inflated quantitative criteria and rarely considered client or attorney satisfaction. Staff turnover was high, volunteers were difficult to retain, and programs lacked integration with the public interest bar (Lardent, 1989). The solution to this problem was seen in concentrating efforts in large law firms.

The Organized Bar Responds

Leaders in the ABA *pro bono* community saw that large law firms had resources that could be put to use to strengthen *pro bono* as a delivery

---

[4] In the social movement literature the classic work on framing is Snow and his colleagues' (Snow et al., 1986) reworking of Goffman's *Frame Analysis* (1974). In building and sustaining social movements, social movement organizations appeal to potential recruits by making a compelling argument that a social problem exists, that they have a vision for an alternative outcome, and suggest a strategy for achieving that outcome. See also Merton (1971) on the definition of a social problem.

system for legal services for the poor. As important, they realized that those same large firms could gain from embracing *pro bono* programs. Large firms had the advantage of considerable resources in terms of labor (both attorneys and support staff), capital, and experience coordinating large numbers of attorneys. They also had command resources: the ability to assign attorneys and other personnel through persuasion or direct order. *Pro bono* offered large firms several advantages as well. For law school graduates who had decided not to pursue full-time public interest careers, large firms that encouraged *pro bono* had a recruiting advantage over those that did not. It also gave associates opportunities for client contact and courtroom experience, often years before they would otherwise receive them. It improved large firms' public relations at a time when lawyers and their firms were subject to popular skepticism or downright hostility. Having large firms manage attorney involvement in *pro bono*, as opposed to having individuals involve themselves in *pro bono* activities, rationalized a process that could otherwise be chaotic. Central coordination allowed firms to control costs, monetary and otherwise, and reap benefits.

Large law firms continued to grow in the 1980s and 1990s. In 1979 the fifty largest U.S. law firms had an average number of 321 attorneys. In 1991 that number increased to 475. In 2001 the top 100 firms averaged 621 attorneys (Cummings, 2004: 35, 37). Law firms became more specialized, and attorneys working within large firms practiced in narrower fields. Since the 1970s, corporate litigation increased, but routine work for corporations tended to be performed by their in-house legal departments. The growth of those in-house departments meant that there was closer monitoring of outside firms, with corporations often spreading their legal work among many firms (Galanter and Palay, 1995: 30). Competitive pressures increased, but because law firms generally are driven by revenue rather than by cost, they increased staffing to capture more business (Bower, 1987). Hiring greatly expanded, and large firms dismantled hiring barriers to groups such as Jews, women, and racial minorities. Firms hired from a wider range of schools and went further down the class ranks in choosing associates (Abel, 1989: 109-10; Epstein et al., 1995; Heinz and Laumann, 1982).

The Pro Bono Challenge: The Ford Foundation Targets Large Firms

Once again the Ford Foundation was at the forefront of a major development in encouraging the legal profession to provide services to the poor. It is significant, though, that Ford's efforts relied upon the private sector. In the past, it looked to the nonprofit sector and government to tackle the problems of low-income people in gaining access to the courts. In 1993, the ABA-sponsored Law Firm Pro Bono Project, with funding from the Ford Foundation, initiated the Law Firm Pro Bono Challenge. Targeted at the nation's 500 largest firms, the Challenge enlisted 155 firms at its inception, each of which agreed to commit itself to provide *pro bono* services equivalent in time to three or five percent of their annual billings. Over half of those *pro bono* services had to be devoted to the poor. The Challenge encouraged firms to have a majority of attorneys donate services. For firms that opted for the three percent level (eighty percent of those that originally signed on), it was anticipated that attorneys would average about fifty hours per year. In keeping with ABA ethical rules, the goals were aspirational – the Challenge pledged to keep the number of *pro bono* hours and compliance with the goals at the firm level confidential. The initiative represented a major shift from obliging individual attorneys to fulfilling their service goal, to having firms take responsibility for providing *pro bono* (*Legal Times*, May 3, 1993: 3; *National Law Journal*, May 10, 1993; *New York Law Journal*, May 24, 1993: 3).

The Challenge found recruiting signatories difficult. From its beginning only three of the ten richest firms (as measured by profits per partner) joined the Challenge. Spokesmen from Cravath, Swaine and Moore noted that the *pro bono* requirements were onerous: charitable activities such as fund-raising and administrative work with legal services organizations were excluded A co-chairman of the management committee of the New York firm Fried, Frank, Harris, Shriver and Jacobson who sat on the ABA committee sponsoring the Challenge explained that his firm did not sign on because of the pledge's requirement that half the *pro bono* work should be done for the poor. A partner at one prominent firm objected to the requirement that a majority of attorneys in a firm participate, noting his firm does not "believe that it is necessarily wiser to encourage reluctant lawyers to participate in *pro bono* activities rather than sponsor the work by enthusiastic participants" (*American Lawyer*, June 1993: 26; *New York Law Journal*, May 6, 1994: 3).

Yet, despite the difficulties that the Law Firm Pro Bono Challenge encountered, efforts to find an organizational home for *pro bono* in large firms increased. Firms continued to create *pro bono* committees, often hiring full-time personnel – although frequently non-lawyers – to direct the efforts. Firms expended greater resources to publicize their efforts, issuing publications devoted to *pro bono* efforts, enlisting publicity departments to tout their activities, and building intra-firm commitment by recognizing attorney *pro bono* work with annual awards (*National Law Journal*, August 7, 1995: D8).

The Expanding Scope of *Pro Bono*

In conjunction with an increasing institutionalization of *pro bono* in large firms the scope of *pro bono* activity expanded. On the supply side, as large firms grew to meet the staffing needs of an increasingly competitive market, there was a tendency to over-hire. When the economy was growing, lawyers specializing in bankruptcy were in low demand; when corporate consolidation was waning, merger and acquisition specialists found themselves with free time. Law firms were reluctant to dismiss associates when business contracted. It hurt morale and made subsequent recruiting difficult. In addition, large firms had expanded non-litigation practice areas since the 1970s. They had a supply of young attorneys specializing in transactional law who were available to do *pro bono* work and often eager to work with clients, opportunities they rarely had at an early stage in their careers.

On the demand side, public interest law moved in new directions. Responding to the scourge of AIDS, social service agencies redirected resources, and new organizations arose in the 1980s and 1990s. These agencies often called on multifaceted legal interventions and were able to take advantage of the talents and resources of large firms and their attorneys. Public interest organizations embraced community economic development, an area that required transactional legal expertise. Cummings (2001: 400, 403) estimates that "community economic development emerged as the dominant approach to poverty alleviation," and, as a result, public interest lawyers and an increasing number of *pro bono* attorneys have engaged in transactional legal assistance in the areas of real estate, tax, and corporate law to bolster community organizations' efforts at neighborhood development (Perry, 1998; Simon, 2001).

Community economic development proved a fertile ground for large firm *pro bono* endeavors. An increasing social skepticism of welfare policy, a growing acceptance of free market policy solutions by academics and decision-makers, and a devolution of funding and social policy from the federal level to the state and local level all created an ideological atmosphere conducive to and political opportunities for new public interest initiatives. Nonprofit neighborhood groups and community organizers shifted their emphasis from making demands on the state to fostering entrepreneurial activities. Demand increased for the types of skills that large-firm lawyers who specialized in transactional work could provide. Knowledge and experience in corporate law, tax, real estate, and finance were lacking in many public interest settings and often thought to be irrelevant by the activist lawyers who cut their teeth on the social movements of the 1970s and 1980s (Trubek, 2002; Southworth, 2004: 263).

Conclusion

As the organization of *pro bono* comes to reside increasingly in large firms, the potential for conflicts in institutional logic (Friedland and Alford, 1991) between commercialized law firms and charitable public service also increases. To remain economically competitive, law firms have to increase billable hours, especially among associates. Firms do this by growing: increasing the number of associates and practice areas (Galanter and Palay, 1991). Real and positional conflicts of interest potentially narrow the areas in which firms can offer *pro bono* services. While *pro bono* opportunities are assiduously marketed to attract that group of potential hires who want opportunities to serve the less fortunate or effect political change, firms have to keep the interests of their paying clients uppermost. They have also to consider how fulfilling the service ideal comports with the firm's efficient use of its resources. Regardless of the intentions and commitments of large firm lawyers to *pro bono* practice, the firm's *raison d'être* is selling legal services.

The institutional logic that flows from the legal profession's service ideal is different from that of large firms. The service ideal combines an orientation to altruism, a commitment to expertise, and a respect for democratic inclusion. Altruism privileges a concern for the well-being of others over those of one's self and most immediate family or confreres. A commitment to expertise over which lawyers have a socially sanctioned monopoly, means that they alone can provide advice on legal matters.[5] Finally, to maintain the legitimacy of the legal system in a democratic polity, lawyers must provide, if not guarantee to some extent, equal access to the courts and other aspects of the law to those who otherwise lack it.

Decisions to create *pro bono* departments, moves to appoint partners to direct them, and other signs of firms' commitment to *pro bono* are largely symbolic exercises aimed at external audiences. They are used mostly to boost a firm's reputation, improving its ability to recruit lawyers. They also represent preemptive attempts to forestall greater *pro bono* accountability. The seeming paradox that some of the most vocal advocates for large firm involvement in *pro bono* service are also publicly opposed to mandatory *pro bono* (Lardent, 1996; see also Atkinson, 2001) is easily understood if *pro bono* is seen as a form of currency in the symbolic economy of the large firm. Mandatory *pro bono* would devalue the currency by removing *pro bono* from a moral economy of scarcity.

Until *pro bono* activity is mandatory, the symbolic capital associated with it represents for its advocates a resource that can be used to offer more free legal services. Given the profession's lukewarm support for the service ideal and public interest law, *pro bono publico* may be in the words of Atkinson, "a decidedly second-best means of delivering legal services to the poor." Nevertheless, it is one provider, if not the largest, of civil legal services in the United States.

---

[5] On the ability of professions as opposed to markets or bureaucracies to provide expertise, see Freidson, 2001.

7

ENTREPRENEURIAL LAWYERING

The 1960s was a decade of political ferment in the United States and much of the world (Freeman, 1975; Caute, 1988; Ali and Watkins, 1998; Branch, 2006). The long decade began with the lunch counter sit-ins in Greensboro, N.C. in February 1960 and ended symbolically well into the 1970s with the exit of the last people from the American embassy in Saigon, Vietnam, in May 1975. Active movements on behalf of black and women's liberation, against the war in Vietnam, in favor of environmentalism, and relating to a number of other political and social issues mobilized millions of Americans to demand fundamental change. Virtually no sector of society was unaffected. The public interest bar and left-wing members of the legal profession were busy (1) defending civil rights activists in the South, (2) providing indigent defense (*Gideon* (1963) and other Supreme Court rulings expanded the rights of criminal defendants), (3) representing the poor in civil matters (the War on Poverty recognized limited rights to access to the courts as a matter of governmental policy), (4) counseling "draft dodgers" and rebellious GIs, and (5) mounting vigorous defenses of anti-war protesters and self-identified revolutionaries.

In this chapter, I will explore a third type of public interest practice, *entrepreneurial lawyering*, that had its origins in the 1960s, appearing as the response of a sector of the legal profession to the changing political climate. A confluence of factors facilitated the creation of entrepreneurial lawyering. These included middle-class social movements reacting to the economic dominance of the large corporation and its close relationship to government and advocating an extension of public goods. In addition, there was a supply of eager young law school graduates, the availability of foundation funding, a sympathetic federal court, and the commitment of lawyers to challenging the dominant political ideology of pluralism.

While the NAACP and the ACLU had been forced to the courts to carry out their work, the entrepreneurial lawyering movement eagerly undertook litigation as their primary strategy for political change. From the mid-1960s to the mid-1970s, a largely middle-class political movement, believing that power was increasingly out of the hands of the "public" but disdaining the confrontational politics of the New Left and poor people's movements, found expression in a congeries of law firms, research centers, lobbying groups, and membership associations. These groups gathering together what Simon Lazarus called the "Genteel Populists" (1974) were an attempt to limit the power of business. They were part of a long American tradition of the "common people" standing up against entrenched elites (Pollack, 1962; Vogel, 1980-81: 607).

The Scope and Organization of Public Interest Law Groups

In 1969, there were twenty-three public interest law centers with fewer than fifty full-time attorneys. In 1975 there were 600 public interest lawyers practicing in 108 tax-exempt public interest law centers. By 1984, there were 154 groups employing 906 full-time lawyers. Reflecting social movements' commitment to legal action, the first wave of law centers, which appeared between 1969 and 1975, served consumers, the elderly, prisoners, workers, and gays and lesbians. What we now call the "public interest movement" included new or revitalized groups such as the Natural Resources Defense Council, the League for Conservation Voters, Consumers Union, the Union of Concerned Scientists, and Public Interest Research Groups. Between 1975 and 1984 there was a growth in groups that counseled the disabled and were concerned with international human rights. In addition, multi-issue organizations such as the Center for Law in the Public Interest (CLIPI) and New York Lawyers for the Public Interest came into being. A number of groups that were interested in public goods began to develop litigation strategies; they included the Center for Science in the Public Interest, the American Council for the Blind, the Conservation Law Foundation of New England, and many of the Public Interest Research Groups (PIRGs). The distribution of groups was bi-coastal: the cities with the most organizations were Washington, D.C. (45), New York (30), San Francisco (13), and Los Angeles and Boston (9 each) (Aron, 1989; 27-31).

Much as the direct service lawyering of the public interest bar sought to overcome the failure of markets to guarantee access to the courts and political mobilization lawyering sought to force the government to obey the Constitution, a major preoccupation of entrepreneurial lawyering has been to force the government to regulate in the interests of the public. This new public interest movement was one of numerous historical responses to the economic dominance of the large corporation. In the Progressive Era the untrammeled power of monopolistic corporations was met with reformers' urge to regulate. The Interstate Commerce Commission (1887), the Pure Food and Drugs Act (1906), the truth in advertising movement of the 1910s, and the Federal Trade Commission (1914) were all attempts to have government rein in the power of big business. In the 1930s, the labor movement exerted a counterweight to the nation's leading corporations. Yet the business community captured the regulatory agencies of the Progressive Era and eventually turned 1930s labor law against the working class. The 1960s public interest movement was another attempt to control the power of capital, but in keeping with the generalized distrust of all large institutions and perhaps with an eye to previously failed efforts, it also sought to end government's cozy relationship with business (Vogel, 1980-81).

The Entrepreneurial Law Firm

The term "public interest" as a type of lawyering that sought to give voice and power to the poor and disenfranchised only appeared in the late 1960s, and it designated a narrower field of practice than the types of law that this study covers (Esquivel, 1996: 336). This new form of practice consisted of environmental and consumer lawyers and generally those legal advocates who worked "at the intersection of corporate power and governmental responsibility." They had expertise in the procedures and routines of administrative and executive agencies where decisions affected large numbers of citizens. They brought the adversarial process into the regulatory system and acted as a counterweight to the corporate bar (Halpern, 1976: 159). In addition, they hoped to move beyond a purely litigious stance toward politics – they wanted to be taken seriously in the corridors of power – and included "programs that focus on policy-oriented cases, where a decision [would] advance a major law reform objective or affect large numbers of people..." Public interest lawyers shared a common set of goals: "to make government more accountable to the public and more responsive to the concerns and needs of unrepresented persons; to increase the power of citizens' groups; to insist on a place at the bargaining table; and to ensure that the development of public policy be open to public scrutiny" (Aron, 1989: 4).

The new public interest lawyers had a more expansive definition of who their clients should be. It was not just the poor who had been excluded from governmental and other decision-making processes. In the realm of consumer product safety, environmental degradation, and public services, the legal system had not acted as a neutral arbiter. Instead it functioned as a forum where corporate power trumped the underrepresented voices of citizens.

Attorneys interested in pursuing legal practices that challenged the influence of corporations in the public realm set up tax-exempt groups such as the Center of Law and Social Policy (CLASP) or created traditional partnerships (Berlin, Roisman and Kessler) dedicated to pursuing this new form of public interest law. The private partnerships found fee-paying clients "slow coming and slow paying," and the tax-exempt groups initially received little support from the foundation world. CLASP survived through the early lean years with the support of former Supreme Court Justice Arthur Goldberg, who had returned to private life. He helped them assemble influential legal insiders for their board of trustees, and, as a result, several small foundations provided early grants. CLASP initiated clinical programs in conjunction with some of the nation's most prestigious law schools: Penn, Yale, Stanford, UCLA, and Michigan. It also gained credibility through its work on the Alaska Pipeline and DDT cases. A year after its founding, the Ford Foundation guaranteed its immediate survival through a grant of $375,000.

Advocates set up public interest firms and organizations in Washington, D.C., New York, Chicago, San Francisco, and Los Angeles. Some organizations such as the Citizens Communication Center, which intervened in federal communications policy, dedicated themselves to specific and somewhat arcane areas of the law. The Natural Resources Defense Council did the same for environmental law. Others took as their mandate local (Stern Community Law Firm) or state (Center for Law in the Public Interest) matters. The Environmental Defense Fund, like CLASP, started from scratch but built a membership base and initiated litigation in its own name. The Sierra Club Legal Defense Fund and Consumers Union Law Firm aligned themselves with existing organizations to carry on legal advocacy for their underrepresented constituencies (Halpern, 1976:161).

Entrepreneurial Founders

One aspect of entrepreneurial lawyering that differentiates it from the earlier forms of direct service and political mobilization lawyering is the role that individuals have played in the founding of these organizations. The early legal aid movement had Arthur von Briesen of the New York Legal Aid Society and Reginald Heber Smith of the Boston Legal Aid Society. Roger Baldwin directed the ACLU for thirty years, and Thurgood Marshall guided the NAACP-Legal Defense and Education Fund through its most important years. They were crucial to the growth of their respective organizations and left their imprints on them, but only Baldwin was at the founding of his group. Each of these leaders (although Baldwin is a partial exception) inherited a fairly well established organizational form. In addition, of the organizations this study has most closely examined, lawyers founded none except Boston Legal Aid.

In contrast, several of the public interest law centers founded in the 1960s and 1970s were the brainchildren of politically impassioned lawyers or those lawyers who had moved beyond the limits of their previous organizations. Edward Sparer, who would spearhead the efforts for a constitutional right to social benefits, left Mobilization for Youth to found the Center on Social Welfare Policy and Law. Charles Halpern began the Center for Law and Social Policy. They shared an important feature of entrepreneurialism: the ability to put together a novel combination of resources and "get things done" (Schumpeter, 1991: ch. 10). Part of their entrepreneurialism was identifying a social need on which the law could have an effect. Gary Bellow observed that "attorneys in Washington tend to first establish a firm, and then focus upon developing a constituency" (citing Bellow, Comment, 1970: 1086).

Many public interest law centers drew their inspiration from Ralph Nader, a Harvard Law School-educated government lawyer who became a public figure in 1966 after the publication of *Unsafe at Any Speed* (1965). General Motors attempted to deflect criticism from his exposé of the dangers associated with the Corvair automobile by investigating Nader's personal life and trying to discredit him. With the more than $200,000 he received in the judgment against the auto giant for spying on him, he founded the Center for the Study of Responsive Law (CSRL) in 1969. The Center employed six full-time lawyers, a political scientist, and a physician. Nader was known as an indefatigable ascetic – much like Roger Baldwin without the baggage of a blue-blood heritage. His busy schedule of public speaking and impassioned advocacy for the middle class against big business and its junior partners in government paid off handsomely. During the summer of 1970 CSRL recruited 196 graduate student interns from medicine, law, engineering, and other fields.

Nader gained further attention when CSRL published a series of critical studies on the Federal Trade Commission, Interstate Commerce Commission, Agriculture Department, and Food and Drug Administration. He hoped that by exposing the failure of government agencies to fulfill their mandates and showing how power was concentrated in corporations, citizens would see their basic values were being undermined. He is reputed to have said, "who needs Marxist-Leninist rhetoric when you can get them on good old Christian Ethics?" In 1970, he founded the Public Interest Research Group. As sole proprietor, Nader employed 13 full-time attorneys at minimum salaries to use a variety of legal techniques to make large institutions accountable to the public. The attorneys he recruited tended to be from elite law schools and often were near the top of their classes (Comment, 1970: 1105, 1103; Trubek, 2002: 578).

Nader's ability to recruit the best and the brightest and to establish public interest law centers, either through inspiration or directly setting them up, speaks to his charismatic authority as well as his entrepreneurial abilities. The influence he had over the public interest movement during the 1960s and 1970s would be difficult to overstate. Whether the movement would have existed without him makes for interesting speculation, but, as Stinchcombe points out, echoing Weber, "entrepreneurship is both a matter of innovation and a matter of nontraditional authority, and a flow of innovations without nontraditional authority does not revolutionize a productive system" (Stinchcombe, 1965: 161).

According to Weber, charisma is a property of individuals or institutions, which can disrupt traditionally and rational-legally legitimated systems of authority. They claim legitimacy through their direct experience of divine grace. Charisma need not be tied to divinity or religion, though. It can adhere to "creative, expansive, innovating personalities who are regarded as 'extraordinary' even though they neither claim to possess divine grace nor have it imputed to them." They are those who by example and command point to a different way of life, who show by their commanding forcefulness or exemplary inner state that there is an alternative mode of being. The norms of charismatic authority reside within existing culture, but they are incompatible with the routines of that culture. They derive from ultimate sources of legitimacy. Charismatic figures or institutions deny the value of actions motivated by desire for status, personal affection, pecuniary gain, or other proximate ends (Shils, 1968: 387). Lacking a market framework or profit motive, Weber supplies a sociological understanding of how motivations provide mechanisms for Schumpeter's schema for "getting things done." Nader, the crusading and entrepreneurial ascetic, offered a model and rationale for talented law students who could otherwise command top salaries in the labor market to embark on careers in the public interest.

The Supply of Law School Graduates

Entrepreneurial leadership was insufficient for producing a public interest bar that could supplement direct service and political mobilization lawyering. A new public interest bar needed a supply of lawyers who had an affinity for such work. The legal profession grew considerably during the 1960s at the same time as entrepreneurial lawyering took off. Between 1960 and 1970 the number of lawyers nationwide increased by almost a third from 210,000 to 278,000. Over the next ten years the number grew by eighty-nine percent to 525,000. Even more impressive growth occurred in law schools. In 1960, approximately 44,000 students enrolled in law school; student enrollments almost doubled to 86,000 in 1970 and increased again by fifty percent in 1980 to 129,000. The growth in the new sector of public interest law was dramatic, but it remained a miniscule proportion of the profession as a whole. Aron estimates that between 1969 and 1984 the number of attorneys at public interest law centers, which included long-standing organizations such as the ACLU and NAACP-LDF, jumped from fewer than fifty to 906. It is for that reason it is important to examine the changing political attitudes of law students to see why they entered the arena of the public interest (Abel, 1989: 278-79, 281; Aron, 1989: 27).

Changing Society

Robert Stevens (1973) in his study of law school students at six campuses – Boston College, Connecticut, Iowa, Pennsylvania, University of

Southern California, and Yale – in two cohorts, one from the early 1960s and the second in the early 1970s, found that by the 1970s a substantial percentage of students expressed a desire to change society. The desire "to restructure society" grew in importance from the class of 1960 to the class of 1972. At Yale, the change was dramatic: those of the class of 1960 who had a "great" desire were thirteen percent; in the class of 1970, thirty-seven percent responded similarly. From the class of 1972 fifty-seven percent said the desire to restructure society was great. At USC, where social change ranked lowest on the agenda, the difference in attitude was considerable. In the class of 1960, zero percent had a great desire to restructure society. By the class of 1970, eighteen percent had a great desire for social change (Stevens, 1973: 579).

Between 1960 and 1970, students became increasingly liberal or radical, and students in the class of 1972 were even more radical than in 1970. Yale students in 1960 indicated that fifty-six percent considered themselves "liberal" or "far left." In 1972, that percentage rose to eighty, thirty-two percent considering themselves "far left." At the other schools, the number on the left rose, but about half identified themselves as "conservative" or "moderate." A spring 1971 Gallup poll of the general public found that it too was moving to the left. Sixty-five percent of the general population whose politics shifted moved leftward, but in contrast seven percent of the sample considered itself "very liberal" and nineteen percent "fairly liberal." Twenty-nine percent identified themselves as "middle," twenty-eight percent "fairly," and eleven percent "very conservative" (Stevens, 1973: 583-86).

Changes that occurred in the political orientation of law students and their interest in pursuing non-commercial careers had an effect on the hiring strategies of large law firms. The student revolt of the 1960s cut back on the number of graduates willing to enter the most lucrative sector of the profession; at least it was the case at elite schools for a few years. In 1960, sixty-one percent of Harvard Law School graduates went directly into private practice. In 1967 and 1968, that number fell to forty-four percent. In 1973, the percentage of graduates going into private practice rose to two-thirds. Large firms had to offer increased *pro bono* opportunities. Some firms went so far as to provide new associates the opportunity to work in neighborhood legal clinics or, in the case of the Baltimore firm Piper & Marbury, to open a neighborhood law firm that served the poor (Ashman, 1972; Stevens, 1983: 251; see also Chapter 6 above).

Changing Law Schools

The general ferment that took place on American campuses in the 1960s and early 1970s extended to law schools, although in a milder form – law students did not take over administration buildings nor were they known for housing cells of the Weather Underground. Students did organize against racism – they played a prominent role in offering legal counsel to civil rights protesters and voting rights activists – as well as against sexism and the Vietnam War, but law schools were first and foremost institutions of professional training. Their students exhibited understandably contradictory tendencies. As historian Robert Stevens wryly noted, "Professing to envisage a career for themselves as civil rights lawyers, they nevertheless expected to earn as much or often more than their predecessors" (Stevens, 1983: 234; see Greenberg, 2004; Meltsner, 2006).

Much of the "sixties" reform energy found an outlet in clinical legal education. As early as 1959 the National Legal Aid and Defender Association (NLADA) with assistance of the ABA and American Association of Law Schools and initial funding of $800,000 from the Ford Foundation made grants through 1965 of $500,000 to nineteen law schools. Students received a variety of clinical experiences: as clerks in legal aid offices; as interns in juvenile and family courts; in observation or participation in the work of mental health hospitals, social agencies, police departments, and correctional facilities. A successor project, the Council on Education in Professional Responsibility (COEPR), received additional funding of almost $1,000,000 from the Ford Foundation in 1965. It made grants to twenty-one law schools; half of the grants went to fund summer internships with local governments. In the spring of 1968, a $6 million Ford grant went to the recently formed Council on Legal Education for Professional Responsibility (CLEPR). Between 1970 and 1976 the number of clinical programs grew from 169 to 494. In 1975, twenty-four percent of second- and third-year students had clinical experience. Students not only gained important practical experience in traditional public interest areas, but they also received training in policy-making and the by-ways of the regulatory state. An added advantage was that legal clinics drew many of their instructors from the public interest field and as a result provided students with valuable information and social capital (Brickman, 1973: 58-59; Marden, 1973: 6-7; Stevens, 1983: 241; Schrag and Meltsner, 1998).

Sympathetic Federal Courts

The entrepreneurial lawyering movement's leaders put much faith in the ability of their sector of the legal profession to persuade the courts to deliver justice. Outside of the white South, most Americans accepted the court's leadership in the struggle against segregation. The federal courts had expanded individual rights in numerous spheres during the 1960s, and many public interest lawyers thought that the court shared a commitment to their version of substantive justice. They expected the court would expand its liberalism beyond issues of individual rights, as it had done in combating segregation. Courts did what Alexander Hamilton said they could not do: "exercise 'influence over the purse' and 'direction of the wealth of society'" (Neier, 1982: 130). Throughout the 1950s and 1960s the Court had come to recognize wealth (or poverty) as a "suspect classification" deserving "strict scrutiny" under the Fourteenth Amendment's equal protection clause. The Warren Court ruled that classifications that resulted in "wealth discrimination" violated the Fourteenth Amendment. It went further and decided that there were certain fundamental rights implicit in the Fourteenth Amendment. These fundamental rights, such as the right to vote in state elections, which was not guaranteed under the Constitution, made "other basic civil and political rights" possible. Advocates for the poor argued that if voting was a fundamental right, then surely material subsistence was also (Bussiere, 1997: 84-98). Lawyers in the new public interest centers did not assert that the "public" deserved strict scrutiny, but they expected that the judiciary, as an independent branch insulated from the power of big business, would fulfill a watchdog function.

Two important cases paved the way for much of the law that the public interest law reform movement relied upon. They gave hope to legal activists that the judiciary might be a model for citizen empowerment in the regulatory state. In *Office of Communication of United Church of Christ v. Federal Communications Commission*, 359 F.2d 994 (D.C. Cir. 1966), the D.C. Circuit Court of Appeals ruled that the FCC must allow members of the public to intervene in hearings because the agency itself could not adequately represent the public interest.[1] In a second historic case, *Scenic Hudson Preservation Conference v. Federal Power Commission* (1965), the court ruled that the Federal Power Commission in its hearings must discharge its duties to consider the public's ecological interests.[2]

---

[1] In *Office of Communication of United Church of Christ v. Federal Communications Commission*, the U.S. Court of Appeals for the D.C. Circuit ruled that a church group and prominent individuals had standing to challenge a Mississippi radio station's application for license renewal. The court reversed the FCC and remanded the case. It held that the Commission should hold evidentiary hearings.

[2] In *Scenic Hudson Preservation Conference v. Federal Power Commission*, 354 F.2d 608 (2d Cir. 1965), *cert. denied*, 384 U.S. 941 (1966), the plaintiffs sought to invalidate a license for Consolidated Edison to build a power plant at Storm King Mountain on the Hudson River. They argued that the site should be preserved for historic, scenic, conservation, and recreational purposes. The Federal Power Commission countered that the plaintiff lacked standing due to insubstantial economic interest in the project. The federal Second Circuit dismissed the agency's argument, holding:

> [T]he Commission has claimed to be the representative of the public interest. This role does not permit it to act as an umpire blandly calling balls and strikes for adversaries appearing before it; the right of the public must receive active and affirmative protection at the hands of the Commission (cited in Rabin, 1976: 226).

Public Goods Lawyers: Challenging the Politics of Pluralism

With the affirmation of the federal courts that the public had the right to be heard in the administrative arena, Ralph Nader and other entrepreneurial lawyers such as John Adams of the Natural Resources Defense Council took up the cudgel and assumed an advocacy role. Lawyers concerned with law reform appropriated academic critiques of laissez-faire liberalism and New Deal policymaking and responded to popular mistrust of bureaucracy. In the political realm, the civil rights movement had provided training and inspiration for many lawyers and the public at large to access the legal sphere for the redress of their rights. Furthermore, with the decision in the case of *Gideon v. Wainwright* (1963), the Supreme Court granted the right to access to the courts and effective implementation of that right was codified in the law. "And, there was that frustrating, unending war – creating an impulse in virtually every stratum of society, lawyers included, to do *something* about access to 'the system'" (Rabin, 1976: 227, emphasis in original).

What Rabin called that "impulse to do something" was more than an inarticulate call to arms. It relied on a critique of American politics that had evolved in the public interest community from a version of public interest law that Trubek and Trubek (1981) have termed the "classic approach." This strategy is based on a pluralist theory of American politics and leads to a more populist attack on the institutions, regulatory agencies, and the vested interests that they purportedly served, that thwarted the public will. In his book *The Governmental Process*, the political scientist David Truman (1951) presented the version of pluralist theory that held sway in the 1950s and 1960s. He argued that the American political system distributed resources and power to *organized* groups according to their ability to bargain with each other and the government for rights and privileges. Pluralism, with its competition between organized interests such as unions and business groups, replaced the idea of laissez-faire liberalism that had been the dominant discourse until the New Deal. What pluralism provided was a description and explanation of cooperative management of the commanding heights of the economy by narrow interests aided by the regulators charged with overseeing them. Lawyers for the poor claimed the poor lacked organization and thus found themselves excluded from decision-making policies. Much of direct service lawyering, including the work of most Legal Services attorneys, engaged in the classic approach, aspiring to represent the disenfranchised in the same manner as private firms represented better-off sectors of the population.

The political and cultural turmoil that were products of the black and women's liberation, antiwar, and other movements raised the question of power for social critics. An academic critique of pluralism provided a tool for public interest lawyers who had been influenced by the social movements of the 1960s to attack government administrative policy and the agencies that conducted that policy. Theodore Lowi in his book *The End of Liberalism* (1969) argued that vested and powerful interests perverted interest group pluralism. With agencies having multiple and conflicting policies, groups with a unity of purpose and resources tended to control the agencies that were meant to control them. To overcome the power of the vested interests that controlled policy Lowi advocated a return to the rule of law. It was rules rather than the directors of agencies that could provide justice. His prescription for what ailed liberalism and democracy had an attraction for reform-minded lawyers, for they had the expertise that could apply the law to the complicated issues of government, especially those that involved governing the economy.

With the eclipse of the welfare rights movement and the Nixonian "law and order" backlash, the poor appeared to decline as a subject of history and became more an object of policy. Direct action and self-organization had run its course by the early 1970s, and there appeared to be a breakdown in the state's ability to implement effective policy. Lowi's critique of pluralism found an audience in U.S. political culture. For consumers and citizens, those concerned with environmental degradation or workplace issues of health and safety, i.e., the "public," the critique of pluralism had resonance.

The major aim of the public interest movement was to increase the power of people over public policy and, in their roles as citizens, consumers, and taxpayers, to give them as much power as business had (Vogel, 1980-81: 622). The power of capital was its wealth, and the public interest movement was no match for its resources. The movement had few resources to compete with capital, and unlike capital which could "strike" by refusing to invest, the public interest movement had little to withhold from society. At this moment, Ralph Nader, with his organization Nader's Raiders, stepped into the breach and took up the battle against pluralism. They positioned themselves to speak for the consumer and pursue the public interest in the administrative arena (Rabin, 1976: 224-25).

If direct service lawyers used legal advocacy to provide social welfare benefits, the ACLU had the Constitution as its client, and NAACP lawyers forced the state to obey the Constitution, then entrepreneurial lawyers might be considered *public goods lawyers*. Public goods, a term borrowed from the economics literature, are goods or services that once they are made available to one person are free to all, and their consumption cannot be denied. They are said to be "non-rivalrous" and "non-excludable," i.e., anyone can consume as much as desired without diminishing the goods available to others. Clean air is a public good because it is generally impossible to prevent someone from breathing it, and one person's consumption does not diminish the supply for others. The public airwaves are another example of a public good because, with the cost of a radio or television affordable to most Americans, anyone can listen to the radio or watch TV; an increase in demand does not mean a decrease in supply. The issue of public goods raises a problem for market economies. As Hume noted in *A Treatise of Human Nature* (1739-40: 538), there are some social tasks which, while unprofitable for any individual to undertake, are still beneficial to society as a whole. For those tasks or functions to be performed, collective, or governmental, action is necessary. Public goods are not free goods, though. The costs of producing and supplying public goods often fall to government (Sandmo, 1987; Hardin, 2003).

Thus, public interest lawyers entered the field of policymaking and litigation to ensure the production of public goods, and they engaged in political struggles over how to equitably distribute their costs. For example, clean air and water are public goods that involve considerable costs to maintain in an industrial society. Organizations such as the Sierra Club, the Natural Resources Defense Council, and various other public interest groups litigated to enforce rules, wrote regulations, and lobbied legislators. They faced opponents in industry who wished to avoid the costs of complying with regulations and government actors who saw few distinctions between the roles of government and private industry (Comment, 1970).

Lawyers advocating in much of the public interest field did not counsel clients as much as represent diffuse constituencies. They advocated for the extension of public goods and because their services were not sold as commodities they faced the free-rider problem. The diffuseness of their constituency – consumers are not an easily identifiable or represented group – was compounded by their lack of organizational unity. The low visibility of corporate and regulatory agency decisions compounded the obstacles these public interest lawyers faced. In response they borrowed much from the repertoire of political mobilization lawyering. Public relations work and education about relevant law were mainstays of these entrepreneurial lawyers. They wrote articles, appeared in the media, and spoke frequently on college campuses. They tended to direct their political energies to the legislative and regulatory arenas, but they frequently lacked the resources to stay on top of various rules and procedures that must be met to affect policy change (Comment, 1970: 1096-98, 1102; Trubek and Trubek, 1981: 135-36).

Entrepreneurial Lawyering and the Legislative Process

The public interest bar's involvement in the legislative process extended beyond its attempts to craft new laws and see them enacted. It used legislation to further its ability to advocate. Lawyers who use the courts for political change face the problem of the limits of the law. What is just and right may not necessarily be legal. In fact, as Weber (1978 [1921-22]) pointed out in the early decades of the twentieth century, in a capitalist society procedural justice more often trumps substantive justice. One approach to using the courts is illustrated in the NAACP and NAACP-LDF campaign to end segregation. *Brown v. Board of Education* (1954) overturned *Plessy v. Ferguson* (1896) by a long march through the courts; it involved defeats, tactical retreats, and a faith in the righteousness of its cause.

In retrospect, *Brown* seemed inevitable, but consider the case of Edward Sparer and his colleagues at the Center on Social Welfare Policy and Law (CSWPL). They along with activist lawyers in the anti-poverty movement sought to establish a constitutional "right to live." Court rulings had successfully challenged the punitive effects of the welfare system by eliminating residency laws, 'man in the house" rules that disqualified mothers who cohabited with men, and midnight raids to check up on recipients. The Warren Court seemed on the verge of ruling for a right to live, but in *Wyman v. James*, 400 U.S. 309 (1971), with Harry Blackmun writing his first opinion, the Supreme Court held that welfare is a gift, not a right (Davis, 1993; Diller, 1995: 1415). The right to live may have been perceived as just in the wealthiest nation, but it was not to be the law.

Public interest organizations on the Left would largely give up faith in campaigns to change the law radically through the courts. Instead, by the late 1960s they moved to the legislative arena, where one of the first orders of business was to enhance their ability to conduct public interest law. It was a move that would pay off handsomely, structurally altering their power to litigate. They pushed for and won legislation such as the 1974 amendments to the Freedom of Information Act that allowed citizens to sue if regulations were not being adequately enforced. To make it easier for attorneys to sue regulatory agencies, they supported a provision in the National Environmental Policy Act of 1969 that required environmental impact statements from administrative agencies. To expand the right of citizens to information, they advocated for "whistle-blower" protection. Laws that prohibited tax-exempt organizations from lobbying restricted public interest organizations in their attempts to influence legislation, and in 1970 fifteen public interest groups formed a coalition to loosen restrictions. The 1976 Tax Reform Act passed with a provision allowing tax-exempt 501(c)(3)'s to spend up to twenty percent of their budgets on lobbying (Vogel, 1980-81: 611-12, 614).

One of the most important efforts to strengthen public interest attorneys' recourse to the courts – and this effort went to the heart of their entrepreneurial spirit – was the struggle over fee-shifting. Recovering court fees from a losing party generally does not occur in the U.S. legal system. Uniquely among industrialized countries, neither side in an American legal dispute generally pays the other side's attorneys' fees. The

"American Rule," as it is known in the legal profession, was established in early Supreme Court decisions and for Federal Courts in the 1853 Fee Bill. An exception is when an opponent has litigated in bad faith; another is when the parties' contract has provided for fee-shifting. Other exceptions have been statutorily established, most importantly in the 1964 Civil Rights Act. Under Title II litigation that challenges racial discrimination in public accommodations, attorneys' fees can be awarded at the court's discretion. In 1968, the Supreme Court in *Newman v. Piggie Park Enterprises, Inc.*, 390 U.S. 400 (1968), ruled that only under special circumstances could the courts deny attorneys' fees for cases litigated under Title II.

In 1974 the D.C. Circuit Court of Appeals ruled that fee-shifting was permissible for any case in furtherance of the public interest even absent specific statutory authority. The following year the Supreme Court overruled the D.C. court in *Alyeska Pipeline Service Company v. The Wilderness Society*, 421 U.S. 240, 250 (1975), asserting that such public-interest fee-shifting could only be carried out with the consent of Congress. Recognizing that the private bar had an important role in enforcing civil rights and the statutory protection of access to public goods, and bowing to pressure from the public interest bar, Congress passed legislation, the Civil Rights Attorney's Fees Award Act of 1976, mandating the award of legal fees and expenses for plaintiffs who prevailed in civil rights litigation. Congress went on to pass laws permitting attorneys' fees in other types of litigation, among which were civil rights, police brutality, consumer and environmental protection, employment discrimination, and privacy/sunshine cases (Aron, 1989: 11-12; Bradford, 1995).

Funding

Unlike either the early legal aid societies started by immigrant mutual aid groups and social service organizations, or the political mobilization lawyering that was carried out by political groups, the new public interest groups of the 1960s and 1970s were entrepreneurial creations. The innovative approaches to law and new organizational forms that their founders delivered required they set up business plans that would address securing a source of capital. Funding for establishing public interest law organizations came overwhelmingly from foundations, especially the Ford Foundation.

Contributions from wealthy individuals and law firm subscriptions supported the early legal aid societies in New York and Boston, and the ACLU benefited from the contributions of a few of its charter members. Most funding for the NAACP's legal work came from membership dues, but foundation funding played an important role as was described in Chapter 4: for example, it received an important grant from the American

Fund for Public Service (the Garland Fund) in the 1920s. In contrast to the entrepreneurial firms of the 1960s and 1970s, foundation funding came well after the organizations had been established. Starting in the late 1950s and picking up steam in the 1960s, foundations began to provide seed capital – and indispensable social connections to other funders – for new forms of public interest law. The Kaplan Foundation, a New York City foundation that dispensed the wealth of New York real estate magnate J.M. Kaplan, provided some initial funds, prior to the Ford Foundation's contribution, to Mobilization for Youth (MFY), an important precursor organization of the Legal Services program. The Russell Sage Foundation provided MFY with valuable connections to NIMH decision-makers and also intellectual support that aided it in receiving funding and the imprimatur of the leading government social science funder (see Chapter 3).

In the 1960s, the NAACP-LDF received relatively small grants from family foundations to continue its work opposing segregation. Contentious politics was still a problem for most foundations, but in 1965 the Ford Foundation, hoping to avoid the appearance that it was funding civil rights groups, granted $1,000,000 to an ostensibly independent organization, the National Office for the Rights of the Indigent (NORI), which was basically a front group of the NAACP-LDF. LDF was the leading public interest law organization in the country and benefited from what Robert Merton (1973) called the "Matthew effect."[3] The money the Ford Foundation gave to LDF provided a fiscal cushion that permitted its legal director Jack Greenberg to hire additional lawyers and move into new areas (Meltsner, 2006: 158). In the 1970s, funding for its capital defense work and the provision of legal training came from the Rockefeller, Carnegie, and other nationally prominent foundations (Greenberg, 2004: 400, 489, 404-05).

Ford made further grants to the public interest bar in the early 1970s, starting with two grants in 1970 to the Natural Resources Defense Council and the Center for Law and Social Policy, which concentrated on environment, consumer affairs, and health problems of the poor. By 1975, Ford made grants to thirteen other firms with total funding from Ford over the five years equaling $12.5 million. Those Ford Foundation-supported firms were or had been in litigation in 370 cases and intervened in nearly 150 administrative proceedings. From 1972 to 1975 seventy-four percent of funding to public interest firms came from foundations, twenty-two percent from the federal government, and one percent from court-awarded legal fees (Ford Foundation and ABA Special Committee on Public Interest Practice, 1976: 14-15, 50-52; Trubek and Trubek, 1981: 124).

---

[3] "For unto every one that hath shall be given, and he shall have abundance: but from him that hath not shall be taken away even that which he hath." Matthew 13:12.

The Council for Public Interest Law in its influential report *Balancing the Scales of Justice: Financing Public Interest Law in America* (1976) envisioned four sources of public interest funding: (1) organized private foundations, (2) the organized bar, (3) court-awarded attorneys' fees, and (4) the government. None of these sources provided sufficient funds to sustain the organizations. The Ford, Carnegie, and Rockefeller Foundations decided in 1975 and 1976 to phase out their contributions as, according to a Ford Foundation spokesperson, "they become self-sustaining." The organized bar failed, as it had in the past (see Chapter 2), in offering financial support to the public interest bar. The ABA gave considerable rhetorical support for the public interest law organizations but never matched it with equivalent financial contributions. For example, in 1977, the Carnegie Foundation offered a $250,000 grant to the Council on Public Interest Law on the condition that the ABA contribute twice that amount through a dues check-off. The ABA refused and Carnegie withdrew its offer. Local bar associations in Los Angeles and Washington, D.C. were more forthcoming, however, and established dues check-off systems: between the two cities, they raised $165,000 (Trubek and Trubek, 1981: 127-28).

Aggregate funding for public interest firms from foundations remained constant from 1975 to 1983, but on average each organization received thirty-six percent less funding. The wealthy were not establishing large foundations at the same rate they had in the past, and large foundations experienced frustration and pessimism about the possibilities of solving social problems. Federal government funding for social and legal services rose slightly between 1975 and 1979 in aggregate and average group terms, but dropped between 1979 and 1983 in aggregate terms by twelve percent and in the average amount going to each group by twenty-nine percent.

With the decline in foundation and federal support, new sources of revenues had to make up the shortfall. By the mid-1980s, almost a third of funding (thirty-one percent) came from individual charitable contributions and membership dues, and court-awarded attorneys' fees made up nine percent of revenues. Foundation grants dropped to twenty-four percent of revenues. Federal grants declined slightly from twenty-two to eighteen percent of funding. Foundation and federal government support were still important to the public interest bar as a whole: eighty-one percent of organizations received foundation grants, seventy-four percent individual contributions, thirty-five percent federal funding, and thirty percent membership dues. In contrast, nonprofit groups that were not engaged in legal services received twenty-eight percent of funding from client services – the IRS forbade nonprofit public interest legal organizations from receiving client funds. In 1983, legal centers received $60 million from philanthropic foundations, less than one-tenth of one percent of the $65 billion of charitable giving (Aron, 1989: 39-40, 52-53, 71).

As funding from foundations, and to a lesser extent the federal government, declined, public interest organizations relied on individual donations, many originating in direct mail campaigns. In the early 1980s the Reagan administration proved a boon to such fund-raising. Figures such as Secretary of the Interior James Watt offered convenient and compelling targets for environmental groups. The National Audubon Society sent out a mass-mailing in 1981 announcing it was "entering a battle" with the federal government and raised almost $1 million. Environmental groups were able to increase the amount of funding they received from individuals so that it provided a majority of their revenues (Aron, 1989: 71). Entrepreneurial lawyering organizations were able to raise funds through direct solicitations because they were organizationally and culturally part of a burgeoning sector of the nonprofit world that formed to address political issues. In addition, they were able to take advantage of the pioneering efforts of the NAACP-LDF in its use of 501(c)(3) tax-exempt status, and in its and the ACLU's use of direct mail (the ACLU set up a 501(c)(3) foundation in 1966).

In the post-war period nonprofit organizations differed considerably from previous national associations. The service clubs (fraternal, sororal, veterans, and patriotic) found themselves eclipsed by national mass membership organizations such as the National Audubon Society and American Association of Retired Persons. While the pre-war organizations – the Shriners, Masons, and women's clubs – were built on sociality (often mixed with a heavy dose of exclusivity), the new organizations rarely met face to face. The mutual support that the New York German Society encouraged and that led to the New York Legal Aid Society was replaced by advocacy groups more in line with the social structure of the welfare state. For individuals, membership and/or contributions became an act of political identification. If the granting of tax-exempt status did not exactly confer governmental authority on public interest organizations, it nonetheless gave them entrée into the organizational field of public decision-making (Hall, 2003: 370). Of course, being admitted to the field was necessary but not sufficient. Large foundation partnerships, government funding, and successful use of the courts helped as well.

* * *

Entrepreneurial public interest lawyering came to occupy a niche that neither direct service nor political mobilization lawyering could easily fill. The everyday workings of legal services in which a mass of the poor received fairly repetitive counseling weighed heavily on the attention spans of the best and the brightest law school graduates. At the same time, nurturing innovation in the field strained the resources of even the wealthiest foundations. Furthermore, Legal Services found itself continuously subject to political control from above. Political mobilization lawyering faced the problem of what to do when its social movements declined or had less use for lawyers who organized. Both the ACLU and the NAACP had been forced to the courts, and they stayed there, adapting to a new political era that required fewer political skills but increasing legal expertise and specialization. Entrepreneurial lawyering created more organizations and employed more full-time public interest lawyers engaged in law reform than ever before. It expanded on political technologies of direct mail and grantsmanship that the NAACP-LDF and ACLU had pioneered. Finally, it identified a myriad of legal opportunities that delivered legal reforms, frequently as public goods, to a diffuse constituency.

Entrepreneurial lawyering relied upon a high degree of legal expertise and insider knowledge of the workings of the regulatory state. It combined this expertise with a diffuse commitment to an expanded sense of democracy and access, not just to the courts but to the political system: what T. H. Marshall (1992) would consider a necessary condition for the fulfillment of social citizenship. This combination of expertise and populist politics allowed entrepreneurial lawyering to take root and flourish in a context of liberal politics. At the same time, however, it was unmoored from a political base and lacking a constituency or "natural clientele" outside of the fickle world of foundations. This has meant that it has largely been unable to sustain its strengths – a base of intellectually and politically committed individual lawyers – in the face of a legal system moving increasingly to the right.

The myriad of present-day public interest law organizations consist of small staffs of highly trained attorneys located in the corridors of power (Southworth, 2002) and attuned to opportunities to affect the law. These organizations are part of the legacy of entrepreneurial lawyering. The 2000s and 2010s are not the 1970s, though, and with a very different political climate, entrepreneurial lawyering's promise of opening government to the "people" remains unfulfilled, a consequence of the narrowing of the political opportunity structure (Eisinger, 1973: 11; McAdam, 1982: 40). Like much of the public interest bar, the fortunes of entrepreneurial lawyering have depended on the ebb and flow of social movements and the expansion and contraction of possibilities for political liberalism. Shifting interests of foundations affect funding: no organization has taken the place of the Ford Foundation in setting an agenda for wide-ranging policies of legal reform. Other areas of the opportunity structure (Merton, 1995) remain open, however. The supply of law students interested in careers in public service remains strong and has the institutional support of law schools that provide training. There are still occurring various public and private efforts to change the financial disincentives to entering the public interest bar.

8

CONCLUSION

This study has explored various institutional responses of lawyers to the problem of providing legal services when those services are typically sold as commodities. I have described three different forms of practice that have sought to meet citizers' demands for substantive justice: direct service, political mobilization and entrepreneurial lawyering. These three forms of lawyering serve the public interest in that they offer legal counsel to individuals who cannot afford it, represent groups whose social or economic marginality make them the target of abuse or neglect, advocate to increase citizens' democratic participation in society, and challenge government programs, policies, or actions as unlawful. Finally, public interest lawyering seeks remedies intended to benefit a broad class of persons rather than simply individual plaintiffs (Aron, 1989: 4; Jacobs, 2003: 1).

Direct Service Lawyering

Direct service lawyering was an outgrowth of the legal aid movement. It began not with lawyers but developed from immigrant mutual aid organizations and groups of social workers and reformers that wanted to use the legal system to ameliorate conditions of urban poverty. They were responding to the problems of urbanization and industrialization as they affected a population of immigrants and rural migrants. Lawyers from the corporate bar and members of the philanthropic and political elite came late to the movement, but through the legal aid societies they institutional-ized a specific form of service based on noblesse oblige, good government, and a form of citizership that stressed order and conformity to wage labor. Lawyers, or at least the elite of the bar, came late to the legal aid movement in part because the social problems of the poor did not appear as legal problems. In the eyes of the legal elite, the difference between "social standards and social actualities" (Merton, 1971) was not a structural feature of capitalist development – the need for a low-wage, disciplined workforce that could be reproduced on the cheap (Engels, 1993 [1845]; Chused, 2000) – or social integration in a period of rapid industrialization (Durkheim, 1984 [1893]; Weebe, 1967). The leaders of legal aid came late to the movement because they saw demand for services as the result of moral failure; tenants would drink away their rent or abandon their wives, or petty capitalists would abscond with wages. Legal aid for the urban poor became a widely accepted solution when political remedies threatened to displace the courts. Legal aid societies brought together "good government" reformers and their cities' most prominent citizens to offer an alternative to lower-class lawyers, often closely associated with political machines (Anthes, 2000), or the doctrines of anarchism and socialism.

Early advocates of public interest law attempted to reconcile a commitment to the providing the poor with access to the courts and making those same courts more efficient. The largest legal aid societies relied primarily on full-time staffs of attorneys and thus replicated an emerging form of legal organization, the corporate law firm, that prized functional specialization – legal aid attorneys were the nation's first "poverty lawyers" – and economies of scale.

Like many active in Progressive Era reforms, the leadership of the legal aid movement was appalled by the conditions of urban working class life. They expressed ambivalence about the causes of poverty and injustice, but their service ideal was refracted through an ideology of individual moral worth. They knew that a necessary, and many believed a sufficient, condition for individual escape from poverty was work and sobriety. The early legal aid societies combined their service ethic with ethical obligations.

The institutionalization of indigent civil and criminal legal services in legal aid societies in addition relieved the bulk of urban lawyers from fulfilling their professional ethical obligations to provide access to the legal system. Corporate lawyers, who almost exclusively represented the organized bar, could continue providing their clients with zealous advocacy while the poor enjoyed a form of legal practice that stressed compromise and education rather than adversarial conflict. Reginald Heber Smith, in *Justice for the Poor* (1919), argued:

> There is a direct relationship between legal aid organizations and the members of the bar, both as individual attorneys and as a collective body. Out of this relationship there spring reciprocal obligations.... While the responsibilities are bilateral, the performance is still very much one-sided... [T]he lawyers are only dimly aware that they owe a debt to legal aid work, and as yet they have not taken the part which may fairly be expected of them....
>
> [I]n all their work, [legal aid societies] are relieving the bar of a heavy burden by performing for the bar its legal and ethical obligation to see that no one shall suffer injustices through inability, because of poverty, to obtain needed legal advice and assistance. Each case which a legal aid organization undertakes puts the bar in debt to it, for in the conduct of that case, it is doing the work of the bar for the bar. (Smith, 1919: 243, 246.)

"The result of these practices." in the words of Michael Grossberg, "was the establishment of a new professional responsibility and the legitimation of a two-tiered legal system that sanctioned adversarial solutions for those who could pay, and alternative forms of dispute resolution for those who could not" (Grossberg, 1997: 307).

The consequences of a two-tiered legal system could be seen most fully in the system of indigent criminal defense. The early legal aid pioneers, New York, Chicago, and Boston, generally eschewed criminal defense. Their reluctance to embrace criminal defense should not be too surprising. They set the standard for representing the "deserving poor," and were able to take over existing organizations from immigrants and social reformers by their ability to tap into "Eastern establishment" money. They went so far as to reject public financing for indigent criminal defense. When they represented the poor in criminal proceedings, they often worked closely with the police and prosecutors.

Federal law, legal precedents, and the willingness of politically motivated lawyers and organizations to defend the most stigmatized members of society combined to increase the rights of criminal defendants. Although not enforced in the states until the 1960s, the Sixth Amendment guaranteed the right to retain counsel in criminal cases. Starting in the 1930s the federal courts, in a number of cases that featured black defendants battling Southern "justice" with the aid of NAACP and other politically engaged lawyers, building on precedent and an increasingly liberal reading of the due process clause of the Constitution expanded the rights of criminal defendants to access to the courts and required they receive effective counsel. The culmination of the "due process revolution" in criminal defense was *Gideon v. Wainwright* (1963) and several other cases decided by the Warren Court. The constitutional guarantee to the right to counsel spurred the states to institutionalize and expand public defender offices. Those cases also raised the importance of the provision of effective counsel, an ideal that brought to the fore a quest for substantive justice for the poor in the criminal and civil courts.

The impetus for federally funded legal services for the poor came not from extant legal aid organizations or leaders of the bar but from a variety of actors outside of or at the margins of the legal profession. Several of the early forays into providing legal services outside of the Legal Aid model originated from private foundations, especially the Ford Foundation, federal agencies, and even the remnants of the settlement house movement. They provided early financing, ideas, political support, and inspiration to those who would lead the efforts to create what eventually became the Legal Services Corporation (LSC). Early leaders of this movement were social workers and lawyers, yet the lawyers saw legal services for the poor not as an end in itself, but as a means to end poverty. Their alliance with social workers and government agencies resulted in conflicts over how lawyers would fulfill their service ideal. The young leaders of New Haven's Community Progress, Inc. and New York's Mobilization for Youth insisted on representing their clients with zealous advocacy regardless of whether it conflicted with other actors in their nascent anti-poverty programs. Interpreting the service ideal to embrace both client advocacy and professional autonomy, they argued that their duties to their clients redefined their organizational roles. In MFY they saw themselves as legal counselors and political advocates.

When advocates for a federally funded legal services program took up the challenge of getting legislation passed, they had to widen their political horizons. In their insistence on professional autonomy they shared a concern with the elite of the organized bar that interference from non-lawyers had to be avoided at all costs. From the beginning of the process they had strong backing from figures high in the Johnson administration, and when Johnson won the 1964 election with strong Democratic victories in congressional races, the Administration enjoyed an extraordinary mandate and the ability to overcome recalcitrant conservatives of both parties. Local bar and legal aid society opposition had still to be overcome. Legal Services advocates sought a federally funded program of neighborhood law offices precisely because they would not resemble legal aid societies: they felt the legal aid societies were less than thorough advocates and were under the influence of conservative lawyers whose main loyalties were to local elites. Solo practitioners and small-firm lawyers, especially in urban areas, opposed Legal Services because they feared they would present unfair competition. Legal aid groups took umbrage at the way in which Legal Service partisans characterized them, but hard opposition from the National Legal Aid and Defender Association managed to eliminate itself from any future role in influencing the program's plans.

To secure the backing of the ABA, Legal Services' architects had to turn over to them control over the LSP structure and grant-making process. With those powers they were able to enlist legal aid societies and overcome local opposition. The active support of national bar leaders insured passage of necessary legislation and thwarted conservative attempts to undermine the program through the 1970s, but it came at a price. Those parts of the program meant to involve the poor were effectively marginalized to but a few sites. Projects had to pass muster with state and local bars and state judiciaries, and those entities looked askance at projects that engaged in group representation and community advocacy. Moreover, the process of seeking annual appropriations meant Legal Services' funding was permanently politicized. With the eclipse of liberalism starting in the mid-1970s Legal Services came under threat. Funding for the program reached its peak in constant dollars at $321 million in FY 1981 when there were

6,000 LSC lawyers: one lawyer for every 5,000 poor people. In 2007, the Senate Appropriations Committee set proposed funding for LSC at $390 million. An equivalent amount in 1981 dollars would be approximately $171 million (Johnson, 1999: 30; *LSC Updates*, July 5, 2007, available at http://www.lsc.gov/press/updates_2007_detail_T158_R14.php).

The model of direct service lawyering that the early legal aid movement instituted resembled much of what we would now call "welfare." It was means tested; its benefits varied by locality; it was often provided by private organizations, what Alan Wolfe called the "franchise state"; it was incomplete in comparison with other advanced industrial states; and attached to its provisions were strong moral judgments. Legal aid attorneys were constantly aware of the need to restrict it to the deserving poor (Katz, 1996: x). During the early years of the Legal Services Program, an alternative to public interest direct service lawyering that promised "maximum feasible participation" by the poor and was part of a concerted policy to end poverty seemed a possibility. The demise of the judicial activism of the Warren Court, waning support from the bar, and a drastic shift to the right by the populace has meant diminished political support for legal services for poor individuals. Funding cutbacks and increased restrictions on government-funded civil and criminal legal services threaten to turn the poor's ability to secure substantive justice back to a century-old era. The moral strictures placed on legal aid clients have been replaced by a different set of markers for the "deserving poor." Legal Services attorneys – the largest group of public interest lawyers – must now ask whether their clients are immigrants or prisoners. They must refuse to file amicus briefs, litigate issues related to abortion, represent clients facing eviction from public housing where drugs are an issue, or undertake class action suits. Attorneys, of course, can still counsel clients on such matters, but they must do so as a matter of charity. In our legal system the poor are being re-stigmatized. It hardly seems a coincidence that in 1996, the year in which President Clinton ended "welfare as we know it," he also signed into legislation onerous limitations on the ability of Legal Services attorneys to practice law, restrictions that, were they to be placed on private attorneys, would never pass constitutional review.

Political Mobilization Lawyering

Political mobilization lawyering began with the ACLU and the NAACP. Like the legal aid societies its founders were socially homogenous, but they were also well connected in the higher echelons of national political society. Like many of the early legal aid societies, neither the ACLU nor the NAACP had many lawyers among its founding membership. Both organizations had activist agendas: anti-militarism and defense of civil rights, in the case of the ACLU; and anti-discrimination at the NAACP. Neither group considered itself a legal organization – the NAACP focused on building membership and the ACLU on public education and aiding strategic campaigns related to labor – but both from their beginning expended considerable resources addressing constituent concerns in the courts. By the 1920s it was clear to the leaders of the ACLU and the NAACP that their personal connections could deliver few, if any, political benefits; use of the courts would be strategic to their organizational existence.

The combination of representing a largely disenfranchised constituency that had not organized itself politically or economically, and having a mission – representing legally oppressed citizens – that went to the heart of the legal system, forced the NAACP into the courts. The NAACP's legal work was initially done in an ad hoc fashion and relied on highly respected and prominent members of the national bar. Like many of the supporters of the early legal aid movement, these white attorneys were motivated by noblesse oblige and embraced their *pro bono* legal work as an obligation to the legal profession. At the same time, like their colleagues in the ACLU, they gravitated toward political lawyering because they saw upholding the service ideal as upholding the Constitution. The ACLU's initial trajectory was similar to the NAACP's. It too began representing a constituency, war resisters and labor radicals, that confronted a hostile majority. Facing government repression from the executive branch it, too, was forced into the courts.

The legal strategies of both organizations developed in tandem with their ongoing political work. Court cases supplemented the organizing and educational work of the ACLU and NAACP. In the hostile political context in which they operated, successful litigation represented some of the few tangible results to their memberships and the larger society. The NAACP increased its membership numerically and across a wide expanse of the country, so that it began resembling a mass organization. Still, not until the end of the 1930s was it able to shed its image as a middle-class group. The ACLU was much slower in creating a national membership; it tended to rely more on well-connected and well-off influentials who could deliver its message to the media or members of the political establishment. To carry out their legal work, both groups had to rely on a supply of lawyers eager and able to engage in litigation. Building networks of sympathetic lawyers was not always easy. Maintaining a sufficient supply of cooperating attorneys would be a challenge for the ACLU, especially when it ventured outside of large urban areas. The NAACP would face an even more daunting task when it had to call on black lawyers in the Deep, and not-so-Deep, South.

The NAACP could hardly rely on white attorneys in the South; most were firmly allied with the Jim Crow power structure, and those who were not mostly feared bucking it. Pressure from the organization's middle-class membership and an emerging supply of black attorneys created the conditions for blacks to invent a whole new field: civil rights law. In the 1920s, a group of African American lawyers studied constitutional law under the tutelage of Harvard Law School professor Felix Frankfurter. These attorneys provided the human and social capital that was to train and equip a generation of black civil rights lawyers. The key institutional setting in which this was done was Howard University Law School, which became the largest source of black attorneys well into the 1960s.

Internally generated funds and outside foundation funding were instrumental in the legal strategies of both organizations. In the 1930s the Garland Fund provided money to the NAACP to embark on a legal strategy to improve Negro life. That initial capital allowed it to hire Charles Houston as general counsel and later Thurgood Marshall who planned a litigation campaign to desegregate education that culminated in *Brown v. Board of Education* (1954). Much as the run-up to *Brown* represented a breakthrough legal strategy attacking segregation in incremental steps, the ACLU likewise entered new legal terrain when, as in the case of its campaign against Boss Hague, it pioneered the use of injunctions to prevent the state from curtailing freedom. Local chapters of the NAACP continued to agitate on issues of importance to their membership. From 1940 to 1960, the LDF's first two decades of independence from the NAACP, it had four or five lawyers on staff. That changed in the 1960s when responding to the upsurge in civil rights protests, opportunities to litigate employment discrimination under Title VII of the Civil Rights Act of 1964, and an influx of funds from foundations, the staff expanded to a high of thirty attorneys. During roughly the same period, the number of black attorneys in the South grew considerably and the LDF developed an extensive network of cooperating attorneys who were reimbursed a modest fee for LDF-authorized litigation. In 1975 the LDF had an active docket of about 200 employment discrimination cases.

The ACLU also stressed membership building and had a decentralized form of organization. Local chapters had almost complete autonomy and undertook legal campaigns with volunteer attorneys and little aid from the national office. As late as 1960, the ACLU had a staff of five permanent lawyers. During the 1950s and 1960s campaigns to counter government encroachment on the Bill of Rights proved powerful recruitment tools: membership doubled about every five years. In 1974, membership passed 275,000 in 375 local chapters in forty-nine states. Five-thousand volunteer lawyers worked with a full-time staff of thirty-four attorneys in nineteen local offices and twenty-five lawyers in three ACLU national offices. The national office reduced its use of volunteer attorneys. Staff attorneys also moved away from their previous roles as "generalists" directing volunteer litigators. They became project attorneys in areas such as juvenile, women's or prisoner rights, abortion, or sexual privacy. These projects received their funding from private foundations. The organization also shifted gears away from a policy of filing amicus briefs to direct representation of clients.

Entrepreneurial Lawyering

A third group were the public interest law firms. They included the various groups of "Nader's Raiders," environmental groups such as the Sierra Club Legal Defense Fund and Natural Resources Defense Counsel, and other firms such as Citizens Communication Center and Center for the Law and Public Interest. They typically had three to six attorneys, recruited them from elite law schools, and received their initial funding and logistical support from the Ford Foundation. Ford gave them guaranteed funding and considerable tactical autonomy to carry out litigation strategies. The groups were primarily interested in providing "the public" with access to federal regulatory agencies. With foundation support these lawyers were able to devote considerable time to gaining expertise in highly complex regulatory areas and thus litigate on equal terms with federal agencies or the most prestigious corporate firms. According to Robert Rabin, foundation support

> made possible a new departure – litigation directed at social change with the benefits of a corporate law firm structure: centralized control over caseload, stimulating collegiality, a full-time professional staff, and the opportunity to specialize. At the same time, foundation subsidization abrogated the limitations of corporate practice tied to client control. Moreover, the hazardous painstaking endeavor to build a membership base that so markedly characterized, and limited, the growth of earlier litigation-oriented law reform organizations was circumvented (Rabin, 1976: 236).

In addition, they had independence from political pressures that eventually restricted what Legal Services Corporation grantees could and could not do. Without a membership base they could never escape the problem of external funding, and the political changes they sought were all the more precarious because their constituencies tended to be foundations or the organizations themselves.

Pro Bono Publico in Large Firms

Most of this study has treated the public interest bar as operating in a "separate sphere" of the legal profession (Heinz and Laumann, 1982). This sphere differentiates itself from the for-profit sphere by adhering to non-commercial values and largely exists outside of the logic of the market. I have attempted to show that the public interest bar is not entirely divorced from the larger profession. It has shared personnel, institutions of training and socialization, and, in a variously attenuated manner, an ideal of service that recognizes concepts of democracy and justice. In the practice of *pro bono publico* the organizational separation of the public interest and commercial spheres breaks down. I have argued in part that political and financial pressures have channeled public interest lawyering, especially direct service lawyering, back to an era of charitable service. The institutionalization of *pro bono* lawyering in large firms, on the other hand, represents a commercialization of charity. It is as if at the commercial heights of the profession, the service ideal has been colonized by the profit motive.

A confluence of factors encouraged large firms to participate in a massive shift in how *pro bono* services were delivered. During the 1960s the legal profession grew with an influx of young lawyers, including women and minorities entering the previously exclusionary ranks of the large corporate law firms. Those firms offered high salaries but they found themselves during a time of political and cultural turmoil in an increasingly disadvantageous position in recruiting the "best and the brightest" law school graduates, who often opted for positions in the public interest bar. Faced with (1) the need to recruit and retain attorneys, (2) demands from the courts for mandatory *pro bono*, and (3) pressure from the ABA and other bar associations to make up for cuts in government funded legal services, large firms became active sites for the recruitment of *pro bono* lawyers. Finally, in the 1980s and 1990s when the wealth and venality of large law firm attorneys symbolized unbounded self-interest, firms increased *pro bono* service to head off populist distrust of the profession.

Several consequences followed from the institutionalization of *pro bono* in large firms. The nature of *pro bono* as an individual obligation of service shifted, so that fulfillment of the service obligation is now organized by each law firm. It now represents one of the largest providers of legal services to the poor and disenfranchised. In terms of the number of personnel, a greater number of practitioners come from the *pro bono* sphere than any other component of civil legal services. Third, large firms found that it was conducive to their bottom lines, or, at least no large firm could compete without alerting the profession and the public to its charitable efforts.

The historical transformation of *pro bono* from an individual obligation to corporate charity had several steps. In the late 1960s and 1970s firms felt the pressure to offer public interest opportunities to recruit recent law school graduates. They felt pressure from young associates who had already decided on corporate practices to be given time and opportunities to practice in public interest fields. In large cities associates banded together, often with the assistance or at least acquiescence of the elite bar associations, to create groups that would lobby firms for greater participation and coordinate case referral and legal education efforts. Cuts in the Legal Services Corporation beginning in the early 1980s reduced the number of direct service lawyers for the poor at the same time as state courts were expanding the rights of the poor to certain types of legal representation. The Reagan administration entered office with the goal of eliminating federally–financed Legal Services, but opposition from the bar thwarted their effort. Instead, a provision to the Legal Services Corporation charter that would have profound effects on the growth of *pro bono* services passed in 1981. That year legislation mandated that every LSC grantee spend the equivalent of one-eighth of its LSC funding on private attorney involvement (PAI). LSC grantees could use those funds to pay private attorneys as a form of Judicare, or (and this is what most Legal Services organizations did) they could set up programs to recruit and train volunteer attorneys and coordinate their efforts with low income clients. Between 1980 and 1985, the number of *pro bono* programs (typically run by or with the assistance of local bar associations) coordinating *pro bono* attorneys and clients increased from 88 to over 500. Furthermore, in the 1980s, large salary increases for commercial law firm members in addition to highly publicized scandals put the legitimacy of the profession under close scrutiny.

In the 1990s, the ABA and the Ford Foundation launched an effort to increase *pro bono* legal services by specifically targeting large firms. These firms had the advantage of considerable resources in terms of labor (both attorneys and support staff), capital, and experience coordinating large numbers of attorneys. They also had command resources, the ability to assign attorneys and other personnel through persuasion or direct order. At one time the Ford Foundation had looked to the nonprofit sector and government to deliver legal services to the poor, but in 1993 it funded an ABA-sponsored Law Firm Pro Bono Project that targeted the nation's 500 largest firms. Signing on firms was difficult, though. Several partners from prestigious firms who served on the board of the Project were unable to convince their own firms to join the effort. Yet, despite the difficulties that the Law Firm Pro Bono Project's Challenge encountered, efforts to find an organizational home for *pro bono* in large firms increased. Firms continued to create *pro bono* committees, often hiring full-time personnel to direct the efforts. Firms expended greater resources to publicize their efforts, publishing brochures and designing web pages devoted to *pro bono* efforts. They also enlisted publicity departments to tout their activities and built intra-firm commitment by recognizing attorney *pro bono* work with annual awards.

The commercialization of the service ideal risks undermining the ideal itself and the role of the profession as an alternative to business. It is not that it is wrong for law firms to be involved in facilitating legal services for the poor. However, in locating the largest proportion of those civil legal services in organizations that follow an institutional logic (Friedland and Alford, 1991) different from that of a democratic legal system, the possibility of escaping a two-tiered system of law is not advanced.

Opportunities for public service among lawyers (fewer jobs, less funding, fewer connections to vibrant social movements) have created corresponding changes in ideologies of service (diffuse commitments to service, restricted ambitions of law reform, more cynical attitudes to the efficacy of the legal system). Politically, what constitutes public interest is broader than the field of civil rights and civil liberties, and the opportunities that individual lawyers now have to identify new clientele and innovate in the delivery of legal services are greater than ever. The institutional support for public interest law is much narrower – increasingly reliant on wealthy individuals and foundations – and less accountable to the poor or citizenry.

BIBLIOGRAPHICAL REFERENCES

Abel, Laura K. and David S. Udell. 2002. "If You Gag the Lawyers, Do You Choke the Courts? Some Implications For Judges When Funding Restrictions Curb Advocacy by Lawyers on Behalf of the Poor." *Fordham Urban Law Journal.* (February) 29: 873-906.

Abel, Richard L. 1985. "Law Without Politics: Legal Aid Under Advanced Capitalism." *UCLA Law Review.* (February) 32: 474-642.

Abel, Richard L. 1989. *American Lawyers.* New York: Oxford University Press.

Acheson, M. W., Jr. 1926. "The Situation in Pennsylvania." *The Annals of the American Academy of Political and Social Science.* (March) 124: 161-162.

Albert-Goldberg, Nancy and Marshall J. Hartman. 1983. "The Public Defender in America." in McDonald, William F. (ed.) *The Defense Counsel.* Beverly Hills, CA: Sage Publications.

Ali, Tariq and Susan Watkins. 1998. *1968 – Marching in the Streets.* New York: The Free Press.

Anthes, Louis. 2000. "Bohemian Justice: The Path of Law in Immigrant New York, 1870-1940." Ph.D. diss., New York University.

Aron, Nan. 1989. *Liberty and Justice for All: Public Interest Law in the 1980s and Beyond.* Boulder, CO: Westview Press.

Ashman, Allan. 1972. *The New Private Practice: A Study of Piper & Marbury's Neighborhood Law Office.* Chicago: National Legal Aid and Defender Association.

Association of the Bar of the City of New York and National Legal Aid and Defender Association, A Special Committee. 1959. *Equal Justice for the Accused.* Garden City, NY: Doubleday & Co.

Atkinson, Rob. 2001. "Historical Perspectives on *Pro Bono* Lawyering: A Social-Democratic Critique of *Pro Bono Publico* Representation of the Poor: The Good as the Enemy of the Best." *American University Journal of Gender, Social Policy & the Law.* 9: 129-170.

Auerbach, Jerome S. 1976. *Unequal Justice: Lawyers and Social Change in Modern America.* New York: Oxford University Press.

Babson, Steve. 1999. *The Unfinished Struggle: Turning Points in American Labor, 1877 – Present.* Lanham, MD: Rowman & Littlefield.

Belfrage, Cedric. 1973. *The American Inquisition, 1945-1960.* Indianapolis, IN: Bobbs-Merrill.

Berg, Manfred. 2004. "Individual Rights and Collective Interests: The NAACP and the American Voting Rights Discourse." in Berg, Manfred and Martin H.

Geyer. (eds.) *The Quest for Inclusion and Participation: in Modern America and Germany*. New York: Cambridge University Press.

Bergstrom, Randolph E. 1992. *Courting Danger: Injury and Law in New York City, 1870-1910*. Ithaca, NY: Cornell University Press.

Berman, Jerry and Edgar Cahn. 1970. "Bargaining for Justice: The Law Student's Challenge to Law Firms." *Harvard Civil Rights – Civil Liberties Law Review.* 5: 16-31.

Bower, Ward. 1987. "Strategies for Profitability." *Legal Economics.* 13 (October).

Bradford, William A. Jr. 1995. "Private Enforcement of the Public Rights: The Role of Fee-Shifting Statutes in Pro Bono Lawyering." in Katzman, Robert A. (ed.) *The Law Firm and the Public Good*. Washington, DC: The Brookings Institution.

Branch, Taylor. 2006. *At Canaan's Edge: America in the King Years, 1965-68*. New York: Simon and Schuster.

Brickman, Lester. 1973. "CLEPR and Clinical Education: A Review and Analysis." in *Clinical Education for the Law Student: Legal Education in a Service Setting*. New York: The Council on Legal Education for Professional Responsibility, Inc.

Brinkley, Alan. 1991. "Great Society." in Foner, Eric and John A. Garraty. (eds.) *The Reader's Companion to American History*. New York: Houghton-Mifflin.

Brown, Esther Lucille. 1948. *Lawyers, Law Schools and the Public Service*. New York: Russell Sage Foundation.

Brown, Peter Megargee. 1989. *Rascals: The Selling of the Legal Profession*. Indianapolis, IN: Benchmark Press.

Brownell, Emery E. 1951. *Legal Aid in the United States: A Study of the Availability of Lawyers' Services for Persons Unable to Pay Fees*. Rochester, NY: Lawyers Co-operative Publishing Co.

Burtman, Bob. 2002. "Criminal Injustice." *Independent Weekly*. (Durham, NC). October, 16.

Bush, Rod. 1999. *We Are Not What We Seem: Black Nationalism and Class Struggle in the American Century*. New York: New York University Press.

Bussiere, Elizabeth. 1997. *(Dis)Entitling the Poor: The Warren Court, Welfare Rights, and the American Political Tradition*. University Park, PA: Penn State Press.

Cahn, Edgar S. and Jean C. 1964. "The War on Poverty: A Civilian Perspective." *Yale Law Journal*. (July) 73: 1317-1352.

Caplan, Lincoln. 1993. *Skadden: Power, Money and the Rise of a Legal Empire*. New York: Farrar Straus Giroux.

Cash, W.J. 1941. *The Mind of the South*. New York: Alfred A. Knopf.

Caute, David. 1988. *The Year of the Barricades: A Journey Through 1968*. New York: Harper and Row.

Chused, Richard H. 2000. "Landlord-Tenant Courts in New York City at the Turn of the Twentieth Century." in Steinmetz, Willibald. (ed.) *Private Law and Social Inequality in the Industrial Age.* New York: Oxford University Press.

Clarke, Claude E. 1926. "Legal Aid by Privately Supported Organizations." *The Annals of the American Academy of Political and Social Science.* (March) 124: 54-58.

Comment. 1970. "The New Public Interest Lawyers." *The Yale Law Journal.* (May) 79:6, pp. 1069-1152.

Cortner, Richard C. 1988. *A Mob Intent on Death: The NAACP and the Arkansas Riot Cases.* Middletown, CT: Wesleyan University Press.

Council for Public Interest Law. 1976. *Balancing the Scales of Justice: Financing Public Interest Law in America.* Washington, DC: Council for Public Interest Law.

Cummings, Scott L. 2001. "Community Economic Development as Progressive Politics: Toward a Grassroots Movement for Economic Justice." *Stanford Law Review.* (December) 54:6, pp. 399-493.

Cummings, Scott L. 2004. "The Politics of *Pro Bono.*" *UCLA Law Review.* 52:1, pp. 3-149.

Curran, Barbara A. and Clara N. Carson. 1994. *The Lawyer Statistical Report: The U.S. Legal Profession in the 1990s.* Chicago: American Bar Foundation.

Davis, Martha F. 1993. *Brutal Need: Lawyers and the Welfare Rights Movement, 1960-1973.* New Haven, CT: Yale University Press.

Davis, Martha F. 2001. "Our Better Half: a Public Interest Lawyer Reflects on *Pro Bono* Lawyering and Social Change Litigation." *American University Journal of Gender, Social Policy, and Law.* 9:1, pp. 119-27.

Diller, Matthew. 1995. "Poverty Lawyering in the Golden Age." *Michigan Law Review.* (May) 93: 1401-1432.

DiMaggio, Paul J. and Walter W. Powell. 1983. "The Iron Cage Revisited: Institutional Isomorphism and Collective Rationality in Organizational Fields." in Powell, Walter W. and Paul J. DiMaggio. (eds.) *The New Institutionalism in Organizational Analysis.* Chicago: University of Chicago Press.

Drachman, Virginia G. 1998. *Sisters in Law: Women Lawyers in Modern American History.* Cambridge, MA: Harvard University Press.

Durkheim, Émile. 1984 [1893]. *The Division of Labor in Society.* New York: The Free Press.

Durkheim, Émile. 1995 [1912]. *The Elementary Forms of Religious Life.* Glencoe, IL: The Free Press.

Edwards, Lee. 2004. *Bringing Justice to the People: The Story of the Freedom-Based Public Interest Law Movement.* Washington, DC: Heritage Books.

Eisinger, Peter K. 1973. "The Conditions of Protest Behavior in American Cities." *The American Political Science Review.* 67:1 (March), pp. 11-28.

Eisler, Kim Isaac. 1990. *Shark Tank: Greed, Politics, and the Collapse of Finley Kumble, One of America's Largest Law Firms*. New York: St. Martin's Press.

Emanuel, Anne S. 1996. "Lynching and the Law in Georgia Circa 1931: A Chapter in the Legal Career of Judge Elbert Tuttle." *William and Mary Bill of Rights Journal*. 5: 215-48.

Engels, Friedrich. 1993 [1845]. *The Condition of the Working Class in England*. New York: Oxford University Press.

Epstein, Cynthia Fuchs. 1993 [1981]. *Women in Law*. Urbana, IL: University of Illinois Press (repr. 2012, Quid Pro Books, New Orleans).

Epstein, Cynthia Fuchs. 2002. "Stricture and Structure: The Social and Cultural Context of Pro Bono Work in Wall Street Firms." *Fordham Law Review*. (April) LXX: 5, pp. 1689-1698.

Epstein, Cynthia Fuchs, Robert Sauté, Bonnie Oglensky, and Martha Gever. 1995. "Glass Ceilings and Open Doors: Women's Advancement in the Legal Profession." *Fordham Law Review*. (November) LXIV: 2, pp. 291-450.

Esquivel, David R. 1996. "The Identity Crisis in Public Interest Law." *Duke Law Journal*. (November) 46: 327-51.

Fairclough, Adam. 2001. *Better Day Coming: Blacks and Equality, 1890-2000*. New York: Viking.

Falk, Carol. 1970. "Many Lawyers Take Up Political, Social Causes on Their Firms' Time." *The Wall Street Journal*. May 20: 1, 15.

Ford Foundation and American Bar Association Special Committee on Public Interest Practice. 1976. *Public Interest Law: Five Years Later*. Chicago and New York: American Bar Association and Ford Foundation.

Freedman, Monroe. 1975. *Lawyers' Ethics in an Adversary System*. Indianapolis, IN: Bobbs-Merrill.

Freeman, Jo. 1975. *The Politics of Women's Liberation: A Case Study of an Emerging Social Movement and Its Relation to the Policy Process*. New York: McKay.

Freidson, Eliot. 2001. *Professionalism: The Third Logic*. Chicago: University of Chicago Press.

Friedland, Roger and Robert Alford. 1991. "Bringing Society Back In: Symbols, Practices, and Institutional Contradictions." in Powell, Walter W. and Paul DiMaggio. (eds.) *The New Institutionalism in Organizational Analysis*. Chicago: University of Chicago Press.

Friedman, Lawrence M. 1993. *Crime and Punishment in American History*. New York: Basic Books.

Galanter, Marc and Thomas Palay. 1991. *Tournament of Lawyers: The Transformation of the Big Law Firm*. Chicago: University of Chicago Press.

Galanter, Marc and Thomas Palay. 1993. "Public Service Implications of Evolving Law Firm Size and Structure." in Katzmann, Robert A. (ed.) *The Law Firm and the Public Good.* Washington, DC: The Brookings Institution/The Governance Institute.

Gariepy, Marguerite Raeder. 1926. "The Legal Aid Bureau of the United Charities of Chicago." *The Annals of the American Academy of Political and Social Science.* (March) 124: 33-41.

Goffman, Erving. 1952. "On Cooling Out the Mark: Some Aspects of Adaptation to Failure." *Psychiatry: Journal for the Study of Interpersonal Relations.* 15 (November), pp. 451-63.

Goffman, Erving. 1974. *Frame Analysis: An Essay on the Organization of Experience.* New York: Harper.

Goldman, Eric F. 1955 (Revised Edition) *Rendezvous With Destiny: A History of Modern American Reform.* New York: Vintage.

Goldman, Mayer C. 1919 (2nd Edition). *The Public Defender: A Necessary Factor in the Administration of Justice.* New York: G. P. Putnam's Sons.

Goldstein, Robert Justin. 1978. *Political Repression in Modern America: 1870 to the Present.* Cambridge, MA: Schenkman.

Goode, William J. 1963. *World Revolution and Family Patterns.* New York: The Free Press.

Gordon, Jennifer. 2005. *Suburban Sweatshops: The Fight for Immigrants Rights.* Cambridge, MA: The Belknap Press of Harvard University Press.

Greenberg, Jack. 2004. *Crusaders in the Courts: Legal Battles of the Civil Rights Movement, Anniversary Edition.* New York: Twelve Tables Press.

Grossberg, Michael. 1978a. "Altruism and Professionalism: Boston and the Rise of Organized Legal Aid, 1900-1925, Part I." *Boston Bar Journal.* (May) 22: 21-28.

Grossberg, Michael. 1978b. "Altruism and Professionalism: Boston and the Rise of Organized Legal Aid, 1900-1925, Part II." *Boston Bar Journal.* (June) 22: 11-24.

Grossberg, Michael. 1997. "The Politics of Professionalism: The Creation of Legal Aid and the Strains of Political Liberalism in America, 1900-1930." in Halliday, Terence C. and Lucien Karpik. (eds.) *Lawyers and the Rise of Political Liberalism.* New York: Oxford University Press.

Hall, Peter D. 2003. "The Welfare State and the Careers of Public and Private Institutions Since 1945." in Friedman, Lawrence J. and Mark D. McGarvie. (eds.) *Charity, Philanthropy, and Civility in American History.* New York: Cambridge University Press.

Halpern, Charles. 1976. "The Public Interest Bar: An Audit." in Nader, Ralph and Mark Green. (eds.) *Verdicts on Lawyers.* New York: Thomas Y. Crowell.

Hardin, Russell. 2003. "The Free Rider Problem." in Zalta, Edward N. (ed.) *The Stanford Encyclopedia of Philosophy* (Winter 2003 Edition). Available at http://plato.stanford.edu/archives/win2003/entries/Hardin/.

Heinz, John P. and Edward O. Laumann. 1982. *Chicago Lawyers: The Social Structure of the Bar*. New York: Russell Sage Foundation.

Helfgot, Joseph. 1974. "Professional Reform Organizations and the Symbolic Representation of the Poor." *American Sociological Review*. (August) 39:4, pp. 475-92.

Helfgot, Joseph. 1981. *Professional Reforming: Mobilization for Youth and the Failure of Social Science*. Lexington, MA: Lexington Books.

Hilbink, Thomas M. 2002. "Defining Cause Lawyering: *NAACP v. Button* and the Struggle over Professional Ideology." *Studies in Law, Politics, and Society*. 26: 77-107.

Hoffman, Lily M. 1989. *The Politics of Knowledge: Activist Movements in Medicine and Planning*. Albany, NY: State University of New York Press.

Houseman, Alan W. 1995. "Political Lessons: Legal Services for the Poor – A Commentary." *Georgetown Law Journal*. (April) 83: 1669-1709.

Houseman, Alan W. and Linda E. Perle. 2003. *Securing Equal Justice for All: A Brief History of Civil Legal Assistance*. Washington, DC: Center for Law and Social Policy.

Houston, Charles Hamilton. 1928. "Tentative Finding Re Negro Lawyers: A Report to Dean Roscoe Pound of the Harvard Law School." (February) Available at http://www.law.cornell.edu/houston/survey.htm.

Hume, David. 1978. [1739-40]. *A Treatise of Human Nature*. New York: Oxford University Press.

Igra, Anna R. 2000. "Likely to Become a Public Charge: Deserted Women and the Family Law of the Poor in New York City, 1910-1936." *Journal of Women's History*. (January) 11:4, pp. 59-77.

Irons, Peter. 1982. *The New Deal Lawyers*. Princeton, NJ: Princeton University Press.

Jacobs, Daniel S. 2003. "The Role of the Federal Government in Defending Public Interest Litigation." *Santa Clara Law Review*. 44: 1-56.

Jacobs, James B. 1977. *Stateville: The Penitentiary in Mass Society*. Chicago: University of Chicago Press.

Jepperson, Ronald L. 1991. "Institutions, Institutional Effects, and Institutionalism." in Powell, Walter W. and Paul J. DiMaggio. (eds.) *The New Institutionalism in Organizational Analysis*. Chicago: The University of Chicago Press.

Johnson, Earl, Jr. 1974. *Justice and Reform: The Formative Years of the OEO Legal Services Program*. New York: Russell Sage Foundation.

Johnson, Earl, Jr. 1999. "Justice and Reform: A Quarter Century Later." in Reagan, Francis, Alan Paterson, Tamara Goriely, and Don Fleming. (eds.) *The Transformation of Legal Aid: Comparative and Historical Studies*. New York: Oxford University Press.

Jones, Douglas Lamar, Alan Rogers, James J. Connolly, Cynthia Farr Brown, and

Diane Kadzis. 1993. *Discovering the Public Interest: A History of the Boston Bar Association*. Canoga Park, CA: CCA Publications.

Katkin, Kenneth. 2005. "'Incorporation' of the Criminal Procedure Amendments: The View from the States." *Nebraska Law Review*. 84: 397-468.

Katz, Jack. 1982. *Poor People's Lawyers In Transition*. New Brunswick, NJ: Rutgers University Press.

Katz, Michael B. 1996 (2nd Edition). *In the Shadow of the Poor House: A Social History of Welfare in America*. New York: Basic Books.

Kelman, Mark. 1987. *A Guide to Critical Legal Studies*. Cambridge, MA: Harvard University Press.

Kilwein, John. 1999. "The Decline of the Legal Services Corporation: 'It's Ideological, Stupid!'" in Reagan, Francis, Alan Paterson, Tamara Goriely, and Don Fleming. (eds.) *The Transformation of Legal Aid: Comparative and Historical Studies*. New York: Oxford University Press.

Kluger, Richard. 1976. *Simple Justice: The History of Brown v. Board of Education and Black America's Struggle for Equality*. New York: Alfred A. Knopf.

Kozol, Jonathan. 2005. *The Shame of the Nation: The Restoration of Apartheid Schooling in America*. New York: Crown.

Kronman, Anthony T. 1983. *Max Weber*. Stanford, CA: Stanford University Press.

Lardent, Esther F. 1989. "*Pro Bono* in the 1990's: The Uncertain Future of Attorney Volunteerism." paper presented at the Conference on Access to Justice in the 1990's. Tulane Law School.

Lardent, Esther F. 1996. "The Case Against: Just Say No ... To Mandatory Pro Bono." *The American Lawyer*. available at http://www.probonoinst.org/pdfs/justsayno.pdf.

Larson, Edward J. 2006. *Summer for the Gods: The Scopes Trial and America's Continuing Debate over Science and Religion*. New York: Basic Books.

Larson, Magali Sarfatti. 1977. *The Rise of Professionalism: A Sociological Analysis*. Berkeley: University of California Press.

Lazarus, Simon. 1974. *The Genteel Populists*. New York: Holt, Rinehart and Winston.

Leuchtenburg, William E. 1963. *Franklin D. Roosevelt and the New Deal: 1932-1940*. New York: Harper & Row.

Levi, Edward H. 1963. *An Introduction to Legal Reasoning*. Chicago: University of Chicago Press.

Lewis, Anthony. 1964. *Gideon's Trumpet*. New York: Vintage Books.

Lin, Elbert. 2003. "Case Comment: Korematsu Continued..." *Yale Law Journal*. (April) 112: 1911-18.

Lipsky, Michael. 1980. *Street Level Bureaucrats: Dilemmas of the Individual in Public Services*. New York: Russell Sage Foundation.

Lowi, Theodore J. 1969. *The End of Liberalism: Ideology, Policy, and the Crisis of Public Authority*. New York: Norton.

Luban, David. 1988. *Lawyers and Justice: An Ethical Study*. Princeton, NJ: Princeton University Press.

MacDonald, Dwight. 1953a. "The Defense of Everybody – I." *The New Yorker*. July 11, pp. 31-55.

MacDonald, Dwight. 1953b. "The Defense of Everybody – II." *The New Yorker*. July 18, pp. 29-55.

Maguire, John MacArthur. [1982] 1928. *The Lance of Justice: A Semi-Centennial History of Legal Aid Society, 1876-1926*. Littleton, CO: Fred B. Rothman & Co.

Marden, Orison S. 1973. "CLEPR: Origins and Program." in *Clinical Education for the Law Student: Legal Education in a Service Setting*. New York: The Council on Legal Education for Professional Responsibility, Inc.

Marshall, T. H. 1992. "Citizenship and Social Class" in Marshall, T.H. & Tom Bottomore (eds.) *Citizenship and Social Class*. London: Pluto Press.

Massey, Douglas S. and Nancy A. Denton. 1993. *American Apartheid: Segregation and the Making of the Underclass*. Cambridge, MA: Harvard University Press.

Maute, Judith L. 2002. "Changing Conceptions of Lawyers' *Pro Bono* Responsibilities: From Chance Noblesse Oblige To Stated Expectations." *Tulane Law Review*. 77: 91-162.

McAdam, Doug. 1982. *Political Process and the Development of Black Insurgency, 1930-1970*. Chicago: University of Chicago Press.

McBurney, Meredith. 2003. "The Impact of Legal Services Program Reconfiguration on *Pro Bono*." ABA Center for Pro Bono. available at http://www.abanet.org/legalservices/probono/impact_reconfiguration.pdf.

McCann, Michael W. 1986. *Taking Reform Seriously: Perspectives on Public Interest Liberalism*. Ithaca, NY: Cornell University Press.

McCann, Michael W. 1994. *Rights at Work: Pay Equity Reform and the Politics of Legal Mobilization*. Chicago: University of Chicago Press.

McConville, Michael and Chester L. Mirsky 1989. *Criminal Defense of the Poor in New York City*. New York: Center for Research in Crime and Justice at New York University School of Law.

McIntyre, Lisa J. 1987. *The Public Defender: The Practice of Law in the Shadow of Repute*. Chicago: The University of Chicago Press.

McGerr, Michael. 2003. *A Fierce Discontent: The Rise and Fall of the Progressive Movement in America, 1870-1920*. New York: The Free Press.

McLeod, Jacqueline A. 2005. "Persona Non-Grata: Judge Jane Matilda Bolin and the NAACP, 1930-1950." *Afro-Americans in New York Life and History*. (January). 29:1.

Meier, August and Elliott Rudwick. 1976. "Attorneys Black and White: A Case Study of Race Relations within the NAACP." in Meier, August and Elliott Rudwick. *Along the Color Line: Explorations in the Black Experience.* Urbana, IL: University of Illinois Press.

Meltsner, Michael. 2006. *The Making of a Civil Rights Attorney.* Charlottesville, VA: University of Virginia Press.

Merton, Robert K. 1957 [1949]. *Social Theory and Social Structure: Toward the Codification of Theory and Research.* New York: The Free Press.

Merton, Robert K. 1971. "Social Problems and Sociological Theory." in Merton, Robert K. and Robert Nisbet. (eds.) *Contemporary Social Problems.* (3rd Edition). New York: Harcourt, Brace, Jovanovich.

Merton, Robert K. 1973. "The Matthew Effect in Science." in *The Sociology of Science: Theoretical and Empirical Investigations.* Edited and with an introduction by Norman W. Storer. Chicago: University of Chicago Press.

Merton, Robert K. 1995. "Opportunity Structure: The Emergence, Diffusion, and Differentiation of a Sociological Concept, 1930s to 1950s." in Adler, Freda and William S. Laufer. *Advances in Criminological Theory: The Legacy of Anomie Theory.* (Vol. 6). New Brunswick, NJ: Transaction Publishers.

Morris, Jeffrey B. 1997. *"Making Sure We Are True to Our Founders": The Association of the Bar of the City of New York, 1970-1995.* New York: Fordham University Press.

Moynihan, Daniel P. 1969. *Maximum Feasible Misunderstanding: Community Action in the War on Poverty.* New York: The Free Press.

Nader, Ralph. 1965. *Unsafe at Any Speed: The Designed-in Dangers of the American Automobile.* New York: Grossman.

Neier, Aryeh. 1982. *Only Judgment.* Middletown, CT: Wesleyan University Press.

New York Lawyers for the Public Interest. 1991. *Celebrating 15 Years.* New York: New York Lawyers for the Public Interest.

Nonet, Philippe and Philip Selznick. 1978. *Law and Society in Transition: Toward Responsive Law.* New York: Harper & Row.

Note. 1971. "The Right to Effective Counsel and New York City Legal Aid." *New York University Review of Law and Social Change.* (Spring) 1:1, pp. 1-58.

Orfield, Gary and Chungmei Lee. 2007. *Historic Reversals, Accelerating Resegregation, and the Need for New Integration Strategies.* Los Angeles: Civil Rights Project/*Proyecto Civiles*, UCLA.

Parsons, Talcott. 1954 [1939]. "The Professions and Social Structure." in Parsons, Talcott. *Essays in Sociological Theory, Revised Edition.* Glencoe, IL: The Free Press.

Parsons, Talcott. 1954b. "A Sociologist Looks at the Legal Profession." in Parsons, Talcott. *Essays in Sociological Theory, Revised Edition.* Glencoe, IL: The Free Press.

Patterson, James T. 1994 (2nd Edition). *America's Struggle Against Poverty, 1900-1994*. Cambridge, MA: Harvard University Press.

Perry, Maribeth. 1998. "The Role of Transactional Attorneys in Providing Pro Bono Legal Services." *Boston Bar Journal*. (May/June) 42:16-27.

Pious, Richard M. 1971. "Policy and Public Administration: The Legal Services Program in the War on Poverty." *Politics and Society*. 1: 365-391.

Piven, Frances Fox and Richard A. Cloward. 1966. "The Weight of the Poor: A Strategy to End Poverty." *The Nation*. (May 2).

Piven, Frances Fox and Richard A. Cloward. 1971. *Regulating the Poor: The Functions of Public Welfare*. New York: Vintage Books.

Piven, Frances Fox and Richard A. Cloward. 1977. *Poor People's Movements: Why They Succeed, How They Fail*. New York: Pantheon Books.

Pollack, Norman. 1962. *The Populist Response to Industrial America: Midwestern Populist Thought*. Cambridge, MA: Harvard University Press.

Powell, Michael J. 1988. *From Patrician to Professional Elite: The Transformation of the New York City Bar Association*. New York: Russell Sage Foundation.

Rabin, Robert L. 1976. "Lawyers for Social Change: Perspectives on Public Interest Law." *Stanford Law Review*. (January) 28: 207-61.

Rabinowitz, Victor. 1987-1988. "The National Lawyers Guild: Thomas Emerson and the Struggle for Survival." *Case Western Reserve Law Review*. 38: 608-617.

Raynor, Gregory K. 1999. "The Ford Foundation's War on Poverty: Private Philanthropy and Race Relations in New York City, 1948-1968." in Langemann, Ellen Condliffe. (ed.) *Philanthropic Foundations: New Scholarship, New Possibilities*. Bloomington, IN: Indiana University Press.

Rice, Elmer. 1963. *Minority Report: An Autobiography*. New York: Simon and Schuster.

Rosenberg, Gerald N. 1991. *The Hollow Hope: Can Courts Bring About Social Change?* Chicago: University of Chicago Press.

Rossinow, Douglas C. 1998. *The Politics of Authenticity: Liberalism, Christianity, and the New Left in America*. New York: Columbia University Press.

Rudolph, Frederick. 1950. "The American Liberty League, 1934-1940." *American Historical Review*. (Oct.) 56:1, pp. 19-33.

Sandefur, Rebecca L. 2006. "Lawyers' *Pro Bono* Service and American-Style Civil Legal Assistance for the Poor." Unpublished manuscript, Department of Sociology, Stanford University.

Sandmo, Agnar. 1987. "Public Goods." in Eatwell, John, Murray Milgate and Peter Newman. (eds.) *The New Palgrave: A Dictionary of Economics*. London: Macmillan Press.

Sarat, Austin and Stuart Scheingold. (eds.) 1998. *Cause Lawyering: Political Commitments and Professional Responsibilities.* New York: Oxford University Press.

Sarat, Austin and Stuart Scheingold. (eds.) 2005. *The Worlds Cause Lawyers Make: Structure and Agency in Legal Practice.* Stanford, CA: Stanford University Press.

Scheingold, Stuart A. 1974. *The Politics of Rights: Lawyers, Public Policy, and Political Change.* New Haven, CT: Yale University Press.

Scheingold, Stuart A. and Austin Sarat. 2004. *Something to Believe In: Politics, Professionalism, and Cause Lawyering.* Stanford, CA: Stanford University Press.

Schmitt, J.T. 1912. *History of the Legal Aid Society of New York.* New York: The Legal Aid Society of New York.

Schrag, Phillip G. and Michael Meltsner. 1998. *Reflections on Clinical Legal Education.* Boston: Northeastern University Press.

Schrecker, Ellen. 1986. *No Ivory Tower: McCarthyism and the Universities.* New York: Oxford University Press.

Schwartz, Bernard. 1993. *A History of the Supreme Court.* New York: Oxford University Press.

Selznick, Philip. 1969 *Law, Society, and Industrial Justice.* New Brunswick, NJ: Transaction Books.

Shamir, Ronen. 1995 *Managing Legal Uncertainty: Elite Lawyers in the New Deal.* Durham, NC: Duke University Press.

Shils, Edward. 1968. "Charisma." in Sills, David L. (ed.) *International Encyclopedia of the Social Sciences.* New York: Macmillan Co. & The Free Press. 2: 386-90.

Simon, William H. 2001. *The Community Economic Development Movement: Law, Business, and the New Social Policy.* Durham, NC: Duke University Press.

Smith, Reginald Heber. 1919. *Justice and the Poor: A Study of the Present Denial of Justice to the Poor and of the Agencies Making More Equal Their Position before the Law with Particular Reference to Legal Aid Work in the United States.* New York: Carnegie Foundation for the Advancement of Teaching.

Snow, David A., E. Burke Rochford, Jr., Steven K. Worden, and Robert D. Benford. 1986. "Frame Alignment Processes, Micromobilization and Movement Participation." *American Sociological Review.* 51: 464-81.

Solomon, Rayman L. 1992. "Five Crises or One: The Concept of Legal Professionalism, 1925-1960." in Nelson, Robert L., David M. Trubek and Rayman L. Solomon. (eds.) *Lawyers' Ideals/Lawyers' Practices: Transformations in the American Legal Profession.* Ithaca, NY: Cornell University Press.

Southworth, Ann. 2004. "Representing Agents of Community Economic Development: A Comment on Recent Trends." *Journal of Small and Emerging Business Law.* (Summer) 8: 261-72.

Special Committee of The Association of the Bar of the City of New York and The National Legal Aid and Defender Association. 1959. *Equal Justice for the Accused.* Garden City, NY: Doubleday & Co.

Stevens, Robert. 1973. "Law Schools and Law Students." *Virginia Law Review.* (April) 59:4, pp. 551-707.

Stevens, Robert. 1983. *Law School: Legal Education in America from the 1850s to the 1980s.* Chapel Hill, NC: The University of North Carolina Press.

Stinchcombe, Arthur L. 1965. "Social Structure and Organizations." in March, James G. (ed.) *Handbook of Organizations.* Chicago: Rand McNally and Co., pp. 142-93.

Taylor, Charles. 1990. "Invoking Civil Society." *Working Papers and Proceedings of the Center for Psychosocial Studies,* no. 31. Chicago: Center for Psychosocial Studies.

Trubek, Louise G. 2002. "Public Interest Lawyers and New Governance: Advocating for Health Care." *Wisconsin Law Review,* pp. 575-603.

Trubek, Louise G. and David M. Trubek. 1981. "Civic Justice Through Civil Justice: A New Approach to Public Interest Advocacy in the United States." in Cappelletti, Mauro. (ed.) *Access to Justice and the Welfare State.* Alphen aan den Rijn: Sijthoff.

Truman, David B. 1951. *The Governmental Process; Political Interests and Public Opinion.* New York: Knopf.

Tushnet, Mark V. 1987. *The NAACP's Legal Strategy Against Segregated Education, 1925-1950.* Chapel Hill, NC: University of North Carolina Press

Tweed, Harrison. 1954. *The Legal Aid Society of New York City, 1876-1951.* New York: The Legal Aid Society.

Unger, Irwin, 1996: *The Best of Intentions: The Triumphs and Failures of the Great Society Under Kennedy, Johnson, and Nixon.* New York: Doubleday & Co.

Veysey, Laurence R. 1965. *The Emergence of the American University.* Chicago: University of Chicago Press.

Vogel, David. 1980-81. "The Public Interest Movement and the American Reform Movement." *Political Science Quarterly.* (Winter) 95:4, pp. 607-27.

Voluntary Defenders Committee. 1917. "Prospectus of New York Voluntary Defenders Committee." *New York Law Journal.* (March 19).

Walker, Samuel. 1990. *In Defense of American Liberties: A History of the ACLU.* New York: Oxford University Press.

Wasby, Stephen L. 1984. "How Planned is 'Planned Litigation'?" *American Bar Foundation Research Journal.* (Winter) 5: 83-138.

Watkins, John Elfreth. 1906. "Where the Poor Get Legal Advice Free." *Ladies' Home Journal.* (November) XXIII: 12, p. 45.

Weber, Max. 1978 [1921-22]. *Economy and Society: An Outline of Interpretive Sociology.* Roth, Guenther and Claus Wittich (eds.). Berkeley, CA: University of California Press.

White, G. Edward. 1986. "Felix Frankfurter, the Old Boy Network, and the New Deal: The Placement of Elite Lawyers in Public Service in the 1930s." *Arkansas Law Review.* 39: 4, pp. 631-66.

Wiebe, Robert. 1967. *The Search for Order, 1877-1920.* New York: Hill and Wang.

Williamson, Oliver. 1975. *Markets and Hierarchies: Analysis and Antitrust Implications.* New York: The Free Press.

Willrich, Michael. 2003. *City of Courts: Socializing Justice in Progressive Era Chicago.* New York: Cambridge University Press.

Ylvisaker, Paul N. 1963. *Community Action: A Response to Some Unfinished Business.* New York: Ford Foundation.

Zeiger, Robert H. 1995. *The CIO, 1935-1955.* Chapel Hill, NC: University of North Carolina Press.

qp

Visit us at *www.quidprobooks.com*.